More Praise for *Living Beyond T*

Again and again in her new book, Dr. Konvisser illustrates the gift of choice, not "Why me?" but instead "Why not me? What do I do now with my freedom to go forward from this moment?" In human profile after profile, the author poignantly shows her readers how some individuals allow their circumstances to shatter them while others are ennobled by their responses and endurance. Dr. Konvisser's gift to you is an intimate challenge to choose hope and healing in your own life.

Viktor Frankl reminds us that "man is that being who invented the gas chambers of Auschwitz; however, he is also that being who entered those gas chambers upright, with the Lord's Prayer or the Shema Yisrael on his lips." I join Zieva Konvisser in asking which one is your choice.

Robert C. Barnes, PhD, President, International Board of Directors,
Viktor Frankl Institute of Logotherapy

If human resilience in the face of overwhelming trauma has baffled you, this book is the key to unlock the inspiring complexities of the little-understood phenomenon...of posttraumatic growth.... If terrorism aims at breaking the spirit of a civilian population, Dr. Konvisser's unique book, packed with stories of resilience, proves terrorism has failed. The powerful stories of healing and hope in this volume are a reflection of how remarkable the human spirit is. This book is a must-read for anyone facing the darkness of tragedy.

Eli Somer, PhD, Clinical Professor of Psychology, University of Haifa;
Past President, European Society for Trauma and Dissociation and
International Society for the Study of Trauma and Dissociation

The words of these survivors help to illuminate the process of posttraumatic growth, so that others may have a better idea of what gifts may be found as they struggle to cope with devastating events.

Lawrence Calhoun, PhD, and **Richard Tedeschi, PhD**,
Department of Psychology, UNC Charlotte;
co-authors, *Posttraumatic Growth in Clinical Practice*

Zieva Konvisser has ensured that we will not forget the heroism of the terror survivors and the men and women who have guided them on their tough journey. With intelligence and compassion, she has given us valuable insights into these previously uncharted waters.

Barbara Sofer, Israel Director of Public Relations
and Communications for Hadassah

Zieva Konvisser's *Living Beyond Terrorism: Israeli Stories of Hope and Healing* takes us into the hearts and minds of people who have miraculously survived politically motivated bombings in Israel. On the basis of interviews exploring what resilience means to them years after the events, she illuminates the components of the "ability to thrive" after horrific experiences. Konvisser includes lengthy quotations from these interviews, so readers can tease out useful details. These reveal how the survivors represent both general patterns and unique individual responses. This book is a must-read in our age of terrorism and its aftermaths.

Shulamit Reinharz, PhD, Jacob Potofsky Professor of Sociology;
Director, Hadassah-Brandeis Institute and
Women's Studies Research Center, Brandeis University

In the compelling narratives she has assembled, Zieva Konvisser opens for us the world of people who have survived terrorist attacks. Through her insightful presentation, their suffering and resilience are given voice, and we readers learn how such trauma can be managed and meanings created. This well-written and deeply empathic book puts a human face on what terrorism can mean to ordinary citizens and their lives.

Ruthellen Josselson, PhD, Fielding Graduate University;
co-editor, Narrative Study of Lives series

These brave survivors remind us that in Israel too many parents buried their children, too many victims are still suffering from their injuries, and too much blood was spilled. Zieva Konvisser redeems their names and suffering. Her splendid book is about life winning over death. It shows why Israel will win her centennial war against terrorism.

Giulio Meotti, author of *A New Shoah*

Living Beyond Terrorism

Key Israeli Cities and Locations of Attacks

LIVING
BEYOND
TERRORISM

Israeli Stories of Hope and Healing

Zieva Dauber Konvisser, PhD
Foreword by Danny Brom, PhD

 GEFEN PUBLISHING HOUSE

Cover design: Leah Ben Avraham/Noonim Graphics
Typesetting: Irit Nachum
Map illustration on page iv: Alex Lumelsky/SKY Creative
Author photograph: Monni Must
Back cover photograph of the memorial to Egged bus no. 37 bombing, Moriah
Boulevard, Haifa: Zieva Konvisser

Quotes from *Man's Search for Meaning* by Viktor E. Frankl, copyright © 1959,
1962, 1984, 1992, 2006 by Viktor E. Frankl, reprinted by permission of Beacon
Press, Boston, and *Man's Search for Meaning: The Classic Tribute to Hope from the
Holocaust* by Viktor E. Frankl, published by Rider Books, reprinted by permission
of The Random House Group Limited.

Quotes from "Parents' Experience and Meaning Construction of the Loss of
a Child in a National Terror Attack," by Chaya Possick, Ruth Ann Sadeh, and
Michal Shamai, *American Journal of Orthopsychiatry* 78, no. 1 (2008): 97–99,
by the American Orthopsychiatric Association, reproduced with permission of the
American Psychological Association via Copyright Clearance Center.

ISBN: 978-965-229-643-6

1 3 5 7 9 8 6 4 2

Gefen Publishing House Ltd.
6 Hatzvi Street
Jerusalem 94386, Israel
972-2-538-0247
orders@gefenpublishing.com

Gefen Books
11 Edison Place
Springfield, NJ 07081
516-593-1234
orders@gefenpublishing.com

www.gefenpublishing.com

Printed in Israel

Send for our free catalog

Library of Congress Cataloging-in-Publication Data

Konvisser, Zieva Dauber, 1943- author.
Living beyond terrorism : Israeli stories of hope and healing / Zieva Dauber Konvisser,
PhD ; foreword by Danny Brom, PhD.
    p. cm.
Includes bibliographical references and index.
ISBN 978-965-229-643-6
1. Terrorism—Israel.   2. Terrorism—Israel—Psychological aspects.   3. Victims
of terrorism—Israel—Psychology.   4. Victims of terrorism—Israel—Personal
narratives. I. Title.
HV6433.I75K66 2014
363.325095694—dc23
                                    2013043093

Dedication

Tikkun olam – repairing the world

Tikkun halev – repairing the heart

Tikkun haneshama – repairing the soul

Tikkun hador – repairing the generation

In loving memory of my dear parents, Dina Wirshup Dauber, *z"l*, and Emanuel Dauber, *z"l*, who instilled in me the values of education, *tikkun* (repairing or healing), and good deeds.

In honor of the extraordinary people who have created meaning from their experiences as survivors of terrorism in Israel, making a difference by sharing their stories to remind the world of "never again."

In recognition of my family members and friends who have struggled with highly challenging life circumstances and, in that struggle, confronted their trauma-related thoughts, feelings, and images and moved forward with dignity and courage to exemplary deeds and actions.

Our paths have touched and we have been strengthened and enlightened by each other.

"We must never forget that we may also find meaning in life even when confronted with a hopeless situation, when facing a fate that cannot be changed. For what then matters is to bear witness to the uniquely human potential at its best, which is to transform a personal tragedy into a triumph, to turn one's predicament into a human achievement. When we are no longer able to change a situation... we are challenged to change ourselves."

– Viktor Frankl, *Man's Search for Meaning*[1]

---

1 Viktor E. Frankl, *Man's Search for Meaning*, trans. Ilse Lasch (Boston: Beacon Press, 2006), 112.

Contents

Letter from the Publisher

It is with a sense of gravity that Gefen Publishing House presents *Living Beyond Terrorism*. The world over, modern terrorism has changed our lives. While it is true that not every Muslim is a terrorist, it is also true that almost all terrorist attacks are planned and implemented by Islamic extremists. They attack all mankind and among the inflicted people are Muslims, Christians, Jews, and members of every faith upon the globe.

In *Living Beyond Terrorism*, Zieva Konvisser has taken a critical look at the consequences of terror attacks, showing how their effects ripple beyond the victims and their families to wider family, social, and professional circles. Terror reaches across time, too; the incidents that the public may forget within days are felt for years, even across generations. While the country may breathe a sigh of relief when the headline reads "No Casualties" after a bomb goes off in an empty school, for hundreds of youngsters it may translate into a psychological trauma that they will be dealing with for years to come.

Nearly every Israeli is affected by terrorist attacks on his or her extended family. We in Israel feel a special responsibility when it comes to terror, not only because we have so many of our own citizens to take care of in the wake of these attacks but also because we are able to offer our hard-won expertise in these matters to the rest of the world. Who in the twenty-first century has not felt the repercussions of terrorism? The intensive security checks that we are all subjected to in airports worldwide, costing billions of dollars, amply illustrate the pernicious influence of terror. In the wake of 9/11 and the Boston Marathon bombing, America too has had bitter experience with the effects of terrorism. We hope this compendium of Israeli experiences will help others as so many around the globe confront the realities of the all-pervasive threat of terror in the modern world.

Ilan Greenfield
Publisher

Foreword: The Narrative of Terrorism

Human beings are capable both of causing tremendous suffering to each other and of withstanding, coping, and growing from horrific experiences. The majority of traumatic experiences are caused by what human beings do to each other. "Politically motivated violence," which is the topic of this book, is an example of this. Most people, and certainly survivors, call this kind of violence "terrorism," but this word implies a political choice and the author has taken the scientific stance to try to not become a partner in the narrative of survivors, but to study it. She has courageously and deeply listened to the stories of forty-eight survivors and family members of victims of politically motivated violence – a narrative study through qualitative research that makes high demands of the researcher.

I first met Zieva Konvisser in 2003 when she began her research with survivors of terrorism. At the time, during the Second Intifada, we at the Israel Center for the Treatment of Psychotrauma in Jerusalem, along with other trauma professionals throughout Israel, were immersed in the treatment and intervention of trauma responses resulting from exposure to terrorism. In that situation, tending to many affected populations, the reality of posttraumatic growth seemed far from us. Nevertheless, we did recognize and understand the need for Zieva's research perspective on the possibility of posttraumatic growth coexisting with posttraumatic stress. We warmly welcomed her into our community and supported her desire to learn how Israeli civilians overcame the overwhelming psychological effects of such indiscriminate and horrific attacks.

The resulting stories that people tell in this book are frightening. Violence that comes at unexpected times and places. Death and injury in front of the eyes of people who go about their daily lives. How do they adapt to this reality? How do they deal with the memories that will accompany them from the time of the attack? How can they and we maintain a balance between fear and calm that will allow continued functioning and at the same time acknowledgement of the reality of terrorist attacks? It is not only the directly exposed people who need to cope with this, but the whole society, including us, mental health professionals. These questions are central to the field of terrorism and trauma and are discussed in a growing body of research.[1]

Living for many years with the fears of encountering a suicide bomber, the question of terrorism's influence on the psychological wellbeing of the civilian population naturally comes up. While it is important to recognize the damage that continuous fears might create, it is equally important to recognize that people also might feel they gained from the experience. Historically, the psychological literature on terrorism and trauma and its consequences has focused heavily on the negative consequences. Intuitively this makes sense, as most people react to the word "trauma" with fear and aversion. The idea of posttraumatic growth has only started to appear in the past twenty years, suggesting that traumatic experiences might not only have negative consequences, but that people might learn important and meaningful lessons from their experiences.

One of the main and well-recognized tasks that survivors confront is to find meaning in what has happened to them. Survivors have to deal with questions, such as: Why did this happen to me? And now that it did happen to me, what does this mean for my life? Construction of meaning has been shown to occur by two separate and independent pathways as part of the psychological adjustment process to threatening experiences.[2] First, one has to make sense of the event by answering the questions of what happened, how, and why. Second, one has to find personal significance in the event or gain from the experience for one's present life.

Research has shown that there is a correlation between the degree to which people appraise their symptoms as negative, perceive other people's reactions as negative, and believe their trauma has had a

---

1   Y. Danieli, D. Brom, and J. Sills, *The Trauma of Terrorism: Sharing Knowledge and Shared Care: An International Handbook* (New York: Haworth, 2005).

2   S. Joseph and P. A. Linley, "Positive Adjustment to Threatening Events: An Organismic Valuing Theory of Growth through Adversity," *Review of General Psychology* 9 (2005): 262–280.

permanent negative effect on their lives on the one hand, and their experiencing posttraumatic stress disorder (PTSD), on the other.[3] This means that there is a complicated relationship between the search for meaning of the event, the meaning people attribute to their symptoms, and the actual symptoms they suffer from.

In addition, one of the main challenges of traumatic experiences is the clash between the new information of the experience and the existing cognitive schemata. According to the cognitive processing theory of trauma, the bigger the gap between the new information and the existing attitudes and inner knowledge, the more difficult it is to process the experience. Elsewhere, we have described the process of meaning-making as a learning process.[4] In that learning process, successful coping can be operationalized as "minimal learning," i.e., the people who manage to leave their cognitive schemata largely intact and succeed in limiting the scope of the change in their view of the world and of themselves as a result of their experiences are those who have the least symptoms. Thus, the cognitive framing of the event and its meaning is a crucial factor in allowing people to rebuild their lives and create a worldview in which basic trust in life can be restored.

The literature's focus on negative consequences has strengthened the implicit assumption that posttraumatic symptoms, such as re-experiencing the event, avoiding reminders of the event, and symptoms of hyperarousal, are the most important consequences of terrorism. Although there is research showing that the consequences are much more diverse, such as the increase of traffic accidents in the aftermath of terrorist incidents[5] and the increase of risk-taking behavior in adolescents

---

3   Halligan et al., "Posttraumatic Stress Disorder Following Assault: The Role of Cognitive Processing, Trauma Memory and Appraisals," *Journal of Consulting and Clinical Psychology* 71, no. 3 (2003): 419–431.

4   D. Brom and R. J. Kleber, "Resilience as the Capacity for Processing Traumatic Experiences," in *Treating Traumatized Children: Risk, Resilience and Recovery*, ed. D. Brom, R. Pat-Horenczyk, and J. Ford (New York: Routledge, 2009), 133–149.

5   G. Stecklov and J. R. Goldstein, "Terror Attacks Influence Driving Behavior in Israel," *Proceedings of the National Academy of Science, USA* 101, no. 40 (2004): 14551–14556.

who experienced terrorist incidents,[6] there is a need to explore many more aspects of human experience and behavior in the aftermath of trauma. The contribution of narrative and qualitative research for this exploration is of crucial importance. The author of this book is contributing to the study of the consequences of politically motivated violence by documenting many of the challenges that confront people who experience such violence and by elucidating the many ways people find to overcome the horrors of their encounter with deadly violence. Equally, this book contributes to the development of the concept of posttraumatic growth, which is a concept that needs more clarification and empirical support. The message of "hope and healing" that is being transmitted by this book is one that is important for survivors and all those who are supporting them in their journey.

> Prof. Danny Brom
> Founding Director
> Israel Center for the Treatment of Psychotrauma
> Herzog Hospital, Jerusalem

---

6   Pat-Horenczyk et al., "Adolescent Exposure to Recurrent Terrorism in Israel: Posttraumatic Distress and Functional Impairment," *American Journal of Orthopsychiatry* 77, no. 1 (2007): 76–85.

Preface: Defy Darkness – Spread Light

"Smoke, darkness, blood, burning flesh, fire, heat… It's a picture I won't forget my entire life."

Who could forget? The devastating aftermath of a suicide bomber detonating in a crowded bus is unforgettable. But what happens to the survivors of such indiscriminate and horrific attacks? Will the physical and emotional scars overwhelm them or will they be able to transcend the traumatic experience and lead healthy and fulfilling lives?

Many of those who survive are able to grow and thrive: "In the beginning it has to destroy you in order for you to survive; the fight is the crucial one and afterwards it's okay.…" "There is life after the terror act.…" "I became better in my head, in my soul, in my heart.…" "I can see much more clearly what is important and what is not important.…" "I can do everything in life; I have the power.…" "I can do it; I will do it.…" "I am a survivor, not a victim, of terror.…"

Listening to the very human stories of Jewish and Arab civilians who survived suicide bombings, shootings, and rocket attacks in Israel since the late 1990s, I heard distress and despair as well as hope and optimism. The powerful stories they shared gave order, structure, and meaning to their experiences and are testimony to their inner strength and determination.

The people I interviewed discussed their remarkable life journeys – from terrorism to hope and optimism and from grief to meaning and healing; they spoke not just of *moving on* with life as usual, but of *moving forward* with new purpose, contributing to society, and turning tragedy into action. They bear witness to their experiences in order to make sense of them as best as they can, and to help others understand the sources of their strength to survive.

While death and distress are all too present in these stories, the focus of this book is on *resilience* or *recovery* and *posttraumatic growth*, so that life after the event, at least in some areas, is somehow better than before.[1] *Living Beyond Terrorism* emphasizes that hope and meaning can be found after struggling with and surviving a terrorist attack – or any life crisis.

We can learn and be inspired by the stories of these terrorism survivors. The stories can help us meet the challenges in our lives and make choices that will help us live healthier, more purposeful, and more fulfilling lives.

My Story

My interest in terrorism survivors in Israel began years ago as I heard the extraordinary stories of Holocaust survivors, in particular those few members of my family who survived. More than thirty of my relatives – my grandmother's parents, brothers, and sisters, and their families, as well as six of my grandfather's seven brothers and sisters and their families, and numerous cousins – were murdered in Vilna, in what is now Lithuania.

Most of my family members who survived left Europe for Palestine or the United States in the early 1930s, including my mother's parents – Aharon Wirshup and Esther Judith Golomb Wirshup. They were ardent Zionists and moved to Jerusalem with their three children – Yisroel, Nachum, and my mother Dina. Their legacy includes six grandchildren, fifteen great-grandchildren, and eighteen great-great-grandchildren.

A few cousins remained behind and lived to tell their stories. Sima Shmerkovitz Skurkovitz documented her experiences in the book *Sima's*

---

1   Although the term is new, the idea that great good can come from great suffering is ancient, appearing in literature, philosophical inquiry, and religious thinking. The term *posttraumatic growth* was introduced by Lawrence Tedeschi and Richard Calhoun in the 1990s to refer to the positive psychological change experienced as a result of the struggle with a highly challenging life circumstance – a traumatic event of seismic proportions that severely shakes or destroys some of the key elements of the individual's important goals and worldview. It describes the experience of individuals who have developed beyond their previous level of adaptation, psychological functioning, or life awareness (Richard G. Tedeschi, Crystal L. Park, and Lawrence G. Calhoun, *Posttraumatic Growth: Positive Changes in the Aftermath of Crisis* [Mahwah, NJ: Lawrence Erlbaum Associates, 1998], 2, 3, 227).

Songs: Light in Nazi Darkness.[2] As a seventeen-year-old girl, she lived through the hell of the Vilna Ghetto and Nazi concentration camps but managed to survive without losing her humanity. Her singing gave hope to her companions in the terrible darkness.

Izaak Wirszup, his wife Pera, and her daughter Marina also survived the Holocaust. Izaak lived through the Vilna Ghetto and the camps and came out believing that he was spared in order to make a difference. He encouraged me and others to "try for the maximum." Out of their struggle came a survivor's love of life and a legacy. Izaak expressed it this way: "When you alone remain alive, you have to justify yourself. Pera and I have seen firsthand the desecration of life. We have witnessed the organized annihilation of millions of innocent, wonderful human beings. We have seen giants collapse – morally and physically – within days, when subjected to inhuman conditions. But we have also encountered people who would make any sacrifice, heroes whose like we had seen before only in the scriptures. We have seen how love, friendship, and help can transform the most fragile souls into individuals stronger than steel."

But my need and desire to understand Holocaust survivors – their voices, their faces, and their passions – went well beyond my own family history.

In the summer of 1995 I joined together with almost 375 people from different religions, generations, nationalities, communities, and social and professional backgrounds at the Turning Point '95 International Leadership Intensive[3] held in Poland at Auschwitz-Birkenau, the extermination and labor camps that had been liberated fifty years earlier.

---

2   Sima Skurkowitz and Norma Archbold, *Sima's Songs: Light in Nazi Darkness*, rev. and expand. ed. (Jerusalem: Christian Friends of Israel, 1993).

3   The intensive was sponsored by a French organization, ACC International Institute (Au Coeur de la Communication – At the Heart of Communication, now known as Learning as Leadership and based in San Rafael, California, http://www.learnaslead.com/). It is dedicated to creating healthy communication between individuals, families, and communities and to making a difference for all humankind, and was founded by a remarkable French woman, Claire Nuer – who survived the Holocaust as a hidden child and was a survivor (and ultimate victim) of cancer.

Together we confronted and explored how our individual, family, and social histories interacted with the dynamics and realities that helped make Auschwitz possible, and how we could apply the lessons of Auschwitz to our lives. Touring the camps with three survivors – two Jews and a communist resistance fighter – offered me a personal and concrete dimension to a tragedy that is still difficult to comprehend.

As a second-generation witness, I deeply sensed and identified with the horror and the pain. At the same time, I felt the hopes of those who had not only suffered such horrendous events, but who had thrived in spite of them. It became something that happened not just to *them*, but also to *us*! I came away with an important question: *How can we learn from our experiences to prevent genocide?*

The more I studied the Holocaust the more closely I examined my own reactions to what I learned. I noted that many of these people – survivors, resisters, and rescuers – shared their extraordinary stories in the hope of creating meaning from their experiences and making a positive difference in the world.

The lessons of Viktor Frankl, the noted neurologist, psychiatrist, and Holocaust survivor, as laid out in his autobiographical *Man's Search for Meaning: An Introduction to Logotherapy*, especially resonated with me. The book documents how personal strength, wellness, and other positive outcomes can result from the struggle with a trauma or life crisis. His humanistic and existential approach to psychotherapy – *logotherapy* – stresses the freedom to transcend suffering and the defiant power of the human spirit to make choices and embrace life.

Frankl wrote: "What matters is to make the best of any given situation" and to be optimistic "in the face of tragedy and in view of the human potential which at its best always allows for...turning suffering into a human achievement and accomplishment."[4] While you cannot control what happens to you in life, you can always control what you will feel and do about what happens to you. In other words, while we may not all find the "why" of our survival, there is strength to be found

---

4   Frankl, *Man's Search for Meaning*, 137–138.

in the search itself – in the actions taken, by loving another human being, and by the attitude one takes toward unavoidable suffering.

A trip to Israel in October 2002, at the height of the Second Intifada (Palestinian Uprising), helped me connect what I had learned about Holocaust survivors to Israel, Palestine, and the Middle East conflict. My husband and I chose to visit Israel for two weeks – a big step in those days of frequent terrorist bombings – in order to show our support for peace and to observe and experience firsthand what it was like to live with the threat of terrorism.

As I talked to family, friends, and new acquaintances and listened to government officials, tour guides, doctors, therapists, and terrorism survivors, I observed the strength of the human spirit to cope with tragedy and uncertainty. Once again, I reflected upon my earlier question: *How can we learn from our experiences to prevent genocide?* In addition, a new question began to take shape: *How can we move beyond the trauma of such an event?*

To answer these questions, I knew I had to listen more. So between 2004 and 2010 I traveled to Israel eight times for extended stays to collect the stories that make up this book. This experience strengthened my belief in the incredible power of the human spirit.

In 2004 I spoke with twenty-four survivors of terror acts and seventeen family members, bereaved family members, and injured soldiers. The twenty-four survivors made up the research study sample for my doctoral dissertation.[5]

In 2007 I revisited these individuals to engage them in an ongoing and widening conversation, to probe for changes in levels of functioning – positive and negative – and factors facilitating sustained or continued positive growth, and to learn the impact of the 2006 Israel-Hezbollah/

---

5   See Appendix A for an overview of the research methodology and findings, as fully documented in my doctoral dissertation "Finding Meaning and Growth in the Aftermath of Suffering: Israeli Civilian Survivors of Suicide Bombings and Other Attacks" (PhD dissertation, Fielding Graduate University, 2006), available at ProQuest/UMI Dissertations/Theses, publication number 3234197. See also Zieva Dauber Konvisser, "Themes of Resilience and Growth in Survivors of Politically Motivated Violence," *Traumatology* 19, no. 4 (2013): 292-302, doi:10.1177/1534765613477500.

Lebanon War.[6] Seven other survivors and bereaved family members were also interviewed. In addition, I interviewed fifteen Arab Israelis – Christian, Muslim, and Druze – who also directly experienced the effects of terrorism. In total, I interviewed sixty-three individuals.

In 2013 the individuals in this book were again requested to reflect upon and describe any important and meaningful changes that they might have experienced in their family, work, health, and/or outlook in life since the interviews.

These stories brought me back full circle to my original interest in understanding and knowing the voices, faces, and passions of Holocaust survivors who created meaning from their experiences and made a difference. Just as some stories of Holocaust survivors told of moving forward to extraordinary action, so have some of these otherwise ordinary people who personally experienced acts of terrorism shown that they too can prevail by the positive attitude and perspective they adopt in the face of tragedy. As Sima found light in Nazi darkness, they too demonstrate the power to light up the darkness of terrorism, refusing to allow the terrorists to stop their way of life.

Living Beyond Terrorism: The Stories

This book is a result of rigorous scholarly research and analysis of hundreds of hours of survivor testimony and thousands of pages of transcribed interviews, as well as detailed background questionnaires and survey responses. It contains thirty-six compelling stories, as told by forty-eight survivors and family members of survivors and victims primarily between 2000 and 2006. One story by a victim's family from 1996 is included because, as they told me, "for the people who are left behind, it's exactly the same thing."

In total thirty-three incidents are described (see Appendix B). In twenty-seven of them, ordinary people – riding in buses, dining in restaurants, shopping in markets, studying at college, visiting hotels, or walking along the street – suddenly find themselves victims of suicide bombings, shooting attacks, or rocket attacks in Israel and in the West

---

6   See Appendix A.

Bank. Four attacks killed or wounded soldiers. Two were the result of rocket attacks on northern Israel during the 2006 Israel-Hezbollah/Lebanon War.

As a researcher, not as a clinician or journalist, I was careful not to cross either of those lines but to document the stories as told in the voices of the survivors and families. As Henry Greenspan wrote in *On Listening to Holocaust Survivors*, "the sufficient reason to listen to survivors is to listen to survivors. No other purpose is required."[7] The stories explore how these trauma survivors understand what has happened to them and the meaning they take away from their experience. The accounts vividly portray the feelings, thoughts, and actions of these individuals before, during, and after the attack – their suffering and losses, and more importantly, their hopes and dreams and the sources of their strength to survive.

The stories are important both so that others know what happened and for further research so that we can understand and strengthen the factors that help people survive trauma. Telling their stories was therapeutic and, for most, it was an important way to obtain a measure of closure. In recording their stories and sharing them with us, the survivors provide living testimony to the importance of their lives and the lives of those they lost.

Listening to their stories affords us historic memory and connection. As Chaim Potok wrote: "Without stories there is nothing. Stories are the world's memory. The past is erased without stories."[8] This is what we have learned about the importance of collecting the stories of survivors of the Holocaust; so too shall these stories of survivors of terrorism be a reminder to the world that there should *never again* be a world that could breed another holocaust for any people.

Sharing these stories from the Second Intifada is still highly relevant and important ten years later. In Israel, every time the warning siren sounds or the Iron Dome leaps into action to intercept an incoming

---

7   Henry Greenspan, *On Listening to Holocaust Survivors: Beyond Testimony*, 2nd ed. (St. Paul, MN: Paragon House, 2010), 211.

8   Chaim Potok, *Old Men at Midnight* (New York: Alfred A. Knopf, 2001), 74.

rocket…or in New York when a bomber plans to leave a bomb in Times Square where sixteen hundred children are watching *The Lion King* at a nearby theater…or in Boston when a bomb-laden package is left at the finish line of the Marathon, a sports event meant to celebrate human achievement and not to destroy existence, we must remember that at the end of the day, they are all victims of terror. It doesn't make any difference that they were killed ten years ago or maybe two years ago, or in Jerusalem, Tel Aviv, New York, or Boston. For the people who are left behind, the pain is always there…and for the world, it's yet another example of man's continuing inhumanity to mankind.

Lessons Learned

In spite of the ultimate hope many of the stories inspire, they are also moving, heartbreaking, painful, and, for some, even overwhelming. As you read these compelling stories of finding meaning and growth in the aftermath of suffering, you will learn how these individuals *live next to* and *move forward with* their feelings of grief, pain, and helplessness, overcoming suffering and moving forward from terrorism to hope and optimism and from grief to meaning and healing.

While each story is unique, some common qualities that enable growth and positive outcomes evolved from the analysis of these stories. These important themes will be emphasized throughout the book and summarized in the conclusion:

- struggling, confronting, and ultimately integrating painful thoughts and emotions
- adjusting future expectations to fit the new reality and focusing on the important things in life
- calling on inner strength, core beliefs, and values
- staying in control and not falling apart
- moving forward with strength gained from past experiences and prior adversity
- grappling with fundamental existential questions through religion and spirituality
- staying healthy and focusing on body image

- finding the silver lining and creatively giving back – moving forward with action
- staying connected and seeking outside resources to help survive rough times
- telling their stories and making sense of their lives
- being hopeful, optimistic, and celebrating life
- discovering who they are

While it was difficult ten or more years later to revisit the traumatic memories of the attacks and the emotions that were evoked, these brave individuals have recounted both their struggles and achievements over time. While they may continue to suffer from physical and psychological distress due to their terrorism-related injuries and/or to the natural progression of their and their families' lives, they are doing their best to grow and flourish, as demonstrated by their pride in their blossoming families, their gratitude to God, their personal strength and vision, and their many accomplishments in various domains of their lives.[9]

A Tribute and a Responsibility

This book is a tribute to those who survived attacks with or without disability or loss, as well as the family members of those who perished. Their stories help to personalize and contextualize historical events, humanize the people who have survived or perished, and establish real faces in an overwhelming sea of facts and statistics. By telling and retelling their stories, we *celebrate their lives* as people – as human beings – not simply as players in a larger story or as numbers. By telling their stories we bear witness.

This book also honors and recognizes the many organizations – governmental, nonprofit, and medical – and individuals, both professional and volunteer, who provided loving care, services, and support to the survivors and families (see Appendix C).

---

9   The 2013 updates for those who responded will generally be found at the ends of their stories.

I have taken on the difficult task of gathering and sharing these remarkable journeys in remembrance of the past and as a responsibility to the future. While this book may be a useful tool for professionals and scholars working in the arenas of trauma and recovery, it is written for a more general readership to appreciate and learn from inspiring true-life stories of courage and hope and from the people who tell them. Although it is primarily about survivors of Palestinian terrorism and is an important addition to the recent literature on the Israeli-Palestinian conflict and the Middle East reconciliation and peace process, this book falls squarely in the tradition of Viktor Frankl's Holocaust memoir, *Man's Search for Meaning*, and its uplifting message applies to survivors of any devastating terrorist attack or genocide, including those in Rwanda, Darfur, and Congo, as well as to anyone struggling with a challenging life crisis.

I hope these stories of triumph and struggle will help all of us to understand how tragedy and loss is endured, remembered, and retold. And I hope these stories will shed a little light on someone else's path through a dark period of life.

Acknowledgments

Just as my personal story is about my parents' legacy of love of education, *tikkun*, and good deeds and the importance of Israel, family, and friends, I wish to acknowledge with deep appreciation the support that I received in all of these domains of my life from so many individuals, communities, and institutions who recognized, valued, and encouraged my research and traveled with me on this ongoing journey of exploration, personal transformation, reflection, and growth.

I am most fortunate to have been inspired by many wonderful people, including: my dear cousin Izaak Wirszup, who survived the Holocaust, believed that he was spared in order to make a difference, moved forward to make a significant contribution in his field, and encouraged me and others to try for the maximum; Claire Nuer, founder of Learning as Leadership, who survived the Holocaust as a hidden child and was a survivor (and ultimate victim) of cancer, and Learning as Leadership for inspiring and guiding my concurrent journey of personal mastery; and the sixty-three survivors and family members of survivors and victims of terrorist attacks, who shared their stories of hope and healing in order to make sense of their experiences as best as they could and to help others learn.

I am most grateful to the Fielding Graduate University community who were excited about and supportive of my research: my doctoral dissertation committee members for their caring and encouragement and for enriching my learning through their mentoring, guidance, and concrete help – Miguel Guilarte, Steven Schapiro, Thierry Pauchant, and Mark Chesler, and especially Laura Huggler for our weekly lunches and frequent phone calls learning from each other; Katrina Rogers, president of Fielding Graduate University, for her continued friendship, sponsorship, and support of my post-doctoral research; the many other members of the Fielding faculty, administration, and staff who shared their knowledge and insights; the students and alums who were with me at the different stages of my journey and enhanced my own learning process; and the Fielding Graduate University for supporting this research and writing by providing me with four student research grants and by appointing me a fellow in its Institute for Social Innovation.

My sincerest appreciation goes to my devoted cousin and research assistant in Israel, Hadassah Fuchs, as we searched for meaning together; my post-doctoral research assistant Ismaeel Hammoud, an Arab-Palestinian citizen of Israel, clinical social worker, and doctoral student, for his trilingual (English, Hebrew, Arabic) translations and transcriptions before, during, and after interviews, and for helping me understand and address unique cultural and relational issues and barriers within the Arab-Israeli population; my nephew Douglas Deutschman for simplifying the statistical tools and analysis; my transcriptionist Sharon Barker for her calmness and smiley faces; Tal Gutkovitch and Ronit Gill for transcribing and translating the last of the Hebrew interviews; and the international posttraumatic growth and logotherapy communities – including Richard Tedeschi, Lawrence Calhoun, Ryan Kilmer, Charles Carver, Stevan Hobfoll, Christopher Layne, Steven Southwick, Robert Barnes, and Gideon and Judith Millul – who welcomed me, answered my conceptual questions, and encouraged me to pursue our mutual interests.

Thank you to the Israeli trauma community – clinicians, researchers, and helping organizations – who warmly welcomed me, recognized the importance of my work, and supported me in numerous ways: Eli Somer and his colleagues and collaborators Eli Buchbinder, Miri Cohen, and Roni Gagin at the University of Haifa School of Social Work and Rambam Medical Center for their gracious help designing and conducting the pilot interviews; Arieh Shalev, Sara Freedman, and Yossi Israeli of Hadassah's Center for the Treatment of Traumatic Stress and Anxiety Disorders for their insights into working with and assessing terror survivors; Audrey Shimron, Barbara Goldstein, and Barbara Sofer of the Hadassah Offices in Israel for their dedicated support of Hadassah's lifesaving work in Israel and for introducing me to many of the study participants; Danny Brom, Naomi Baum, Ruth Pat-Horenczyk, and their colleagues at the Israel Center for the

Treatment of Psychotrauma for their ongoing support and for sharing their expertise on the theory and practice of trauma and resilience from the Israeli experience; Rivka Tuval-Mashiach, Tuvia Peri, Ruthellen Josselson, Amia Lieblich, and the late Dan Bar-On for their lessons on the narrative approach to understanding human behavior and meaning and the therapeutic value of storytelling; Roberta Bernstein *z"l*, Mooli Lahad, Alan Cohen, Mahmud Dawud, Rachel Lev-Wiesel, Rachel Dekel, Eleanor Pardess, Ofra Ayalon, Ilany Kogan, Alan Kirschenbaum, and Talia Levanon for their insights into coping with the trauma of terror; Daniel Gordis and my "soul sisters" Marie Therese Feuerstein, Liza Wiemer, and Donna Rosenthal, who walked similar paths capturing and telling the stories of Israelis touched by terrorism so that together we can make a difference; and many others who have made a tremendous impact on my work and life.

Many of these individuals continued with me on my journey to become an author and transform my research into this important book. Others joined me on this part of my journey: John Hoover and the members of our Book Proposal Writing Workshop (Suzanne Baer, Elizabeth Bewley, Mary Ellen Brantley, Katrina Burrus, Ruth Camp, Katherine Curran, and Belinda Hartnett), who helped me form, structure, and shape my ideas and develop them into a coherent book outline and proposal; Tom Huggler, Phyllis Heintz, and Barton Buechner for their reading and creative suggestions; Don Cohen, who helped refine and polish the words and ideas within the pages of this book and, with Israel advocate Neil Lazarus, reviewed the sections dealing with the historical facts of the Israeli-Palestinian conflict; Lynne Rabinoff for her belief in me and my work; and Ilan Greenfield, Lynn Douek, Kezia Raffel Pride, and my editor Tziporah Levine and indexer Fern Seckbach at Gefen Publishing House for recognizing the importance of this book and its message, for their intimate knowledge of the subject at hand, and for bringing the book to fruition.

Finally, and most importantly, I offer my deepest appreciation, gratitude, and love to my wonderful family who accompanied me on my journey: my husband Marc for his love and nourishment; my sons and daughters-in-law for their pride and for growing our family tree –

Aaron and Diana and Joshua and Juliet; my grandchildren – Madelyn, Natasha, Ellie, and David – for giving up some of their precious early years while Grandma was a student and an author so that they too will appreciate the importance of education, *tikkun*, and good deeds; and all of my family and friends at home, across the United States, and in Israel, who listened, loved, and were there whenever I needed them.

Introduction: The Human Impact of Terrorism

Terrorism and Politically Motivated Violence

I am sensitive to the fact that the topic at hand involves, at least, two subjective histories that are often highly politicized. My goal is to present these matters objectively in a nonpolitical manner. Above all, this book is about people – how they feel and think and act while struggling with horrific experiences – not about politics. Nonetheless, some may question how I use the terms *politically motivated violence* or *political violence* to describe the incidents in this book, or how and when I use the words *terror* or *terrorism*. Wherever possible, I use the actual words of the speaker or writer being quoted, such as the Hebrew word for an attack – *pigua* or *piguim* (plural) – or a more event-specific term – suicide bombing, shooting, or rocket attack. But the words *terror*, *terror attacks*, or *terrorism* are the best terms to use as this is how it is commonly understood, and because the terms best explain the psychological impact on the survivors of these events when describing the psychological aftermath of these events.

Although terrorism has been variously defined, it commonly refers to the intentional use of, or threat to use violence against civilians or against civilian targets, in order to attain political aims. By undermining the sense of security and disrupting everyday life, terrorism intends to harm the target country's ability to function and seeks to drive public opinion to pressure decision makers to surrender to the terrorists' demands. As a result, according to Boaz Ganor, "the population becomes a tool in advancing a political agenda in the name of which terrorism is perpetrated."[1]

---

1   Boaz Ganor, "Terrorism as a Strategy of Psychological Warfare," in *The Trauma of Terrorism: Sharing Knowledge and Shared Care; An International Handbook*, ed. Yael Danieli, Danny Brom, and Joe Sills (Binghamton, NY: Haworth Maltreatment and Trauma Press, 2005), 33.

For suicide terrorism, while the rationale may be diverse – with motives including hate, incitement, revenge, ease of delivery, religious or ideological zeal, and perhaps desperation – such attacks have come to be the preferred mode of operation of terrorists, with staggering consequences, based on "simply the fact that it works!"[2] Suicide attacks are effective because the perpetrator, more often than not, can choose the precise time and place of the attack, causing numerous casualties and damage to the innocent and focusing attention on the terrorists' cause. In addition, the inability of governments to effectively prevent such attacks is a blow to public morale.[3]

For this reason the most popular targets of suicide bombers are concentrations of people in small crowded public spaces such as markets or public transportation. A variety of methods have been used by suicide bombers to ram the desired target – explosive belts or vests, handbags, backpacks, or vehicle bombs carried in cars, trucks, aircraft, and vessels. To increase the killing and casualties, many explosives contain screws, bolts, nuts, nails, and steel ball bearings as shrapnel, sometimes coated with deadly or debilitating chemicals. Most of these methods require an electronic detonation device activated remotely or by the bomber.[4]

Countries with diverse populations and political systems have been targeted by terrorists, including India, Indonesia, Iraq, Israel, Kenya, Pakistan, Russia, Saudi Arabia, Spain, Sri Lanka, Tanzania, Turkey, the United Kingdom, and the United States. These assaults were largely carried out by Islamic extremists or secular national militants. However, no country has endured more systematic terrorism over an extended period than Israel.[5]

---

2   Ophir Falk et al., "The Suicide Attack Phenomenon: The Suicide Terrorism Threat," Institute for Counter-Terrorism, January 10, 2005, http://212.150.54.123 /articles/articledet.cfm?articleid=526.

3   Ibid.

4   Ibid.

5   Leonard A. Cole, *Terror: How Israel Has Coped and What America Can Learn* (Bloomington: Indiana University Press, 2007), x.

"*Hamatzav*" – The Situation

Since Israel's 1947–1949 "War of Independence" and acceptance by the United Nations, life in Israel has been characterized by a seemingly permanent state of conflict, marked by terrorism campaigns and, from time to time, full-blown war (See Appendix B for Chronology of Events). In the years following the start of the Second Intifada in September 2000, Palestinians have attempted thousands of attacks against Israelis – Jew and non-Jew alike, a wave of terrorism unique in Israel's history.[6] Most were prevented, but hundreds succeeded, including over 140 suicide bombings. Between September 2000 and October 2013, 1,236 Israelis lost their lives in attacks on buses, in restaurants, shopping malls, and even private homes, and thousands more were maimed or psychologically scarred for life.[7] In addition, 5,181 Palestinians were killed and 33,117 were injured in the West Bank and Gaza between September 30, 2000, and August 31, 2008, in events precipitating or following such attacks.[8] All of Israel's citizens and visitors have had to live with the day-to-day fear of suicide bombings, shootings, home intrusions, and rocket attacks.

"On the deepest psychosocial level," Julia DiGangi explains, "although the battles over resources and politics exacerbate the situation, the Israeli-Palestinian conflict is a struggle for existence and identity."[9] The search for identity creates a host of other psychosocial

---

6   Wm. Robert Johnston, "Summary of Terrorist Attacks in Israel," http://www .johnstonsarchive.net/terrorism/terrisraelsum.html.

7   Israel Ministry of Foreign Affairs, "Victims of Palestinian Violence and Terrorism since September 2000," http://www.mfa.gov.il/mfa/foreignpolicy/terrorism /palestinian/pages/victims%20of%20palestinian%20violence%20and%20 terrorism%20sinc.aspx. This figure includes eighteen Israelis killed abroad in terror attacks directed specifically against Israeli targets, as well as three American diplomatic personnel killed in Gaza. It does not include the nine IDF soldiers killed during the ground operation against Hamas terror in Gaza (Dec. 27, 2008–Jan. 18, 2009).

8   Palestine Red Crescent Society, "Total Numbers of Deaths & Injuries - West Bank & Gaza," http://www.palestinercs.org/en/reports.php?page=16.

9   Julia DiGangi, "Homeland, Helplessness, Hate, and Heroes: Psychological Dynamics in the Israeli-Palestinian Conflict" in *Terror in the Holy Land: Inside the Anguish of the Israeli-Palestinian Conflict*, ed. Judy Kuriansky (Westport, CT: Praeger, 2006), 4.

problems, including insecurity, anxiety, hostility, revenge, and humiliation. The imbalance of power between Israeli and Palestinian societies complicates reconciliation efforts. Yet, without reconciliation and peace, violence, and the fear of violence, will continue.

Terrorism's Psychological Toll

Modern terrorism, or politically motivated violence, is a form of psychological warfare and is essentially indiscriminate.[10] The actual victims are irrelevant to the perpetrators; what is important is what they represent. As a result, all individuals are instilled with the fear that the next attack may strike them or their loved ones. Terrorism erodes – at both the individual and the community levels – our sense of security and safety and challenges our natural need to see the world as predictable, orderly, and controllable.[11]

Acts of terror also provoke questions regarding the meaning of human intent, good and evil, faith, basic trust, and God.[12] Like other traumatic events, Ilene Serlin and John Cannon tell us, "It threatens our existence, shaking the foundation of who we are. It makes us face our basic helplessness and mortality.... It shatters our sense of coherence and meaning."[13]

According to Rony Berger, as a result, terrorism survivors must struggle with "assimilating the new and often frightening worldview with the old and familiar one, and...integrating the newfound fragile sense of self with the relatively secure one of the past. Overcoming these challenging psychological tasks is necessary...to achieve adaptive functioning, to maintain their well-being, and...to transcend their

---

10 Ganor, "Terrorism as a Strategy of Psychological Warfare," 34.

11 Jessica Hamblen and Laurie B. Slone, "Research Findings on the Traumatic Stress Effects of Terrorism," http://www.ptsd.va.gov/professional/trauma/disaster -terrorism/research-findings-traumatic-stress-terrorism.asp.

12 Danielle Knafo, *Living with Terror, Working with Trauma: A Clinician's Handbook* (Northvale, NJ: Jason Aronson, 2004), 3.

13 Ilene Serlin and John T. Cannon, "A Humanistic Approach to the Psychology of Trauma," in Knafo, *Living with Terror*, 314.

traumatic experience,"[14] As a result of this struggle, they may move from *victim* to *survivor* and *thriver*,[15] and even from *victim* to *victor*.[16]

Historically, Jewish people have had unique exposure to war and other lifespan traumas, e.g. pogroms, persecutions, wars, and ultimately the Holocaust. More recently, unprecedented national security threats in Israel have created a ripple of lingering worry and anxiety. Eli Somer et al. found that "even in those who have never been directly impacted by a terrorist act, terrorism creates varying degrees of anticipatory anxiety, fears of future harm to oneself or loved ones, and functional impairments, such as refusal to ride public transportation."[17]

Traditionally, an Israeli response to stress is reassurance: *Things will be okay.* But this reassurance is not effective when bombs go off on a daily or weekly basis and when parents feel that they cannot protect their children. In the face of terrorism, a new emphasis is placed on the here and now, for there is no tomorrow or next week. But focus on the

---

14 Rony Berger, "Early Interventions with Victims of Terrorism," in Knafo, *Living with Terror*, 237.

15 The use of the term *survivor* is sometimes controversial within Jewish circles; there are some who feel that *survivor* should be used only for those who have survived the Holocaust and not those who have survived terror acts. Although the terms *victim* and *survivor* are often used interchangeably, the terms *victim*, *survivor*, and *thriver* do reflect "attitudinal distinctions" (Glenn R. Schiraldi, "Appendix I: Victim, Survivor, Thriver," in *Post-Traumatic Stress Disorder Sourcebook: A Guide to Healing, Recovery, and Growth* [New York: McGraw-Hill, 2009], 394–395), as we shall hear in the self-identities expressed by many of the speakers in these stories. Schiraldi describes *thriving* as the "realm of living well" (Schiraldi, *Post-Traumatic Stress Disorder*, xii). Charles Carver defines *thriving* as posttraumatic growth, in which a person responds to adversity by not merely returning to the previous level of functioning, but surpassing it in some manner (Charles S. Carver, "Resilience and Thriving: Issues, Models, and Linkages," *Journal of Social Issues* 54, no. 2 [1998]: 246). Carver further describes psychological thriving as representing "a kind of growth: growth in knowledge, growth in skill, growth in confidence, greater elaboration and differentiation in one's ability to deal with the world at large" (ibid., 252–253).

16 Ofra Ayalon, "Healing Trauma with Metaphoric Cards," *Therapy Today*, 2007, 22–24.

17 Eli Somer et al., "Brief Cognitive-Behavioral Phone-Based Intervention Targeting Anxiety about the Threat of Attack: A Pilot Study," *Behaviour Research and Therapy* 43, no. 5 (2004): 677.

present ignores the long-term perspective, and people who may not be suffering at the moment might manifest problems later.[18]

As we will hear in the stories, responses range widely. Some people cope successfully with difficult situations, recovering within a short period of time and functioning normally. A minority of people, however, experience difficulties that linger and disrupt their ability to function. A wide range of ways to cope is also found. At one extreme, some people become numb to constant stress and avoid current events and news coverage. At the opposite extreme, others follow the news closely, hypervigilant and defining every move by the odds of an attack.[19]

Jewish-Israeli Responses

In the face of intense feelings of depression and helplessness, Israeli society and its people cope in several ways: they keep very busy and volunteer to help others, especially when an attack occurs; they become fatalistic and think *when my name is on the bullet, then it's my time*; they become numb to trauma, saying, *life goes on*; they neglect other suffering and/or trauma they may experience; they continuously search for new ways to deal with terrorism and work through the suffering; they respond with increased sensation-seeking and risk-taking behaviors; and they struggle with a disregulation of emotions, constantly seeking a balance between not feeling and feeling too much, which can result in increased intrafamilial and school violence.[20]

Although terrorism disrupts social, economic, and societal functions, evidence exists that the effect of the continuous threat of terrorism on many Israeli civilians is only marginal because individuals, families, and larger social groups have adapted their preparedness behaviors so as to minimize the impact. Israeli researcher Alan Kirschenbaum found that "the survival strategy against terrorism, like many other types of disasters, has been behavioral adaptation…reflected by the cognitive

---

18   Danny Brom, "Coping with Terror: Lessons from Israel," in Kuriansky, *Terror in the Holy Land*, 44.

19   Ruth Pat-Horenczyk, "Terror in Jerusalem: Israelis Coping with 'Emergency Routine' in Daily Life," in Kuriansky, *Terror in the Holy Land*, 68.

20   Brom, "Coping with Terror," 45–46.

acceptance that terror can be expected to continue to be part of daily life."[21] This coping mechanism of preparedness means strengthening their knowledge of emergency procedures, the expected reactions in themselves and in their families, and ways to help themselves and others. Preparedness is also emphasized at more societal and systemic levels, especially in schools, hospitals, and emergency rooms. Despite this preparedness, people cannot prevent suffering entirely.[22]

I am frequently asked *why do they stay* and *how can they put their children's lives at risk?* For Jewish Israelis, the State of Israel was founded as a homeland for the Jewish people. It represents "the hope of two thousand years, to be a free nation in our land, the land of Zion and Jerusalem," as expressed in "Hatikvah" (the Hope), Israel's national anthem. According to Daniel Gordis in *Saving Israel*, "it was hope that Israel restored to the Jews; and it is a hope that would be utterly lost if Israel ever succumbed;"[23] it is this hope that drives Israelis to live and raise their children in Israel, in spite of their fear. I have been told by Jewish Israelis: "It's the lifestyle...." "It's the habits...." "It's the culture...." And, in the end, "It is the safest place in view of all the anti-Semitism in the world, which is so close to what you hear about the Holocaust." Furthermore, they understand that "the goal of terrorism is to interrupt the mental balance and to disrupt the normal course of life," and therefore their resolve is even greater now because "moving is handing them the victory and I don't want to let them win."

Arab-Israeli Responses

Similar to the national narrative of Jewish Israelis, the Arab-Israeli story is permeated by loss and homelessness. One and a half million Arab Israelis make up 20 percent of the population residing within the internationally recognized borders of Israel. Although they are citizens

---

21   Alan Kirschenbaum, "Terror, Adaptation and Preparedness: A Trilogy for Survival," *Journal of Homeland Security and Emergency Management* 3, no. 1 (2006).

22   Brom, "Coping with Terror," 44–45.

23   Daniel Gordis, *Saving Israel: How the Jewish People Can Win a War That May Never End* (Hoboken, NJ: John Wiley, 2009), 14.

of the State of Israel with equal protection under the law and full rights to due process, nevertheless, feelings of discrimination and racism exist and may increase the likelihood of adverse reactions.[24] In addition, the vast majority are not well assimilated into Israeli society and have fewer psychosocial resources than Jewish society.[25] Jewish Israelis fare better than Arab Israelis in quality of life, rates of infant mortality, availability of medical services, socioeconomic status, education, and employment.

According to Alean Al-Krenawi and John Graham, "Palestinians living in Israel have experienced multiple losses – of homeland, political autonomy, economic livelihood, and hope – as well as pressures in daily life from long exposure to curfews and social exclusion."[26] They undergo daily inconveniences and hassles, as they may be scrutinized more thoroughly during routine security checks and may be considered as potential attackers. Additionally, Arabs may fear being targets of hostile reprisals by Jews should they be caught in the vicinity of an attack.[27] Al-Krenawi and Graham continue: "Feelings of worthlessness, helplessness, powerlessness, and being looked down upon, as well as sadness and fear resulting from the confluence of these inequalities, disturb the individual and the family and may plant the seed for resentment and anger toward their neighboring Israelis that inflames the Israeli-Palestinian conflict."[28]

While Arab Israelis also suffer from posttraumatic stress disorder (PTSD) and feelings of vulnerability and helplessness, they experience additional stressors that are not shared by Jewish Israelis. Palestinian Arabs are living in Israel in a society that is closely identified with

---

24 Marc Gelkopf et al., "The Mental Health Impact of Terrorism in Israel: A Repeat Cross-Sectional Study of Arabs and Jews," *Acta Psychiatrica Scandinavica* 117, no. 5 (2008): 2.

25 Sammy Smooha, *Index of Jewish-Arab Relations in Israel, 2003–2009* (Haifa: University of Haifa) in Stevan E. Hobfoll et al., "Trajectories of Resilience, Resistance, and Distress During Ongoing Terrorism: The Case of Jews and Arabs in Israel," *Journal of Consulting and Clinical Psychology* 77, no. 1 (2009): 144.

26 Alean Al-Krenawi and John R. Graham, "Inshallah, Family, Gender Roles, and Other Issues Affecting Mental Health and Therapy for Palestinian Arab Israelis," in Kuriansky, *Terror in the Holy Land*, 219.

27 Gelkopf, "Mental Health Impact of Terrorism," 3.

28 Al-Krenawi, "Inshallah, Family, Gender Roles," 219.

Western values, that affords them a comfortable and secure lifestyle, and where they are granted rights not given in Arab and Islamic nations. Many find it difficult to hold on to the Arab traditions, beliefs, and perceptions that have defined them.[29] As a result, according to researchers Marc Gelkopf et al., they may be affected by "acculturative stress felt when the traditional paternalistic Arab society faces the predominant Jewish culture and western democratic institutions."[30] Al-Krenawi and Graham add that some Palestinian Arabs in Israel "feel socially excluded, leaving them in a conflict of dual identity as both Israeli and Palestinian. Although they live in the State of Israel, their identification has been shown to be more nationally and emotionally connected with being Palestinian and with the Palestinians in the Occupied Territories," especially since many have relatives and family living there and in neighboring Arab countries.[31]

Many Arab Israelis also identify with the Palestinian Uprising (Intifada), creating a stressful dilemma of dual allegiance at personal and community levels.[32] Thus, they feel the pain of being attacked by other Arabs, who are their brothers, rather than by people seen as an external and natural enemy. In addition, while they themselves are under attack and experiencing a life-threatening situation, like the rest of the Israeli people, they also have to worry about relatives and friends who are in the same situation in the surrounding countries or in the Gaza Strip or the West Bank.[33] But, for many Arab Israelis as well, Israel is home. As they told me: "This is my house and my family. How can I leave Haifa, the nicest place in the world?"

---

29 Sammy Smooha, "Arab-Jewish Relations in the Jewish-Democratic State of Israel" (Hebrew), in *Trends in Israeli Society*, ed. Ephraim Yaar and Zeev Shavit, vol. 1 (Tel Aviv: Open University of Israel, 2001), 231–363.

30 Gelkopf, "Mental Health Impact of Terrorism," 2.

31 Al-Krenawi, "Inshallah, Family, Gender Roles," 218.

32 Gelkopf, "Mental Health Impact of Terrorism," 3.

33 Mahmud Dawud, in an interview with the author on October 31, 2007, and in an email message to the author on March 4, 2009.

Part 1

From Terrorism to Hope and Optimism

Life is inevitably stressful, and people respond to and manage life's stressors – particularly traumatic events, such as a serious accident, assault, natural disaster, or recent loss – with tremendous variability. Traumatic circumstances can have negative effects on our thoughts, create distressing emotions, produce negative changes in behavior, and have physical consequences. Most everyone who experiences a traumatic event will report temporary sleep disturbance, irritability, and a re-experiencing of the event through intrusive thoughts or nightmares accompanied by active attempts to avoid reminders of the event. For most people, these symptoms gradually disappear. For some severely traumatized people, time may not be a healer at all; the symptoms may persist and result in chronic distress and disruption of daily functioning (*posttraumatic stress*), and may adversely impact interpersonal relationships. They may never reach a state of resolution about their experiences, and instead may require intense therapeutic treatment.

However, within about two years after a major trauma, most people do not develop significant distress and functional impairment and have returned to their previous level of psychological functioning. They are able to bounce back after experiencing hardship and adversity and move on with life as usual (*recovery* or *resilience*).

For others, struggling with the crises in their lives can provide them with the psychological growth that would not be possible without the challenge of the traumatic event (*posttraumatic growth, growth following adversity*, or *thriving*).[1] Such positive changes can be manifested in several ways. While the encounter with a major life challenge may make us more aware of our vulnerability, it may also change our self-perception, as demonstrated in a greater sense of personal strength (*we have been tested and survived the worst*) and recognition of new possibilities or paths for one's life. At the same time, we may feel a greater connection to other people in general, particularly an increased sense of compassion for other persons who suffer; as a

---

1   Lawrence G. Calhoun and Richard G. Tedeschi, "The Foundations of Posttraumatic Growth: An Expanded Framework," in *Handbook of Posttraumatic Growth: Research and Practice*, ed. Lawrence G. Calhoun and Richard G. Tedeschi (Mahwah, NJ: Lawrence Erlbaum Associates, 2006), 5–6.

result we experience warmer, more intimate relationships with others. An altered sense of what is most important is one of the elements of a changed philosophy of life that individuals can experience. A greater appreciation of life and for what we actually have and a changed sense of priorities of the central elements of life are common experiences of persons dealing with crisis. We may also experience changes in the existential, spiritual, or religious realms, reflecting a greater sense of purpose and meaning in life, greater satisfaction, and perhaps clarity with the answers to fundamental existential questions. We may move forward with action as we search for meaning and understanding of the event's significance in our lives.

For most people, the aftermath of trauma produces a mixture of such negative and positive experiences[2] – and continuing personal distress and growth often coexist.[3]

How each individual experiences a traumatic event, ascribes meaning to it, and takes action is a result of their personal characteristics, past experiences, present context, and physiological state.[4] Some factors appear to be risk or vulnerability factors for poor adaptation; others seem to confer protection or enhance one's ability to successfully negotiate the experience without long-term psychosocial disability; and still others can either support or undermine resilience depending on their quality or quantity.[5] While no single factor or magical combination ensures a positive outcome, certain psychological, behavioral, social, ecological, biological, and spiritual factors have been shown to enhance stress resilience and growth.

---

2   Lawrence G. Calhoun and Richard G. Tedeschi, "The Foundations of Posttraumatic Growth: New Considerations," *Psychological Inquiry* 15, no. 1 (2004): 93.

3   S. Cadell, C. Regehr, and D. Hemsworth, "Factors Contributing to Posttraumatic Growth: A Proposed Structural Equation Model," *American Journal of Orthopsychiatry* 73, no. 3 (2003): 279–287.

4   Carol S. Fullerton, "Shared Meaning Following Trauma: Bridging Generations and Cultures," *Psychiatry* 67, no. 1 (2004): 61–62.

5   Lisa D. Butler, Leslie A. Morland, and Gregory A. Leskin, "Psychological Resilience in the Face of Terrorism," in *Psychology of Terrorism*, ed. Bruce Bongar et al. (New York: Oxford University Press, 2007), 412.

A useful analogy is of trees facing strong winds. Some trees remain standing, undisturbed (*resistance*), while others may be snapped in half (*distress*). Trees that bend to accommodate the wind may, or may not, recover and resume their original upright positions (*recovery*). Other trees change shape to accommodate the winds or make the tree resistant to breaking in future wind storms (*reconfiguration*). Some trees may be destroyed, yet still have the capacity to nourish new growth, while others are lifeless. The composition of the tree – soft and pliable like a willow, or hard and rigid like an oak – and the tree's environment – availability of water and nutrients, composition of the soil, or presence of other trees that might buffer the wind – also significantly impact whether or not it survives.[6]

In these chapters we meet ordinary people riding in buses, dining in restaurants, shopping in markets, studying at colleges, visiting hotels, or walking along the street who suddenly find themselves the victims of a terrorist attack. Their stories reflect several possible patterns of change in response to the trauma of the terror acts, ranging from those who survive with impairment (as in *posttraumatic stress*), to those who bounce back after experiencing hardship and adversity and move on with life as usual (as in *recovery* or *resilience*), to those who move forward, surpassing what was present before the event (as in *posttraumatic growth, growth following adversity*, or *thriving*). A few report little change in their life or outlook (*stress resistance*), and some continue to struggle (*living the attack*).

---

6   Based on an analogy presented by Stephen J. Lepore and Tracey A. Revenson, "Resilience and Posttraumatic Growth: Recovery, Resistance, and Reconfiguration," in Calhoun and Tedeschi, *Handbook of Posttraumatic Growth*, 24–30.

Chapter 1

Jerusalem of Gold

a mosaic of cultures, nationalities, peoples, and
neighborhoods, of old and new... innocent lives destroyed

Jerusalem, the capital of Israel, is located in the heart of the country, nestled among the Judean Hills. The city's ancient stones, imbued with millennia of history, and its numerous historical sites, shrines, and places of worship attest to its meaning for Jews, Christians, and Muslims. Jerusalem's more recent drive for development has encompassed almost every sphere of urban life, proclaiming its hope for the future: many hotels have been erected; neighborhoods have been renewed; dozens of public parks have been planted; and synagogues, churches, and mosques have been restored or built. Modern malls and a number of industrial zones have been developed and several new suburbs have been built on the city's periphery.[1] Yet in the heart of this peaceful city and the surrounding communities, terrorism has struck. Universities, yeshivas (schools for studying Jewish texts), buses, cars, pedestrians, malls, and restaurants have been targeted for attack and innocent lives destroyed in more than sixty fatal attacks between October 2000 and April 2013 – twenty-two of them in 2002.

---

1 Israel Ministry of Foreign Affairs, "Jerusalem, Introduction," http://mfa.gov.il /mfa/aboutisrael/state/pages/jerusalem.aspx; and Israel Ministry of Foreign Affairs, "Jerusalem, Living in Jerusalem," http://mfa.gov.il/mfa/aboutisrael/state /pages/living%20in%20jerusalem.aspx.

Although no place in Israel was completely safe, Jerusalem bore the brunt of the suicide bombings. In this chapter, survivors of attacks in Jerusalem, between February 2001 and September 2003, tell how they cope and move forward with their lives. They are a diverse group of Jerusalemites. Sonia Dibeh is a Muslim woman; the others are Jewish. American-born Sarri Singer alternates living between New York and Israel; American Peggy Kern was visiting her daughter and son, who live in Israel; Shoshana Gottlieb was born in Israel, raised in Africa, and returned to Jerusalem; while Shai Ben Tzur is a lifelong Jerusalem resident.

In Chapter 2, three students at the Hebrew University Mount Scopus Campus in Jerusalem share their stories; and in Chapter 3, we hear from four other survivors of attacks while they were on their way to and from their homes or work in the outlying communities around Jerusalem. In Part 2, we hear the stories of another group of people with ties to Jerusalem – people who tragically lost loved ones in attacks on "the Children's Bus," in the Sbarro Pizzeria, hiking near their homes, driving along the highway, and defending their country.

The remainder of the book is devoted to attacks in the coastal cities of Tel Aviv, Herzliya, Netanya, and Haifa and in more rural areas throughout Israel and the West Bank, including Judea, Samaria, and the Lower Galilee.

Shooting attack on the road from the Atarot Industrial Park:
February 27, 2001

Shoshana (Shoshi) Gottlieb: Victim or Survivor?

"Every bullet has its address."

S hoshi is a fifty-four-year-old happily married woman, mother of four and grandmother of five. A poised, beautiful woman with sparkling eyes and infectious laughter, her life was changed forever by a senseless and horrific terrorism attack. Suddenly, and seemingly effortlessly, she manages her family, household, and job from a wheelchair in her spacious handicap-accessible apartment in Har Nof, a newer community on the westernmost tip of Jerusalem.

Her daughter Rinat best describes Shoshi: "Mom, when you are sitting by a table when we talk to you, it's just like you are the same as everyone else. No one can see there is something wrong with you."

To which Shoshi quickly adds: "I told you that there is nothing wrong with me, even though I understood in the van the minute I saw my legs what was going on. The minute I went to rehabilitation, I started rehabilitating. I won't let anything take over my life. I haven't given up anything. Even walking I haven't given up. I still hope maybe Christopher Reeve's people will find some cure."

She tells her story. It was a normal workday and Shoshi, an import-export manager at a chemical company, and seven other people were on their way home from work in the Atarot Industrial Park on the outskirts of Jerusalem. The industrial zone, located at the edge of an Arab village and right on the border of the Palestinian Authority, was meant as a forerunner of the "New Middle East": Arabs and Jews making money together, not war. Some two hundred companies opened operations there, about forty of which were Arab-owned. Many companies abandoned the park as their employees, many of them Arabs from Jerusalem and the West Bank, experienced gunfire and stonings while driving to and from their jobs.[1]

As usual, Shoshi was running late and dashed into the van with her bins of work to continue at home. Shoshi's husband Eli had packed her a big breakfast of vegetables and fruits, which she hadn't had time to eat at work. She started to eat an orange as the van traveled along the perilous Jerusalem-Ramallah Road.

"Something attracted my attention to the window next to me. I looked sideways and I saw a hole in the window. And then I heard glass breaking from the window behind me. I was sitting at the back. I remember I didn't get up. I was still bent over and I just looked but I couldn't see anything. And then I heard a hollow shooting sound. I was thrown backwards. My legs were pulling me downwards. I said I'd been shot and gave out the phone numbers for my husband, my home, and my sister. And then I just felt peaceful. I felt no pain. I was wearing black so you couldn't see any blood. I didn't scream or shout out. I'm not the type that screams."

Shoshi was the only one in the van who was physically injured. Her spine was completely severed by a bullet; today she is paralyzed from the waist down and wheelchair bound. Her wound healed within two weeks and then she spent eight months in rehabilitation. Her life is changed forever. Nevertheless, she is able to find meaning and growth, not in the tragic event, but in her life, in her deeds, in her choices, and from her past experiences.

Throughout her life, Shoshi's challenge has been to take up whatever comes along and live with it. She has thought a lot about her past experiences and weaves them in to explain her current story. She was born in Israel to parents who were Holocaust survivors. From them she learned important values – how to be decent, never selfish, open, charitable, quiet, patient, considerate, accepting, and how to love learning, reading, and working. She passed these values on to her own children as well. Her later childhood and adolescent years were spent

---

1   Larry Derfner, "An Intifada Casualty Named Atarot," http://www.jewishjournal .com/world/article/an_intifada_casualty_named_atarot_20010323/.

in Africa, where her father worked for an Israeli construction company. As an observant Orthodox Jew in a secular community, she had a lonely and difficult life. "I knew that this was how it had to be," Shoshi says. "We were different. Many things made me a tougher person as I learned to accept things because of the way of life we led." Always a believer in God, she knew what she wanted – to go back to Israel, marry a religious person, and raise children – and that is what she did.

Three years after the attack, Shoshi described how she was strengthened by her life experiences, her connection to God through prayer, her future vision and goals, and especially by her love for her family. She appreciates and lives life to the fullest and understands herself, as well as what is important in life and what is not. She makes choices that will move her forward in a positive way and takes responsibility for her choices.

As soon as she left intensive care, she asked her husband to bring a prayer book and her makeup. "When the doctors came for their rounds, I was already sitting there – hair combed and makeup on, smiling like nothing had happened. We were five women in a room and you should have seen how slowly one started putting on lipstick and another started putting makeup on her face. Every time they saw me they would say, 'Shoshi, just looking at you, it makes our day.' The doctors used to laugh at us. We were the merry room. Because whenever they came in, all of us were painted."

She admits, though, that she sometimes cried in private. "I woke up every morning about four o'clock and I said my prayers and I cried my heart out. By the time the nurses and doctors came, I was already smiling and I never told them that I cried at night. I thought, 'Let them think whatever they want. It's my affair.' But it took a few days until I was okay."

Shoshi feels no need for help from psychologists, social workers, or self-help groups. "In the hospital, I did not want a psychologist to come near me. I always looked at him as someone who needed counseling, not me. And I had a social worker in the hospital. Actually I didn't need her but she had to open a file." The social worker warned her that she would break down one day, and she responded, "We'll wait and see." She is still waiting!

Shoshi expresses herself through tears and by talking. She always found someone to listen to her – her father, her husband, her children, her audiences, and most importantly God. Her belief in God is critical to Shoshi and gives her a lot of strength, as she describes: "Before the *pigua*, I did not pray as much as I needed. Suddenly I had a lot of time and it really helped me. Praying opens up my eyes and relieves me. It gives me a lot of peace. And it comes naturally, not because I have to do it, but because I want to do it. I love praying and find meaning in every word."

Shoshi's family also gives her a lot of strength. She sees her children and grandchildren in a new way: "Having my family around me, I learned to appreciate them much more. I look at them openly. Before, I accepted them. Today I appreciate and enjoy my children and my grandchildren much more. It's not that I spend more hours with them or I talk to them more than before. When they walk into the house, I *see* them. When I look at them, I look into them, not at them from the outside. I look deeply into their souls and that's what gives me joy."

As a result, she learned a lot of things about her family – "things that I would have never known existed in them. There is so much character in my children. It really surprised me to think I would have never known about it. Also my husband, he is so strong. He says he gets strength from me. But I feel that I get my strength from him. Maybe it's mutual."

Shoshi takes from her life's experiences the importance of human encounters, relationships, and love. She has a greater appreciation of life. "Life goes on as usual in all respects. It doesn't matter what I feel inside. I try not to burden my family. I said to myself that I have to continue being a mother to my family. They look up to me and if I fall – and it is very easy to fall after such a thing – but if I fall, I carry with me my whole family and I don't want a depressed family. I want us to continue being a happy family just as before."

So she overcomes the many logistical hurdles to attend all of her children's school functions. One time, the celebration was three floors down – thirty steps – no elevator. She briefly considered not going. "And then my son came home from school and said, 'Mom, you're coming today – we'll take the *scalamobil*.' It's adapted to my wheelchair and it climbs up and down steps. So I said, 'If my son wants me to go so much, I have to go.' So I went and I didn't regret it for a minute."

Shoshi exudes determination, optimism, and hope. Her acceptance is remarkable. She views life with a positive attitude, after being confronted by an unchangeable fate, and accepts what cannot be changed. She chooses to confront past trauma and current tormentors. One of her sons, Moshe, was born with Down syndrome. She treats him like any of her other children. Encouraging him to move forward helped her prove to herself that she could survive – and even thrive: "Maybe once or twice I asked myself, 'Why did it happen to me?' And then I thought of my son, when he was born. I thought I had given birth to a monster. At that time people didn't take the babies home; they were given up for adoption. One of my doctors said, 'Before you decide what you want to do, just spend one hour with these children.' These were the exact words I wanted to hear. I wanted to hear someone say something positive. I took him home, and you should see that boy. Wherever he is, he changes the place for the better. I am proud that God chose us to have such a child and that, through him, we are able to make a better world. What I went through with him made me a stronger person. When this happened to me, I thought, 'Okay, I already went through a hardship before and I survived. I'll survive now, as well.' And that is how I look at life."

She accepts her own limitations and misfortune, "which is very difficult. I do have my ups and downs. But learning to accept the way you are is very important." And she accepts that suffering is necessary to gain valuable knowledge and grow character: "I thought about the other women in the van with me and I know each one of them personally. I thanked God it happened to me and not to one of them, because I didn't believe that any of them would have taken it the way that I did. I never said, 'why did it happen to me and not to this one or this one or this one?'"

Shoshi believes God plans everything and that she was chosen by God for a reason, not by coincidence or by chance: "When the attack happened to me, I said, 'Okay, this is what has to be, then this is what will be.' Maybe twice, I thought maybe it was a punishment but I couldn't remember doing something so wrong that I would have deserved it. I believe it just had to happen. I believe that every bullet has its address. And it doesn't matter where I had been sitting, if it was inside or by the door or in the front next to the driver, I would have been the one that would have been injured. You either believe or you don't believe."

"God chose me, so I accepted. I decided that I have to go on with life. I have my family. I have my children. I have my son in the army. I have grandchildren. And I hope I live to see my children and my grandchildren happily married."

Concentration camp survivor and psychiatrist Viktor Frankl taught – and Shoshi demonstrates – that one of the possibilities for finding meaning in life is by creating a work or by doing a deed. She has a strong work ethic and considers work as something precious. She believes that "work and studying is a cure for all of a person's illnesses."

After eight months of rehabilitation in the hospital, Shoshi came home and immediately went back to her old job, working from home. "I will never give up work unless they fire me. I love my job. I think that on the day that I'll feel that I don't want to take any more responsibility, I'll call my boss up and tell him that I want to quit."

Since the event, she better understands her priorities: "One of the good things that happened is that I now know what I want to do, not what I have to do. I enjoy reading a good book, watching a film, studying, and doing creative things – like painting, stained glass, and ceramics – just something for myself. Sometimes I have so much work, but now I can say to hell with it. I prefer to do something else – I'll do it later."

Shoshi attended some support groups for a while "as a supporter, not as someone being supported, to help whoever needs me." She continues to be available by phone and in person. "I am willing to talk to the children, so that they will see how I live normally, how my children go to all the outings, and how we never stop living." And she shares her story with individuals, organizations in Israel and abroad, media representatives, and other survivors as an inspiration and to raise funds for worthy causes. "It is really wonderful whenever I see people who want to do so much and to give and to be with us."

Shoshi fights for what she believes she is entitled – and what will improve her quality of life and independence – even though it's "hard to fight for my needs because I don't like it when they say no." She convinced Beit Halochem – the Center for Disabled War Veterans – that, as a victim of terrorism, she should be allowed to use their wheelchair-accessible swimming pool because "swimming is one of the things that really helped me recover and because there I feel free. I feel like everyone else. And that sense of freedom is important for me and for every person who is injured."

Later, she convinced Bituach Leumi – the National Insurance Institute of Israel – to provide her with a motorized wheelchair. At first they refused because her hands were healthy. She disagreed because her neighborhood is built on a mountain and trees are planted in the middle of the pavement. She told them: "As much as I exercise, I'm not twenty years old or a man and it is tough. You want us to be independent. My independence is going wherever I want, seeing whatever I want, and not having someone push me from behind. I want my husband and my children beside me, to talk to me, not behind me."

Shoshi demonstrates that distress and growth can coexist. Life may be beautiful, but it saddens Shoshi that she no longer feels the same joy. "On the outside, I smile and I laugh and I am with everyone. But I did lose some of my joy of life. Things excite me, but not as before. But I take it as a fact. I learn to live with this life." Her health, the possibility of inheriting her father's diabetes, and her inability to exercise are concerns; she doesn't want to be a burden on her family. As a mother, she worries about her family, especially about her army-officer son, and about everyone else's son in the army – and the ongoing threat of terrorism exacerbates her fears.

The long months of recovery and the years since the attack have allowed Shoshi time to reflect on the events in her life and to discover who she really is. She first recognized that she was a survivor, not a victim, when she visited the United States Holocaust Memorial Museum on a speaking trip to Washington, DC. She was inspired by the children of all backgrounds who were there as part of their school studies. They were a sign to her that people will not forget. As she was looking at a photograph and thinking about her parents, she was struck by the thought that "in Israel, they call them 'survivors' of the Holocaust – *nitzolei Shoah*. So why am I a victim? And it was there at that instant that I decided to regard myself as a survivor of terror."

Shoshi experienced inhumanity but does not hate. Neither do her children know what hatred is. She never felt the burden of the Holocaust. Of her parents, who lost all of their family in the Holocaust, "never, ever, did we hear any sound of hatred towards the Germans. Even today, I find it very hard to believe that such cruelty existed at that time, but my parents never brought it into the house. They brought us up as a happy family." She also does not hate Arabs. "We had Arab neighbors with whom I grew up until the age of ten – Arab neighbors and Arab friends. There was never hatred."

Shoshi makes sense of her life in the aftermath of the terrorist attack and moves forward with her life. She is healing. In the face of overwhelming disaster, this otherwise ordinary woman calls forth, from the depths of the human spirit, courage she never knew she possessed; she finds meaning from her deeds, experiences and attitudes, and turns tragedy into triumph. She has become a survivor!

Twelve years after the attack, Shoshi continues to be a proud mother and is now the grandmother of seven. Last year, both her sixty-one-year-old husband, Eli, and her thirty-one-year-old son, Yoel, graduated law school, studying together in the same class at the same university. Eli continued his studies and earned a Master of Laws; and Yoel completed his internship, is a lawyer, and is studying to become a battalion commander in the army. Her youngest son Yair was in an army aviation course and is now taking an officer's course in a special army unit.

Sbarro Pizzeria bombing, downtown Jerusalem: August 9, 2001

Peggy Kern: Gail's Story

"Hashem (God), let us live!"

P eggy (a pseudonym), seventy-eight, was visiting her son and her
daughter Gail and their families to attend a grandchild's wedding
and await the birth of a great-grandchild. Gail suggested they have a
day to themselves, do some visiting, and eat out for lunch. "She said,
'You like fast food, let's go to Sbarro Pizzeria.'"

The pizzeria, on the corner of King George Street and Jaffa Road in
the center of Jerusalem, was filled with lunchtime diners, most of them
children and young mothers, enjoying the beautiful summer day. Peggy
and Gail went up to the counter and chose their lunch. Gail said, "I'm
going to go over and get a drink and pay and you go up those three steps
to a little place where we can eat." Peggy had the tray in her hand when
a terrorist, Izz al-Din Shuheil al-Masri, a twenty-three-year-old resident
of the village of Aqaba, north of Tulkarem in the West Bank, dressed as
a tourist and carrying explosives in a guitar case, entered the unguarded
restaurant just before 2:00 p.m. The five- to ten-kilogram (10–20 lb.)
bomb, packed with nails, screws, and bolts, exploded and completely
gutted the restaurant. Fifteen people, including seven children, were
killed and 130 were injured inside the restaurant and on the busy street
outside.[1]

---

1   In most of the stories, as in this story, the basic facts about the terrorist attack –
date, location, numbers killed and wounded, and information about the terrorist
– were retrieved from the Israel Ministry of Foreign Affairs website and its
links to articles within the MFA Library: "Suicide and Other Bombing Attacks
in Israel Since the Declaration of Principles (Sept 1993)," http://mfa.gov.il
/mfa/foreignpolicy/terrorism/palestinian/pages/suicide%20and%20Other%20
bombing%20attacks%20in%20israel%20since.aspx.

This is the story of Peggy and Gail, who survived the attack; in Chapter 11 we hear from Arnold Roth, whose daughter Malki and her best friend Michal Raziel were killed in the same attack.

Peggy heard "not like what you think of, but a whistling whoosh, which lifted me off my feet. I didn't know that I lost my shoe at the time. I didn't know what had happened. I thought that an oven had exploded. So I said to another woman in Hebrew, '*Ma kara?*' (What happened?). She answered, '*Zeh pigua*' (It's a terrorist attack). I said, '*Ma zeh pigua?*' (What's a *pigua*?) 'I'm American.' And she said, 'A bomb.' I said, 'A bomb?… Hashem (God), let us live!'"

Peggy was so disoriented that she headed back inside towards the counter. Gail saw her and led her out of the fiery restaurant through the shattered windows, climbing over the carnage and the dead bodies, including the dead bomber. "I slipped and my other shoe came off. The bottoms of my feet were all cut. And my daughter who weighs about what I weigh, about ninety-five pounds, picked me up – I don't know how – and took me across the street."

From down the block a man came and brought her a pair of shoes from his store. "He said, 'Here are shoes for your feet – you can't walk like that.' He gave me the shoes and said, 'Don't return them. They're for you.' Whenever I feel like I'm getting a little off track, I pick up these shoes and they just remind me what my life is about."

Peggy suffered from terrible ringing in her ears and hearing loss and now wears two hearing aids. The reality of what happened took a few days to set in. At first, Peggy remembers feeling that "it wasn't real. Everyone asked me how I was and I told them that I was okay. When my husband called from the United States after he heard about the bombing on television, I said, 'Oh, I'm fine,' as I was spitting out concrete." She did not realize how traumatized she was until, on the flight home, she was frightened seeing an Arab woman with her head covered and holding her baby in the seat next to her. She burst into tears. "The flight attendant took me like a little baby and said, 'You don't have to be scared to fly, but we happen to have seats in first class – we'll give you a seat there.' And I said, 'I'm sorry, I overreacted. I was just in a terror attack.'

"Emotionally, of course, it affected me very badly, but much more my daughter than me. She will not take a bus. She will only take a cab. She prefers to be at home rather than go out. But she has developed new talents. Just beautiful different things that are absolutely amazing to me." Peggy tells her own story so that she can speak about her daughter, Gail, and how she came through two terrible tragedies in a short period of time – the Sbarro attack and the loss of her thirty-two-year-old son a year later in a car accident.

Although Gail felt that she did not need or want counseling, when the Ministry of Health called and invited her to come to a group session, she went. The participants went around the circle and spoke about how they felt since surviving an attack. When it was Gail's turn, she said, "I see something missing here. I've listened to all of you and you all said the right things. 'I'll be a better person.' 'I love my family more.' But nobody mentioned the word Hashem, that He brought us through this. And to me that is very upsetting." With that, Gail picked herself up and walked out, even though she still was very fearful. After that she did go for counseling, and it did help her.

Peggy continues Gail's story: "About a month after it happened, a cousin saw that Gail was just so lost. She asked her if there were things that she had wanted to do since she was a little kid and had never gotten to do, but that she might be interested in. She said, 'Yeah, I wanted to play the piano.' So we bought her a piano and she takes lessons. She plays beautifully. And she said, 'Mommy, I could play all day if I had time. I love it.' I am very happy that she got that piano."

Peggy herself is full of the joy of life. She is sustained by her own faith and religious background and attributes her positive attitude to "a very great faith in Hashem. I think by it. And I live by it. I pray every morning with meaning, intention, and understanding that what I say is so important. I think that as I get older, I have more of a feeling of what this life is about and what I can do about it. Even if things fall short, I do try." She prays to Hashem to let her continue to live and to do more in life because "He gave me life. I am seeing children, grandchildren, and great-grandchildren. And I think I have much to be thankful for."

She thinks that she became a little more spiritual since the attack. "I think about it so much more – not specifically Sbarro – but about where I am in this world and what I am up to and the life that He has given me. It may not be just about the attack. It may just be age to think that way. But Sbarro definitely was like a stop. Not fear, but much more awareness of one's questions: Where do I go from there? What will happen? And much more awareness and much more thankfulness of what I have. I mean that to see, to hear, to breathe, to think, to walk – they are such gifts!"

Peggy's personal strength also "comes from a very wonderful, very strong, and very loving family. My mother was born in Baltimore in the 1880s and married my father who was from Russia and traveled, selling merchandise to the farms around Maryland. When we started getting older and there were no yeshivas around and we had a *rebbe* who taught us all, he moved the whole batch of us to New York – and he came only for Shabbos (the Sabbath)." Although the family now is spread apart, "it never took away this closeness – this wonderful togetherness. That is just very, very special."

Peggy's first husband died of a heart attack after twenty-two years of marriage and ten years later she married her second husband, Shimmy, a rabbi and an old family friend who "sat on my father's knee to learn the *aleph-bet* (Hebrew alphabet)… So when we got married, it was like a joy for everybody because they all loved him so." After the attack, Peggy was helped by Shimmy, "my great and understanding husband – but he became more fearful for me, even though I'm not more fearful. If I go out at seven o'clock at night to visit friends down the block, he says, 'Could you call me when you get there?' I say, 'Shimmy, I'm not a little baby.' He says, 'I'll feel better.' So I say okay."

Between marriages, at age forty-five, Peggy went to college and became a nursery school teacher, worked for the Head Start Program, and directed a nursery program at the local yeshiva. "Then I retired and then I started again and then I retired." In her eighties, she was still teaching English reading in the Title 1 program for first grade boys. "I go to school every day and am able to use my mind. I walk through the halls and sing to myself, 'I'm the oldest person here. I'm the oldest person here.'"

Widowed again from her beloved husband in 2012, Peggy has celebrated her ninetieth birthday and is "doing very well. I am thankful that I can do and see and think and walk and talk. Thank the Lord, everything He gives me is a gift. I still look at the shoes sometimes and remember… and want other people to understand the impact of such trauma." Peggy just returned from a family wedding in Israel and Gail is enjoying her growing family of children and grandchildren. "She is doing just fine, but still does not go on buses."

Suicide bombing, Jaffa Road, Jerusalem: January 27, 2002

Sonia Dibeh: Quiet

"You have power, intelligence, and you can overcome."

S onia, a twenty-nine-year-old Muslim woman who was born and lives in Jerusalem, had a doctor's appointment in downtown Jerusalem. After the appointment, she and her friend decided to shop at Freiman & Bein, a well-known shoe store on Jaffa Road. The store is just meters away from the sites of two earlier incidents at the Sbarro Pizzeria and at the bus stop where two women were killed and forty people were injured when a Palestinian terrorist opened fire with an M-16 assault rifle on January 22, 2002.

Less than a week later, just as Sonia entered the shoe store, Wafa Idris, a twenty-eight-year-old, divorced Red Crescent paramedic from the Am'ari Refugee Camp in Ramallah, detonated more than ten kilograms (22 lb.) of explosives outside the store. Idris, the first female suicide bomber in the Israeli-Palestinian conflict, killed herself and eighty-one-year-old Pinhas Tokatli and injured more than 150 others.

Sonia recalls the explosion and its aftermath: "I was very close when the bomber exploded. I saw everything flying. People were injured. I saw the body of the woman who exploded herself. It was in my eyes. I was afraid to run away." The police closed the street. "I was very afraid of two things: of the *pigua* itself and of the Jewish people in the store who knew that I was an Arab. I was the only Arab person there and the Jewish people started to shout at me. I wanted to run away from the place." Somehow, after thirty minutes, she was able to leave, found her car, and went back to work.

Even before the attack, "we worried that a bus would explode next to us" and after the Sbarro explosion, "we thought about not going places." A social worker in Talpiot, Sonia worked with the Shekel Association, assisting disabled people in the community with housing, employment, and enrichment groups. "My work with the Jews was *b'seder* (fine). I liked them and they liked me. I worked with them for eight years and it was truly okay – meeting together, traveling, all kinds of things. But after the *piguim* started, my Jewish colleagues started to distance themselves. Although they told me *shalom*, *shalom*, it was especially difficult when there was a terror attack."

After the *piguim*, the clients also started looking at her differently. "*Aravi*, *Aravi*, (Arab, Arab,) they called me. I was very strong. I told myself that it doesn't matter if they call me an Arab; they should relate to me as I am. So I continued." But after two years she had had enough and started working with Arab clients at Caritas Jerusalem – a humanitarian and developmental organization representing the socio-pastoral services of the Catholic Church.

Sonia was traumatized by the *pigua* and was treated by a psychologist. "I suffered from difficulties in sleeping and I had hallucinations. Every loud voice shook me. If I went in a bus or even if I was near a bus, I was afraid. For more than a year I was afraid to go to Jaffa Road. What had happened and what I had seen was in my head all the time. It took me one year in therapy until I was able to talk about it." The therapy helped her. "Now I know what I want from my life. Now I am stronger than I was, not only because of this accident, but also because many things in my life changed. This experience taught me many things. I used to be afraid of people, now I don't let others intrude, I can set boundaries. I passed this period and continue my life, thank God, and hope for better."

While Sonia gets her strength "from myself and from the psychologist, who told me all the time that I should continue and not stop, my family helped me a lot. My mother is like that too, and my father also is strong. He gives me advice and talks to me, and he's someone I can listen to."

She does not think about why it happened to her. "Many people experienced that; I thanked God that it was easy for me compared to others who became disabled." Although she is not religious, she believes. Meditating in a quiet place also helps. "When I go to the sea, nature, or a place with a lot of greenery or flowers, it helps me a lot. I like the quiet – to sit and to think – to look at the sky and the ground below." After the *pigua*, she moved back to her family home in Ramallah, where "there's a good atmosphere and you can look out from our house at all the trees, as opposed to Jerusalem where it's all houses." But then she moved back to Jerusalem.

Telling her story is very difficult. "All the time I try not to think about it and I want to forget this time. What can I do? It's part of my life. I can't forget it. I can't cut it out. But it is good to remember that something happened, to remember how I used to be and how I am now with my life." She did many good things in her life after the attack. "I took many courses in mental health. I changed my job to work with people who were exposed to accidents like these – inside the family or outside. I said, 'I can't die. I should continue. I can't live with anger and depression.' I continued with my life. I have more patience. I take the time to do things in a normal way." On the other hand, she is more cautious. "I try to thoroughly check people around me – if I know them, whether they're good or bad. I don't believe everyone. I'm suspicious."

At work, when Sonia meets with somebody who was traumatized in his or her life, "my message always is that there are difficult things in life and that we should get through them and we should continue. Even with my friends who have crises, I tell them, 'You can't stop; you have power, intelligence, and you can overcome.' I never tell them that I was in a *pigua*. I say that I experienced many difficult things, not the specifics, and I go on." Sonia learned many things about herself from this experience – how to be stronger, and to know her weak points, how to cope with the weakness, and how to reinforce the strengths. She envisions a future in which she will marry and have children.

Eleven years after the attack, Sonia is going through a difficult period. Her mother recently suffered from cancer and "left me for heaven," her father remarried while her mother was in the hospital, and two of her sisters were divorced and came to live with her. Sonia was at the hospital with her mother all the time. Now, "I'm feeling lonely and started working another afternoon at Caritas as a social worker because I can't stay alone without anything to do. I can't remember the good things, except maybe good friends who are still with me and make it easier for me." Although twice men asked her hand in marriage, neither succeeded; she still wishes to marry and have a baby, "but it seems that

God does not allow this yet." On the one hand, "many times I ask God to finish my life because I can't feel any sweetness or goodness in my life"; but on the other hand "I thank God for everything, whether it is bad or good."

Egged bus no. 14 bombing, downtown Jerusalem: June 11, 2003

Sarri Singer: OneFamily, Strength to Strength

"Survivors healing survivors"

S arri worked a few blocks away from the World Trade Center in New York on September 11, 2001, and had she not overslept, "I would have probably been down there, but because I wasn't downtown, I also didn't experience the trauma that a lot of people did who were there. New Yorkers are amazing; they came together and people moved forward. You get back to normal life, but you will always remember what happened." Nevertheless, the event was life-changing for Sarri and, at some point, "I really decided that we're not safe anywhere, so I would move to Israel to help victims of terror and to try and find different volunteer opportunities."

Eighteen months after moving to Israel, Sarri was working in Jerusalem as an administrator in a post–high school program for girls and volunteering for a number of organizations, including OneFamily Overcoming Terror Together.[1] "I went out to the cafés. I went to the mall – everything that every normal person does who lives there. I wasn't on vacation. I took two buses to work in the morning and two buses home. I didn't think of anything – not at all. I was like on speed mode. I did everything. I never thought twice."

When she closes her eyes, Sarri clearly sees the events of June 11, 2003. She had left her office to meet a friend for dinner at Café Hillel on Emek Refaim, the main thoroughfare of the German Colony neighborhood in Jerusalem. She didn't have enough cash for a taxi, so she took a bus to downtown Jerusalem and waited to catch another bus to meet her friend. "The bus was running late and people were antsy and they wanted to get on the bus already and get home. At one point

---

1   OneFamily Overcoming Terror Together, http://www.onefamilytogether.org.

I contemplated taking a cab and stopping at the ATM, but as I went to hail a cab, I saw the no. 14 bus come. So I got on the bus… I was really tired and I saw the last two seats open in the front section of the bus. Usually I would sit on the aisle seat so that I would get up if somebody got on that was older than me and needed to sit. But for some reason, I sat down next to the window – a choice that I know saved my life."

As she called her friend to tell her that she was running a few minutes late, a Palestinian suicide bomber, dressed as an ultra-Orthodox Jew, boarded the bus. He detonated his explosives just outside the Klal building on Jaffa Road in the center of Jerusalem, killing sixteen people, including all those seated around Sarri, and wounding over one hundred. It was one of eleven attacks on buses or bus stops in the Jerusalem area between 2001 and 2008, in which over one hundred people were killed and hundreds more wounded.

Sarri continues her story: "As I went to put my phone into my knapsack, I felt a huge shockwave hit my face as the explosion tore through the bus. My head felt like two pieces of metal that hit so hard against each other that they made my body vibrate. I didn't think that it was a terrorist attack. I thought maybe somebody hit me with something or we got into a bus accident, but the last thing I thought was that someone boarded the bus strapped with explosives to injure and murder innocent people. I remember immediately shutting my eyes – an instinct that saved my sight. I couldn't open my left eye at all – something had hit it, probably from the bus, and it was already swollen shut. I could barely open my right eye, just enough to see the roof of the bus that had fallen in. And then the moment of eerie silence that followed the blast – a silence so frightening of those who were dead in every seat around me. The first thing that I did was to try to feel my face because I wanted make sure everything was there. Then I remember screaming really loud, 'Oh my God! Oh my God!'"

One of her rescuers was a volunteer for ZAKA, a humanitarian volunteer organization responding to tragic incidents in Israel. "He heard the blast and he started running. He yelled to me that I needed to get out of the bus and I said I couldn't. But he and another gentleman were able to pull me out through a small opening. Luckily I was screaming because a few minutes later a small fire broke out and it was hard to know who was alive and who wasn't... They brought me to the side of the road, where I remember an old woman sitting with me, holding me as I was burned, bleeding, and frightened, until Magen David Adom (Israel's national first-aid and disaster-relief organization) came to take me to the hospital. A lot of people say that the experience is not quick, that it's like slow motion. I felt like everything happened very quickly."

Sarri was taken to Hadassah University Hospital–Ein Kerem. "They are unbelievable. The doctors and nurses are amazing." Pieces of metal and glass went through her left shoulder, breaking her clavicle bone; both her legs were cut and bleeding; her face was bruised and burned; and both eardrums were blown out from the impact of the blast. "When I got there, I didn't want them to call my parents in the United States because I wasn't really able to hear anything." So she waited until a friend came and then spoke with them. Since her father was New Jersey State Senator Robert Singer, she received a lot of media attention, but wasn't treated differently. "The hospital arranged a press conference with about thirty international television stations and newspapers. They didn't let anyone show any of my face on any of the cameras when brought into the hospital – the victim is the first priority. Everyone is treated the same, and everybody's story is important." Her father and brother arrived the next afternoon. Sarri asked her mother not to come. "I didn't want her first trip to Israel to be a reminder of a hospital and the attack."

She was released from the hospital after a week and a half and stayed in Israel for an extra five days "just because I didn't want to be afraid to go back to Israel. I went out for about an hour each day – to lunch, to the malls, to a store. And then the last day before I left, a friend took a walk with me up Jaffa Road. I wanted to go back where the attack had happened and I didn't want to be afraid to walk there. So we went there and I lit a candle and said some *tehillim* (psalms). I think it was very good that we did that."

Sarri spent three weeks back in the United States, ironically traveling with twenty Israeli victims of terror whose visit to the United States she had been arranging. "I wasn't supposed to be on the mission.

Unfortunately I was on the bus in Israel and now I was injured as well."
They traveled around the East Coast and spoke in different communities,
including her own community, "which was very difficult. We had an
event with victims of 9/11. We had a meeting with New York Mayor
Giuliani. We tried to join together because we are trying to help each
other with the emotional trauma of going through any kind of terrorist
attack. And we spoke in Washington to some congressional leaders."

At first, "it was so new and I wanted people to understand better. Until
it happens to you or somebody that you can relate to, it doesn't hit home
as much. And being that I am very involved in the Jewish community,
people felt more connected. I think the speaking was something to let
people know that 'yes, I was injured but life goes on. The Jewish people
are so resilient, and we see throughout history how we have been beaten
down but we've never been killed out.' I wanted people to know that I
had been injured but that wasn't going to stop me from being in Israel
and it shouldn't stop them either. I just wanted people not to be afraid.
And the only way for them not to be afraid was for them to hear me
speak about my own story so they would understand what really was
going on."

On September 3, 2003, Sarri returned to Israel to her job and "a
normal way of life," but she was still afraid of getting back on the bus.
"I took on a second job to pay for my cabs." She still felt a little bit of
anxiety, hoping that it would go away with time. However, she finally
decided that, "okay, I need to deal with what really went on because
the scars are there and they are permanent. But how you decide to deal
with it is the issue and so my answer was that I am not going to let it
eat me up." It was not until 2012, however, that Sarri was finally able to
overcome her fear; she boarded a bus and sat on the exact same seat as
nine years earlier for two stops down King George Street.[2]

She thinks of herself as a survivor, not a victim. "I don't let the attack
define who I am. It was something that happened in my life; it was one
incident, but there is so much more about me than just the attack. And

---

2   Hadassah United Kingdom News: "Sarri Singer Takes the Bus Again,"
    http://www.hadassahuk.org/news.asp?intID=199.

I think that a victim or survivor can't let the attack define them because that will destroy them. It will destroy their life." Furthermore, she was not going to succumb or be overcome by fear or anxiety because "then that eighteen-year-old Palestinian accomplishes what he wanted to. And that was a big motivation for me to go back to Israel. I don't want anyone to tell me that I can't be there. And I don't want to give in to that fear. I refuse to succumb to hate, because the only thing hate achieves is the destruction I witnessed on that tragic day. I will not let this experience destroy me or drive me to do terrible things out of the need for revenge. I've moved on, but not past it. It's a part of my life, but it's not going to take over my life completely."

Right after the attack, Sarri had seen a top psychologist, a trauma specialist in Israel "and he seemed to think because I was so vocal about what was going on that I was fine, psychologically. I didn't have flashbacks or nightmares. However, I didn't have any survival skills. I don't think that I was dealing with things properly then because of the media attention." Later, she worked through the trauma with another psychologist to clearly understand and articulate her pathway to recovery. In the beginning, she moved into action to do something for Israel and did not realize that she had been traumatized – "I felt that I had something bigger to do than deal with the actual trauma." But then she recognized that she was suffering from slight posttraumatic stress disorder. Finally, she started thinking of herself, not about everyone else, and saw a therapist in New York (and continues to see her as needed) to treat the PTSD "which is something that just doesn't go away." She also continues dealing with some attack-related medical issues – "thank God, nothing visible" – repairing a piece of bone pushing on a muscle in her shoulder and correcting her teeth that were shifted by shrapnel. She still has pieces of shrapnel in her mouth, but it would be more traumatic to remove them.

Overall, it has been much worse for her dealing with the physical effects and limitations than with the emotional effects "because we all have things that we go through in our lives that are emotional, from childhood up. So I think that emotionally we are able to cope very well – the human brain, the human body, is able to cope with emotional trauma and emotional stress. Somehow we are able to bounce back from things. It's something that happened and life goes on." She acknowledges, though, that it might have been different if she had seen something in the attack, been more seriously wounded, or had survivor's guilt "because it is really hard to digest when a family member or a friend doesn't make it and you do. Thank God, I was not with anyone that I knew on that bus. I think the hardest thing about the situation is that everybody around me was killed."

Since the attack, she has become close with the family of one of the people who did not survive on her bus – Alan Beer, who was originally from Cleveland, Ohio. His nephew, Uzi Beer, has become a close friend from this experience and Sarri has spent time with Uzi's parents and grandmother – Alan's brother and sister-in-law and mother. "It was the first time I felt survivor's guilt, seeing this woman missing her son, yet telling me the first time she met me how happy she was that I was still alive. It's hard to visit her, but I visit whenever I'm in Cleveland and see the pain that still exists every day for this family who lost someone who was so loved and contributed so much to the lives of so many people."

Sarri does not feel that she has changed since the attack because "we are constantly growing and constantly changing and constantly trying to better ourselves" so this is just a part of that continuous growth process. She reflects that she probably is "stronger and a little more aware and less naïve. I definitely have less patience than I used to have and I am definitely more emotional than I was before the attack – but not too different in terms of things I did and involvement in projects and programs and helping. That's always been something that I love to do."

She was raised with certain values and ideas which were strengthened after the attack. "I think I have more motivation and more of a desire to just keep doing – to live up to whatever potential I'm supposed to have. It's taught me that life is very precious and we don't know how much longer we are going to be here. Obviously I have a larger purpose here and there's more that I need to be doing." Her own family and friends have always been priorities, but now she spends more time with them. She tries "not to worry about the smaller things. I look at the bigger picture and try and just relax more." She is more motivated to do something meaningful, although she does not know if these new priorities are related to the attack or to moving to Israel, where a different value is placed on life.

Looking back, Sarri had a great support system. "What helped me is my family and friends and the fact that I probably have really strong genes from my parents." She also had five amazing friends in Israel when the attack happened – the "Lions," as someone called them – protecting her night and day. "Your support system, upbringing, the environment, where you live, and your coping skills all add up to how you get through something traumatic. Those are the things that will either get you through it or keep you in that victim stage."

In addition, Sarri's faith as an Orthodox Jew helped her get through this period "because of who I am." She does not focus on why she was spared. "I think that everything that has happened until now was supposed to happen and these are the events that were supposed to be. I do question it at times." She also believes that "God put me in a certain situation to do something positive. Obviously, I'm still here for a reason. So I want to make sure that I'm living up to whatever I'm supposed to be doing while I'm still here. I have to keep going and moving."

She also believes that "every Jewish person has the responsibility to help somebody else." In return for the incredible kindnesses shown to her, Sarri is determined to live her life showing kindness to others. Although it was hard, she has taken groups to the hospital and visited survivors of other attacks and their families. "I think it's important for them to know that people care. Unfortunately, we share a bond of something that we'll have for the rest of our lives. And unfortunately, only when you've been through it can you truly understand it."

For Sarri, speaking about the experience is very therapeutic. She has told her story many times, speaking at least on a weekly basis, for Hadassah, OneFamily, and to a lot of kids. As a result, she tells her story in detail, vividly and insightfully, and with lots of laughter throughout. Most importantly, she believes her storytelling has to come from the heart. "I think that what strikes people is the sincerity of the story. When I speak about it, they really understand what I'm saying and they connect to it and relate to it. It reinforces that this is what *we* need to be doing, it's not just what *you* need to be doing."

Sarri was always committed to community service, social justice, and social change. She has tried to take that difficult time and put it to something positive. The attack reinforced "the idea that we have to be doing more." As an American who has been in a terrorist attack in Israel, her personal mission is to bring awareness and understanding of what is happening in Israel and all over the world to others, especially Jewish youth. She hopes to help them develop into future leaders of this country and encourages them to take responsibility for the Jewish homeland.

A year after the attack, Sarri returned to the United States as the East Coast director for OneFamily, working between seventy and ninety hours a week, speaking multiple times weekly, and traveling many weekends. After two years, she finally realized that her body does not function the same way as before the attack and that she had to stop. Leaving OneFamily gave her the sense of "wow, I need to be doing more for myself because this is not what life is about. After being through something so traumatic, you have to take advantage of every second. And I wasn't taking advantage, I was just working and working and not doing anything for myself and not spending time with friends and not going out. And I was just constantly busy with work."

Now she is working at Touro College in New York City, as Assistant Director of Career Services – an opportunity to give back to her alma mater and to guide students in life and career options. Although she still prioritizes the organization, she finds some time to take care of herself – going on vacation, getting a manicure or pedicure, having a free weekend – to just "veg out and enjoy."

In addition, to feed her passion for helping others who like her survived terrorism, Sarri went on to found and direct Strength to Strength,[3] a nonprofit organization based in New York City and dedicated to supporting victims of terrorism and their families. The organization brings together victims around the world and assists with

---

3   Strength to Strength, http://stosglobal.org/.

long-term psychological needs, enabling victims of terrorism to share experiences and empowering them to live life to their best potential and move forward with their lives despite the trauma they have been through. Their motto is *survivors healing survivors*, because "that is what it's all about. It's about knowing that somebody else went through what you've gone through and that they are moving forward in order to ease a little bit of what you've been through. We just want to help people – people who can't help themselves or people who are having a hard time." Having the support of others is the best way that victims of terror can get support and know that they are not alone. "The best way for victims of terrorism to combat the hate that we experienced is to live our lives and move forward."

Sarri has learned many things throughout this journey "and the most significant is to remember what is most important in life, our family and good friends, to never take anything for granted… and to make sure to get rid of things that are not good in our lives." Through her work, she believes that she needs to set an example. "You can't let the terrorists win. If you become that victim, you let them win. So the only way to combat it is to strengthen and heal people and the best way for us to do this is together. Then we'll win the fight."

Café Hillel bombing, German Colony, Jerusalem:
September 9, 2003

Shai Ben Tzur: My Way

"Enjoy your life now."

On September 9, 2003, the Israeli news broadcast warnings that a terrorist had infiltrated Israel; within the space of six hours, a total of sixteen people were killed and over eighty wounded in two suicide bombings. Both bombers were from the village of Rantis in the West Bank and studied together at Bir Zeit University in Ramallah. At 5:40 p.m., one of the bombers, wearing civilian clothes and carrying a leather bag containing a three- to four-kilogram (7–9 lb.) bomb, got out of a car at the hitchhiking post for soldiers outside the main entrance to the Tzrifin army base in central Israel and blew himself up. Nine IDF soldiers were killed and thirty people were wounded.

A few hours later, at 11:20 p.m., a second suicide bomber tried to get into a Pizza Meter restaurant on Emek Refaim Street, but was rebuffed by a security guard. So he went into the crowded Café Hillel next door, where the guard at the entrance to the café tried to prevent him from entering. The bomber managed to get inside before exploding his bomb, killing the security guard and six other people and wounding fifty others, including Shai. Among those killed were Dr. David Appelbaum, who headed the emergency room at Shaare Zedek Medical Center and had often been among the first to reach and treat terrorist attack victims, and his twenty-year-old daughter Nava, who was to have been married the following day.[1]

---

1   This was the third Jerusalem restaurant targeted in a little over two years. It followed the attacks on the Sbarro Pizzeria on August 9, 2001, and the crowded Café Moment at the corner of Aza and Ben-Maimon Streets in the Rehavia neighborhood on March 9, 2002, where eleven people were killed and fifty-four injured when a suicide bomber exploded around midnight on a Saturday night.

A few minutes before the bombing, Shai, a thirty-five-year-old single lawyer, met a friend at Café Hillel. "When we approached the coffee shop, the guard asked me to remove my car from the entrance because he said there had been many warnings of a terrorist in the area, trying to explode himself in a coffee shop." His friend found a table and Shai had just paid for his order at the counter. "As I was bending down to sit, I heard a terrible noise." He was hit in the shoulder by a screw that lodged dangerously close to the main artery and another screw that went through his leg. The change in air pressure from the explosion caused temporary deafness. His whole body was shocked, he couldn't move, and he was very tired.

As the pressure subsided and he regained control, Shai made life-saving decisions for himself and his friend. "I decided to go outside because I thought that there may be another bomb. And I was frightened that the roof was going to cave in. I felt that I could walk. So I stood and I took her with my hand. I told her not to look at the bodies. People began to scream and to panic... We went out from the back of the coffee shop and I sat on the ground, a short distance from the coffee shop." What he thought about first was his brand new car, so he went to the front of the café and told someone to move it. "After that it took us two days to find the person with the keys."

Shai was taken by ambulance to Hadassah University Hospital–Mount Scopus and later transferred to the Ein Kerem facility for surgery. While he was in the hospital recovering from an infection in his leg, he met with dignitaries, was interviewed for television and radio "and a lot of groups came to my bed to speak to me, because I think I was the only one injured who could speak English."

Although he had a few meetings with the staff of the post-trauma department, "I was tired of thinking about it all the time. It was too heavy. I wanted to swallow it by myself. I didn't want to speak about it. It was something private. I wanted to get over it my way. I didn't want someone to push me to his timetable. So I think I dealt with it in my time – step by step." Speaking more impersonally to groups about the attack was helpful for Shai. "I think that because it was light and it was general, it was better for me. And it also helps me now to speak about it."

Shai is more nervous and tense now and when he hears a loud noise, "my whole body is shaken for a while, but in general I came back to regular life. I'm trying, I think successfully." The attack gave him a greater appreciation of life. "It's something that shocks you. It's a time for you to think about everything that is connected to your life, to your society, about the nation, about my place in my nation. If you are just staying in a hospital, you have to think about everything and it slows your life for a while. The little things that used to be important to me are no longer as important as they were."

The attack has affected Shai's faith. "I am a little less religious in my mind, but I try to pray in the synagogue every day – something that I never did before. I used to pray in a synagogue only once a week, on Shabbat. I'm less Orthodox and I pray not in an Orthodox way, but in a Shai way – my way. I don't know why, but praying in the synagogue every morning has given me a lot of energy."

He believes in enjoying life more fully and not to think – or feel – too much: "I'm not saying not to work or do anything, but don't think too much because you can't rule everything. You must enjoy your life now." Shai does not delve deeply within himself or with his loved ones to avoid hurting himself and them. He avoids talking to friends and family about the attack "because I knew they were going to take it very strongly. And I was afraid that maybe they can be hurt only by the knowledge that something could happen to me. After the attack my father was panicked and very angry about everything. I think part of him was shaken. He was in the army before 1948, but it's different when it is your child."

Shai had a girlfriend before the bombing. "This is one of the things that I lost after the bomb. I like my life the way it is. I would like to have a family, but I don't think I would like to pay for that." He is concerned about bringing children into the world to suffer. "So many others can do that instead of me. I'm probably going to do that, but I don't see it as important after the attack, because if I died and was married, my children probably would suffer and wouldn't have any father."

Instead, in the years following the attack Shai directed his energies towards work and altruism. He is grateful that he was not wounded seriously and could "start work quickly and build my office. So it's not just a matter of money, it's a matter of my professional life or death." After the attack, he volunteered to speak with Hadassah groups, represented OneFamily of London to raise funds for building a reception hall at the Abu Kabir morgue for the families coming to identify the bodies of victims, and participated in activities with Hineni, another helping organization. He found meaning in doing these good deeds, providing emotional and instrumental support for others in return for what he had received. "I felt that after I passed such an event, in which I could probably have died, it's nice to volunteer and to donate something to the community in which I'm living. Also I saw many volunteers when I was in the hospital and met many people who came to speak and support me and others. I thought that I would like to be part of this holy work. If I can help in something, it's my pleasure."

In the past, "if I had the time, I was resting. Today, if I have the time, I'm trying to find where to share the time in order to help people and organizations." Instead of setting things aside to do in the future, now he does not wait and does whatever he wants. "Events like this give you a red light; it's saying this is the time, you could have even missed it. So I'm doing whatever I want to do. I'm not waiting for anything. I am not ashamed to think more about what I want to do in my private life. I am more determined to do the things that I want to do. I stopped taking cases that I don't believe in, that are not interesting to me. And I think it's even made me stronger in a way."

Four years after the attack, Shai's focus and career have shifted – maybe or maybe not as a result of the *pigua*. He no longer has his own law firm. "I am more nervous today and I don't have energy for people like I used to. I don't like to be pushed to do things on a schedule. And now, thank God, I don't have to deal with it because I am doing other things." He is working in a lawyer's office helping his retired father with his construction business. "After the bombing, it was hard for me to keep my clients and he offered me to help him manage his business. So I don't have someone on my head, no clients, no boss. My father is very flexible with me. He also trusts me, but for him it is more important that I feel good. And it is good for me also... In life sometimes things go that way. It's not something that you can predict. So maybe the *pigua* helped me in a way to change something. I am enjoying it and hope it is for the good." He does not know if the change is because of the *pigua*. "I don't observe myself every day and wonder whether what I'm doing is connected to the bomb or not connected. Maybe it's also because I'm becoming older."

On January 23, 2011, Shai was dancing traditional and Yemenite dances with no show of disability, laughing as he was held high above the crowd on a chair, holding one end of a napkin, with the other end held by his bride, Yehudit, an auburn-haired sabra from a Polish-Jewish family.

Chapter 2

Hebrew University in Jerusalem

a place of learning and understanding... an attack against Western democratic values and open institutions

Since opening in 1925, the Hebrew University in Jerusalem has a long history of promoting cooperation and coexistence between Jews and Arabs. On Thursday, July 31, 2002, the peaceful environment was shattered by violence when an Arab construction worker from Jerusalem placed a bomb packed with shrapnel among Arab and Jewish students having lunch in the Frank Sinatra Cafeteria on the Mount Scopus campus. Nine people – four Israelis and five foreign nationals – were killed and eighty-five injured, including the three students whose stories are told in this chapter. They reflect the diversity of the university community: Dror Sullaper made *aliya* (the immigration of Jews to Israel) from France; Ariela is a lifelong Jerusalem resident; and Roza is a Muslim woman.

Suicide bombing, Hebrew University Cafeteria: July 31, 2002

Dror Sullaper: The Path of Resuming Life

"In the beginning it has to destroy you in order for you to survive... and afterwards it's okay."

D ror, thirty-one, was studying for an MA in political science and teaching French and political science. That day, he had an appointment for lunch with another young student from France, David Gritz, who had arrived in Israel ten days earlier. David had a scholarship to study Jewish thought at the Hartman Institute and Hebrew at the Hebrew University and was with an Italian girl, Angela, who had a similar scholarship. Dror describes what happened next: "When we arrived at the cafeteria we took our plates, and on the way to our table I stopped to talk with Diego Ladowski, a student from Argentina who had made *aliya* ten years before. He was also a young Israeli diplomat and was supposed to go to the Israeli Embassy in Peru ten days later. He was sitting near his former girlfriend, an Israeli from France. As I was about to wish him *b'te'avon* (enjoy the meal), a bomb exploded."

Dror understood right away that it was a bombing "because of the noise and because I saw that I was full of blood. I didn't feel my right foot. I had the feeling that it was hanging loose. So I told myself, 'Okay, it's a bombing. I'm alive, but I'll have to live with one leg.' At that very moment, David fell over like someone who has lost consciousness. I was of course in a state of shock. I didn't dare to move. I thought that if I turned my head towards the bomb, I would regret it because maybe I would see horrible things. Nevertheless, the curiosity was stronger, and I turned and saw Diego lying on the floor."

Shrapnel hit Dror in his leg and chest and he lost four centimeters (1.5 in.) of leg bone. The shrapnel also tore his esophagus and just missed his main artery, which would have killed him. As he was being anesthetized at Hadassah University Hospital–Ein Kerem, he remembers "seeing a kind of white light and feeling very good. I didn't feel it was a near-death experience, but the strange thing was that I thought to myself, if this is dying, it's not so bad, it's nice." His stay in the intensive care unit "was maybe the worse time of my life because I had physical pains, in spite of the morphine. But the really awful thing in the intensive care unit was the atmosphere of the other people who were injured or in critical condition. I couldn't complain myself because they suffered much more than I did."

He also remembers feeling "like a baby without any strength or defense" and being dependent on nurses, relatives, and his parents. He was most helped by visits from close friends and family, as well as people that he hardly knew and many officials, including the President of Israel. "I had a big opportunity to trust so many good friends, including a friend who stayed every day until the moment that I fell asleep. But when the night came and the visits were not allowed any more, I really had a feeling of solitude and of despair and it was very hard." He also remembers fondly that "a very nice and beautiful nurse took care of me in a very special way; it was really kind of a cliché – the one who was wounded in a kind of war and a beautiful nurse."

For Dror, "it was a very strong experiment in feelings. The bombing was an example of how some human beings can be monsters, and what happened in the hospital showed how others can be humans and can help. I did learn a lot about myself, about life, about how the people around me considered me; but the whole thing of friendship is one of the bottom-line things for me. I discovered that for many people, I was important. Many people wanted me to survive. And you are aware of it only when you are in such an extreme condition!"

Dror made *aliya* to Israel when he was twenty-five from a suburb of Paris "because I felt that my place as a Jew is to be here – it's kind of a feeling of belonging." After his hospitalization, he returned to France with his parents for two months. Then he came back to Israel because "my life is here; my studies are here; and some of my friends are here. Also I appreciated the way the Israeli doctors and nurses took care of me and cured me, and the way so many people came to greet me. I felt that I would be betraying them if I stayed in France. It strengthened my need to live here."

Dror returned to a normal life. "I'm more or less the same for better or for worse. I'm autonomous; I don't need anyone to take care of me. I have two physical disabilities – a shorter leg and hearing loss – and, of course, I have scars everywhere. I don't know if I'm representative of people who were critically wounded, but I really consider myself lucky because I recovered so well, physically and mentally. I live a normal life. I had a new chance, a new life, to be more or less whole."

Psychologically, he is "okay" and not obsessed with the memories of the bombing, nor do the memories come back, although he has "developed fear regarding the bombing or accidents with my leg." Although he suffered himself, he learned a lot from his confrontation with the suffering of other people – the other injured, David's parents, and his own parents. He recognizes that "maybe the bombing was harder for my parents than for me. We were on different paths. My parents were still in shock and didn't realize that for me it was almost over and I was on a path of resuming life. More or less two months after the bombing, my pains disappeared, my strength and energy came back, and I came back to life."

Dror is very much a product of his upbringing. His father Victor is a Holocaust survivor and was in the Jewish underground. "I used to say I have two Jewish mothers, my mother and my father. My father is really like a Jewish mother because he is so careful about me, almost too much actually. I think it's because of the suffering in the war, because he wanted to give his children everything that he didn't get as a child. I grew up with all the stories about the war and, because of that, I think that I have really strong feelings for belonging to the Jewish people."

As a secular Jew, "When I ask myself why did I survive and why did David die, I really get to the conclusion quickly that it's a question without an answer." He believes that "everything that happens here is a result of human behavior and we are responsible for that world – not God. David was killed by the Hamas, he was not killed because God decided his life was over and God decided that I have to live more."

Although other people called his survival a miracle, the word has too much of a religious connotation for Dror. "Yet, I want to believe in something. I don't know that there is a God, but if there is a God, God is greater than humanity." While not religious, he feels close to Jewish culture and tradition. He also has not changed his political views "because if I had changed my mind after this thing, it would have meant that I hadn't considered the previous bombings with the same gravity."

The deaths of David and Diego and other victims of terrorism are difficult for Dror but have not crippled him. "I identify with the suffering of the families – it's more concrete and I feel compassion when I see people in such a critical condition." Dror has built a special relationship with David's parents. "I was really afraid to meet them at first because I was afraid of their pain and I didn't want to add to their pain. I told them about the last moments of their only son's life. For parents, it may be one of the most difficult things you can hear. They knew that I was uncomfortable and they did everything to make me feel comfortable. The more that I know them, the more I love them. But the more I love them, the more I feel sorry for them and for David's death. He was a wunderkind and could have done so many things… We'll never know."

Dror considers "the glass half-full because I got so far and it is behind me now." He works with what life gives him and deals with challenges thoughtfully and sensitively. Thinking about what gives him his strength, Dror responds, "maybe it's my capacity to go through things with a kind of distance and to look at it in almost an intellectual way; also my capacity to speak because I am a very talkative man. And the social worker told me that 'usually the most seriously injured people are the ones who manage to recover psychologically because they don't have any choice. In the beginning it has to destroy you in order for you to survive. And so this fight is the crucial one and afterwards it's okay.'"

Five years after the attack, Dror is studying for his master's degree in political science at Tel Aviv University and works as an editor and reporter for the French language service of Kol Yisrael (Voice of Israel), Israel's public radio network. The job suits him "because I am really interested in everything that is happening in Israel, especially the analysis of the news – not what happened, but why."

The attack is no longer really part of his life. "I healed and I live a normal life. The good things in my life and the bad things in my life are not linked anymore to the bombing. And if they are, it is maybe in a good and positive way. I am stronger than I was before and I have discovered things about myself that I didn't know." Dror describes his life in terms of a few central events "and the bombing is one of them, but it is not one of the more present things. In the same way that there was *before the bombing* and *after the bombing*, there was before and after my *aliya*, before and after my younger brother's death from complications of preleukemia, and before and after I met my wife Yael."

Dror and Yael are the parents of a son Arnon and two daughters, Gilya and Naama. Dror is working for the new Israeli television channel i24 News, broadcasting news from the heart of the Middle East.

Suicide bombing, Hebrew University Cafeteria: July 31, 2002

Ariela: A Decision to Act, Dedicate, Feel, and Do

"Only one good thing came from the attack – the people who I met."

Unlike Dror, Ariela (a pseudonym), a twenty-five-year-old law student at the Hebrew University Mount Scopus, describes the attack very briefly, not wanting to think or feel about it. At the beginning, she was not able to talk about it. "I just acted like nothing had happened," although her hand was crushed and shrapnel injured her leg. She has undergone several operations to repair the damage. "After I got home, it was horrible because every night I would wake up with dreams and I started looking like a zombie. It was a very hard time. My whole life changed after that."

She had a lot of support from "the people I care about – my family and friends and my boyfriend." Ariela's father collapsed running to find her after the attack; he was hospitalized for three weeks and went into debt. Her mother became distressed and "can't bear the thought of me going out. She calls me all the time." Her boyfriend "was amazing. After the attack, he was at the hospital all the time. He didn't go home. He stopped working because I wasn't in good shape. So he passed the test" and they married in August 2004. After she was injured, he joined the police where "he sees the *piguim* from the other side and through my eyes."

After the attack, some of her relationships changed. "I had some friends who disappointed me and didn't seem to have anything in common with me any longer." What helped her most in the early years after the attack was a group of new friends who were all injured in attacks in Jerusalem. They met on a trip to London sponsored by the organization Hineni (Here I Am). "After we came back, it was like we had known each other all our lives. We stayed in touch. That group became a very big part of my life; it was easy with them because they knew what I was talking about. I met with them almost every day, after work in the evening, and we talked about everything. We've been through a lot together, including the death of a good friend in a car accident. Now we talk less about the attacks themselves, because after a long time they move to the background. But we talk about the struggles. I can't imagine how my life would have been without them. It is very helpful to have them."

For almost a year, Ariela could not go back to campus "because I was injured at the place where I had studied. I tried again and again, and every time I got to the parking lot, I started throwing up and crying and shaking. So I stayed at home and studied a year's worth of material by myself. Then I came back and they let me do the exams. And then I started an internship with the legal department of the Knesset (Israeli Parliament). It was very hard, but it's good to move on. All my life was only the injuries; nothing else was important; nothing else had any meaning. But when you get out and you study or work or do something, it feels very good. And it's the only thing that really can take you forward."

Ariela has her good days and her bad days. "I have days when I feel okay and everything is fine. And I have my days when I feel like I'm still struggling to get over it. I feel like somewhere along the way I got stuck; I made major progress in the beginning and then at some point it just stopped and everything stayed the same. I don't know if the situation can be better than it is now."

Two years after the attack, Ariela noted that "everybody says that I'm not the same. I know I've changed. I'm afraid of everything and I'm not as much fun as I used to be. I loved going to discotheques, but I don't have fun there anymore. Whenever I go into a place like that, I just look over my shoulder and remember the attack. I can't do it anymore." On the other hand, "I know that things have gotten better than right after the attack because it used to be even worse. Everything is a lot more loaded. I wish nothing had happened because I could enjoy things then that I can't do now. I try. I go out and I do things and I work. I have a life, but nothing is the same. Only one good thing came from the attack and that's the people who I met." Still, she remained hopeful. "But I think it will get better."

Five years after the attack, her life has changed for the better. "There is no doubt that things have changed. Time also plays its part – for me, my family, my job, and for Israel." She recalls her earlier experiences and her new and demanding job: "After the *pigua* I went through a difficult struggle to complete the entire degree. Then I completed the bar exam. Next, I took some time out – a little break from everything. I just sat at home. I didn't want to work in the profession. A half a year ago, I began to work as a prosecutor. Today I work hard. I entered a difficult job and it's very demanding. I work very late hours, a job where you need to appear in courthouses a lot. In the beginning, there was a lot of pressure, but it's something challenging and fun and it's good for me that I am at a steady job and have structure."

With the passage of time, Ariela is no longer very close with the group of terror victims she met in London. "We were very connected and bonded. It was very good for that time period; we coped together, but it had its hardships. All of the memorials that I attended were around the *pigua*. At a certain point, that connection became looser, and it is no longer something that is a part of my day to day."

But the continuing pain in her hand brings back the memories. "It is very annoying, because it is difficult to do things, like writing, and the appearance is not pleasant. But in some way I've made my peace with it. No day goes by without thinking about it, but it isn't what it was then. Then it was really a part of me, a part of everything and that was it. Today is better." Looking back, "then I really felt stress, anxiety, and fear. And I don't forget that. But today, things have calmed down. I don't wake up at night, I don't think about it to the same degree. In the beginning when I didn't talk about it, everything that was connected to the *pigua* even indirectly would trigger my fears. Today, it's a lot better, even the situation in Israel is much better, and you don't have to deal with it every day like then."

Ariela saw a psychologist and made a decision to move forward. "When I look back, the most difficult time period was the first half year, mostly because of the physical difficulties, but mainly because I refused to talk. Today I know that the treatment I received was very effective. I highly recommend it for people who are holding back something, to go and simply unload. When you have had a really bad experience, no one expects you to lift yourself, to go to work, to go to study. After you recover, you have an excuse. It is comforting and you can stay in it very easily. After a *pigua*, you look at things differently; everything seems very, very small and not meaningful. Why go to work? Why go to school? On the other hand, I can say today, this is a decision. The moment you decide to leave it behind and continue in life, then it's not just a matter of how you feel, it's a matter of what you decide – to act and to dedicate and to feel and to do – what you are doing when you head towards goals."

When her parents saw her come back to her life and put the *pigua* behind her, they did the same. "It was something that everybody goes through. Although it always comes up in all connections, I am now talking from a different place – a place that *was*. Then, the feeling was not that it was, but still *is*."

Suicide bombing, Hebrew University Cafeteria: July 31, 2002

Roza: Two Suicide Bombings – Two Different Experiences

"In the first one I saw everything and in the second I was arrested."

Roza (a pseudonym), a Muslim woman, experienced two *piguim* – suicide bombings – in her native Jerusalem. The first was five years earlier on Jaffa Road in downtown Jerusalem and the second, on July 31, 2002, was at the Hebrew University Mount Scopus campus, where she was a student. "In the first one I saw everything and in the second I was arrested."

She experienced the two bombings in very different ways. "The first time, I heard the boom. It was very close. Everybody shouted and ran and cried and got hysterical, but not me. I didn't know why. I didn't do anything. Finally, I started crying. I saw dead people, blood, and organs. I experienced it and saw everything. I was so young. It was over. I stopped near the window and looked at people without any special feeling, without excitement. I didn't feel that I was suffering. When the *pigua* happened, I was with myself – away from it." This numbing and freezing is characteristic of many traumatized people.

"In the second it was different. When I remember it, I feel anger. It was not exactly traumatic because I had experience." Roza explains: "I had an exam. When the *pigua* occurred, I felt a strong urge to stay and see everything. I don't understand why it was important for me to see everything. I was disappointed when they prevented me. I wanted to see the people who worked with me."

She was rounded up and arrested with all of the other Arabs in the area. "They arrested me and I felt very bad. I don't want to remember it. I felt offended. It was harder than the first time. They saw that I was an Arab and I was arrested. They put us in the sun and we were there for hours. When we wanted to drink or talk on the phone, they wouldn't let us. I felt angry. I couldn't believe it. Since then I understand what the Palestinians experience, and what I see on television I experienced myself."

She remembers that when she returned home, she couldn't sleep. "The next day, I wanted to go to the university, I don't know why. I didn't have anything to do. I liked the university very much, but maybe it's because it was the place where I was harmed."

Roza is perplexed about her feelings: "In the first one, I didn't feel it was difficult, but the second, I felt ashamed to talk about it. I know it was traumatic, but it wasn't against me. I don't know why I wasn't hysterical, or why I was just looking with a very strange feeling, as if I were watching a film on television. I looked at it from afar. Usually when I experience difficult things I see them in a dream, but I didn't even dream about it. But in the *piguim*, I felt like it was the end of the world. I always knew that there were *piguim*, but I always thought that it wouldn't happen to me."

Roza received her MA and works as an educational consultant in the Arab schools. She and her former professor are writing an article about her thesis. "In my thesis I did my research about significant others for adolescents, and one group of significant others were the *shaheed* (martyrs). It also perplexed everyone."

Chapter 3

A Drive for Development

new communities and neighborhoods... daring to dream

After the 1967 Six-Day War, the areas of Judea, Samaria, and Gaza, as well as the Golan Heights and Sinai Peninsula, came under Israeli control. Judea and Samaria, located on the west bank of the Jordan River, are the biblical names for the area now more commonly referred to as the West Bank. Judea refers to the entire region south of Jerusalem, including Gush Etzion and Mount Hebron. The region of Samaria refers to settlements in all areas north and west of Jerusalem. While providing Israel with essential security, they are a hotbed for terrorist cells and attacks on settlements, settlers, and those passing through. Although we hear much about those Jews who move to these areas for ideological or religious reasons, many families have moved outside the major urban area for convenience and economic reasons, traveling back and forth to the cities for work and pleasure.

Especially in the first two years of the Second Intifada, the roads leading to these communities were frequent targets of shooting attacks. Thousands of residents of Jerusalem's "southern gate" communities, including Efrat and Gilo, were targets of daily bombings, land mines, grenade attacks, shootings, and stonings. In this chapter, four ordinary people tell their stories of being the innocent targets of shootings and bombings while they were on their way to and from their homes and work. In the next chapter, we hear from three others attacked in more distant areas.

Jacki Glassman and BD both made *aliya*, Jacki from South Africa and BD from the United States. They live with native Israelis and many other immigrants from the US, Canada, South Africa, England, South America, Russia and elsewhere in Efrat, the principal town of the historic Etzion Bloc region that had been under Jewish control even before the founding of the State of Israel in 1948 and was recaptured in 1967. It is a scenic hilly area fifteen kilometers (9 mi.) south of Jerusalem, and home to almost ten thousand people or seventeen hundred families, the majority of whom are modern Orthodox. Both of their vehicles were shot at by terrorists along two different routes leading in and out of Efrat – the "Tunnel Road" and the "Back Road."

Ronit Elchayani and Ronit Tubul were injured in the same bus bombing on their way to work in the center of Jerusalem. They were traveling from their homes in Gilo, a residential neighborhood of about forty thousand people that lies within the municipal boundaries of Jerusalem. Between 2000 and 2002, during the first two years of the Second Intifada, Gilo's residents were subjected to gunfire and mortar attacks, launched by Palestinian militias shooting from the Christian Arab village of Beit Jala near Bethlehem.[1] Many homes facing Beit Jala suffered extensive property damage and many civilians were injured. The Israeli government eventually built a cement barrier and bulletproofed the outer row of homes in Gilo.

---

1   Israel Ministry of Foreign Affairs, "Pictures from Gilo- Community under Siege-
    December 2000," http://mfa.gov.il/MFA/MFA-Archive/2000/Pages/Pictures%20
    from%20Gilo-%20Community%20under%20Siege%20-%20Decemb.aspx.

Shooting attack, Efrat–Jerusalem roadblock: April 12, 2001

Jacki Glassman: A Time to Focus

"I'd been through a miracle, and had to share the experience with friends and family."

It was the Thursday of the Jewish holiday of Passover. That night, Jacki, a forty-five-year-old dentist who practices in Jerusalem and lives in Efrat, was due to fly to South Africa for his brother's oldest son's bar mitzvah. "It was during the holiday period, so there tended to be a little bit less traffic on the Tunnel Road to Jerusalem from Efrat. I picked up two hitchhikers who were friends of mine, and off we went to Jerusalem. I was driving a Fiat Uno, five seats – a small car. I had nobody next to me because I was giving a bar-mitzvah gift to friends in Jerusalem and the passengers were sitting nicely in the back."

It was quite uneventful until they came to the first tunnel roadblock. "I stopped patiently. Suddenly we heard bullets flying all around and it sounded like we were in the middle of a movie theater. We could see that a short distance away from us, one of the people manning the roadblock had been hit by a marksman from Beit Jala and the others were cowering behind these fairly large concrete blocks. We waited and nothing else happened, so we just carried on our way towards Jerusalem."

Once they got past the second tunnel and into Jerusalem, Jacki "stopped the car at a traffic light, got out of the driver seat, and went to look at the side of the car. A bullet had entered the frame where the two doors meet and it had turned and was caught inside the back door. And inside the door, instead of white paint, there was a bulge where the body of the bullet was."

Later on, "I looked at the top of the car and saw in the middle of the top of the car what appeared to be an entry hole. And at the back of the car, I saw what appeared to be an exit hole. It was unbelievable.

The bullet must have gone into the car and passed between the two of them and through the backseat and into the boot! Clearly we had been through a miracle, but none of us knew that it had affected us in any way."

An Orthodox Jew, with a strong belief in God, Jacki follows the Jewish practice from biblical times that if "you have personally gone through a miracle you have the duty to publicize the miracle. So I had to share the experience with friends and family so they would understand that, although we might be going through difficult times, there is Somebody up there Who is guiding the show and looking after us and we've got to take encouragement from it."

Ever since, on or soon after the nineteenth of every Hebrew month, as he drives past the place where the incident took place, "I give thanks to the One Above Who performed a miracle for me at this place." For Jacki, believing in God is also saying that "everything that happens to us is directed by Him and that the burden that God decides for us is the way that we can most grow. And at the end of the day, the questions are – were we the best that we could be? Did we live up to our own potential?" And that is how Jacki lives his life.

Jacki describes himself as an optimist both before and after the attack and believes that "you can always look at a glass as being half-empty or half-full; so I just saw the fact that my colleagues and I had been spared, not that we could have died." At the same time, he also is realistic and does the best that he can do for the particular situation, "dealing with what you can; and what you can't deal with, trying to contribute and doing the best that you can." The best way he feels he can contribute and give back is as a dentist, helping people of all backgrounds and "trying to make this world a better place."

Jacki was born in Johannesburg, South Africa, and looks at the world as an Anglo-Saxon South African and as a Jew. "Anglo-Saxons expect life to be a game of cricket. If you play badly, you expect to lose; if you play well, you expect to win. We expect things to be fair, but not everybody is dealt the same deck of cards and life isn't always fair. That's hard to accept, because some people have just got a better chance and others just get dealt a lousy deck of cards." As a Jew, "I believe that *kol Yisrael arevim zeh lazeh* – all Israel is responsible one for the other. If there is another Jewish person anywhere, it somehow affects me."

Although the attack was life threatening, Jacki does not know if it has particularly changed his life. "Maybe I'm in denial or whatever. Everybody goes through things. However, I clearly saw the event as a time when I was spared. How that has hit me, I still don't know; maybe I will wake up in the middle of the night with it hitting me." Nevertheless, he does feel that the attack "was a time to focus on doing things the best that I can and trying to help as many people as possible on a daily basis. I try to search for meaning and make the most of every opportunity."

Jacki moved to Israel in 1984 and chose to live in Efrat with his wife and their four daughters "because I believe that this is the right place to be and we should be here and we've got a job to do. The attack certainly hasn't shaken my belief in living here or in being here." However, the attack "probably has had an unspoken effect on the kids. We've all been shaken up and had to adjust to attacks from the First Intifada when we got rocks thrown at our car." There is something unique about being raised in Israel. "Here the kids go to funerals, not just for somebody who was a hero, but also for their friends or their relatives or people who they've known. Nevertheless, they want to be here." And, like Jacki, they feel the need to contribute. His two oldest daughters work with kids who have had siblings or parents badly injured or unfortunately killed, or helping kids who themselves were in an attack; they volunteer at Camp Koby – a program established in memory of a teenager brutally murdered by terrorists in 2001 and providing a special place for children of violence to grieve.

Jacki recognizes that "some people can go through the same thing and come out like complete disbelievers thinking there is no God in the world; while others find that the reality of who they are and what they've got to do is heightened." For Jacki, it has been a reminder "that you've got to make every day count."

On the yearly anniversary of the attack, the three survivors of the attack get together at one of their homes and have a festive meal of thanksgiving "because if somebody does you a favor you've got to say thank you. We invite ten or twenty people and we give thanks to the Lord above. Most of all it gives us a time to reflect and to appreciate what we've been through and what we and our families have thankfully achieved."

Jacki and his family have much to be thankful for. Jacki still enjoys dentistry, and following his wife's encouragement, got his fellowship in implants, and with the help of implant and laser dentistry "has now been placing as well as restoring people's smiles. I remain optimistic, cheerful, and grateful to God for heaping on me and my family all that He has." While his wife Hazel has also started taking an active role in the managing and staff training at his dental office, she continues to work at the Open University in Jerusalem, supervising one of the English language tracks, adding courses in business English, and preparing students for the English part of their university entrance exams.

Their oldest daughter is married and is blessed with two sons; she and her husband are a dynamic couple working in education in the Old City of Jerusalem. Their second daughter is also married with two sons; her husband is finishing his electrical engineering degree and she is passionate about her social work. Their third daughter is in her second year of internal architecture and interior design and loving it. And their youngest daughter has graduated from high school and is about to start her national service working in Tel Aviv with troubled teens.

Jacki sums up his philosophy of life: "As we make our way through the university called life, I try to learn and grow from every challenge – and of course there have been challenges – as well as becoming more focused on appreciating why and for who, we do what we do. I don't always succeed, but I have been blessed with family, friends, and neighbors who make it easier to fulfill the expectations we have of and for ourselves, our community, and our nation."

He concludes with the blessing that his late father-in-law always gave to his family – the priestly blessing:

May the Lord bless you and protect you.

May the Lord shine His face upon you and be gracious to you.

May the Lord turn His countenance to you and give you peace.

Amen!

Shooting attack, Elah Valley, on the road from Efrat to Jerusalem: August 27, 2001

BD: Jewish Destiny

"There is this settler attitude of *we are here, there are sacrifices we have to make.*"

B D was being driven from the airport to his home in the West Bank community of Efrat in Gush Etzion. He describes the attack and immediate aftermath with clear recall: "We chose to drive on the Back Road between Bet Shemesh and Efrat. It's considered the safest route. It doesn't go through very many Palestinian-controlled areas, except one village called Tzurif, which has been a problematic village even since before the founding of the State. We were near the agricultural community of Roglit when the driver suddenly shouted, 'They're shooting at us!'" BD looked out the window and saw three men dressed in black, their faces covered with hoods, aiming rifles at the car. "It was nighttime and I saw at the end of a rifle what looked like fire and bullets began hitting the car. For a second I didn't believe it was happening. It was like watching a movie. I really had this feeling that I wasn't there – that it was just sort of happening. But that just lasted an instant. I realized that I was in huge danger and a lot of people had been killed in this kind of situation."

BD's quick thinking – and his driver's fast actions – saved his life. "I ducked because I felt I presented an awfully good target. I picked up my briefcase and sort of covered my head. And I guess my hand was visible... The driver kept driving, for which I was grateful. I was very aware that the only way to possibly get out of the situation was to just keep going as fast as possible. A moving vehicle makes a little less of a target... But about three or four seconds later they shot out the engine and the car crashed into the side of the hill. I found out later that about fifteen bullets went into the car. The driver was not injured at all and he picked up his mobile telephone and started to call people. He also went out of the car to flag people down to stop as he could see already that I had been hit by at least one bullet. A lot of cars were on the road that night. The first three didn't stop. I'm sure they heard the shooting and they just wanted to get as far away from there as they possibly could, which is a natural thing. The fourth or fifth car stopped. It was actually a medic."

BD was fortunate to survive. His was one of four or five shooting incidents on different roads that night, and in each one of the others somebody died. His right hand was shattered and he had shrapnel in his legs, hands, and arms, which later resulted in infections. He was in Hadassah University Hospital–Ein Kerem for ten days. He has 90 percent use of his hand, although he cannot read his own handwriting now – "But it's not the end of the world. I can use a computer. Maybe my work efficiency even improved a bit because I have to bring a laptop with me to meetings." His scarred hand is a daily reminder of the attack, but "I don't think about it a lot."

BD could not feel sorry for himself. His initial reaction to the attack and his injuries was an overwhelming feeling of gratitude – "I knew that I had come within millimeters of having my head blown off." This feeling was followed by thankfulness and optimism. "It was not very likely that I should have survived. I was just ecstatic. I knew what could have happened." Mostly he was concerned for the important others in his life. His wife was at a dress rehearsal for a play and "I didn't want to call home. I was afraid that I would get one of my younger kids and I just didn't want to upset them." The hardest part for BD is to think and talk about his family in those hours of uncertainty right after the shooting. Even though they heard right away that he was okay, "they didn't know what okay meant."

In the first ten seconds, he knew that he might die and he prayed to God saying the Shema (Hear O Israel) prayer "to protect me and because it is the last thing a Jew should say before he dies." He thinks about that whenever he says the Shema. Also when he prays the Amida, the central prayer of the service which refers to God's mercy, "I think of God's mercy that night." Since the attack, BD's religious practice has increased: he tries as often as he can to pray in a *minyan* (group of ten) instead of alone, he consciously spends more time in the study of Jewish text as a deliberate refocusing, and he places greater value on doing *chesed* (acts of kindness). Like Jacki, every year, BD and his wife host a *seudat hodaya* – a festive meal of thanksgiving – around the date of the attack to give thanks for being saved.

BD never panicked or screamed. He didn't pass out and he tried to stay conscious. In those first couple of minutes, all sorts of thoughts occurred to him. "One, which happens to a lot of people when they survive a terrorist attack is 'okay, this is my terrorist attack. It's over, my family and I have done it and gotten through it. And now we're done.'" Then his thoughts turned regretful. "If I had left the airport just three minutes later, this wouldn't have happened." And, not realizing the severity of his injuries, he wondered how he could make it to a friend's son's wedding later that same week. "I'm not going to want to drive this road at night later this week. Maybe we could go another way."

At the time of the attack, BD was forty-eight years old, married to Ann, and the father of four children who were preteen and teenagers. He is an Orthodox Jew, has a master's degree, and is an economic-development and strategic-planning consultant with clients in the United States and Israel. As such, he is conscious of setting meaningful goals and measuring progress in his personal, as well as professional, life.

He chose to move to Israel sixteen years earlier from the United States because he "felt that Jewish destiny is here in Israel. And I wanted to be part of the destiny of the Jewish people, the future of the Jewish people. I felt a certain obligation to that history, and to God, Who has given the Jewish people an opportunity to reclaim its destiny here in the Land of Israel. God gave this opportunity to my generation and to the preceding generation, so it's an obligation of the Jews to seize that opportunity and to try to make it work." He further chose to live in the hills of Gush Etzion, an area that is so rich in centuries of Jewish life. "You can't take a step without being where two thousand years ago some Jew had stopped on his way from Hebron to Jerusalem." It was meaningful for him "that it be a very, very Jewish area – a real community of involvement and *chesed* and learning."

BD knew from the time he chose to live in Israel that there were risks. And he knew from the point that this Intifada started that there were risks. Nevertheless, he and his family do not think of moving – either to Jerusalem or to the United States – because "bad things can happen to anybody anywhere and you just have to hope for the best." His resolve is even greater now – "Moving is handing them the victory. I don't want to give them the victory. That was very, very strong in my mind – I don't want to let them win. And moving is letting them win." He describes the situation in Israel as "a battleground and a struggle – and struggles are difficult. And people get injured in the case of a struggle, but that doesn't mean to give up." He turns this into a metaphor for his own recovery: "It was very, very important for me not to give up. To give up, is to give up the whole thing."

BD's peace of mind was affected and he "became a little edgier. It's actually hard to know how much of that was my own particular injury and how much was simply because the first two years of this Intifada were so difficult here, so horrendous. It's hard to isolate my own having been shot from all of these other horrible things that were happening, politics, government, etc. It wasn't the injury itself. It didn't make me more stressed. Instead I felt very endangered." For one particularly bad year until the road became safe and the number of violent acts diminished, he and his family would not drive to Jerusalem at night and even wore bulletproof vests on the rare occasions that they had to. When it became too difficult to refrain from going into Jerusalem, they got back to driving at night. "It was a matter of statistics – the odds of winning a lottery are better than that." Then, for a few years after his attack, BD again preferred not to take that road at night. "Not that I think lightning strikes twice in the same exact spot, but it is an eerie feeling to be on that spot at night. I sort of have the same kind of picture. But I don't really think beyond that."

BD's relationship with his family has deepened. His wife is a nurse and she helped treat his wounds at home. "We're a close couple anyway, but I felt an enhanced closeness with her." He insisted that she go on stage on opening night in her leading role in a play because "she had worked so hard the last three months, how could she not. But the other reason was that it would be a very important statement, and it was. It added a tremendous poignancy to the whole production because the whole purpose of the Raise Your Spirits Theatre Company[1] was to raise the spirits of the women of Gush Etzion. Also for her it was a very meaningful thing that they were doing this play and it was going on."

BD heeded the advice of a psychologist who told him that the "best form of therapy is to just talk about it and keep talking about it until you demystify it; you sort of remove the poison from the fangs. And that's probably true. It's not like it's something hidden – something that doesn't surface. Not a day goes by that I don't think about it and I spoke about it a lot, especially in the weeks afterwards, because everybody asked what happened."

He wonders about his kids and if their experiences hold them back in some ways. His then fourteen-year-old daughter washed the blood off his briefcase when it was returned to their home the night of the attack. At first BD didn't believe that she had been traumatized because "it's not her. She had this kind of settler attitude of *we are here, there are sacrifices we have to make, we're still going on, nothing is going to change what happens to us.* And she would never even really be willing to see herself or her family as a victim of anything. Because all right, you were shot – lots of people are shot, lots of people die. She's not going to allow herself to be depressed, upset, scared, or anything… I think if this thing were to start again, she probably would be the most dramatically affected. She now says that she's not willing to go through it again."

When he became of military age, BD's oldest son joined a very elite battle unit in the army and "apparently has no problems related to the *pigua.* He's going through the same tough training just like everybody else." BD thinks his younger two sons were more affected by it. "How that affected our relationship, I can't really say." His youngest son was a little kid. "I don't know if he was going through things because his

---

1   Raise Your Spirits Theatre, http://www.raiseyourspirits.org/.

father was shot or not, but he said it was the result of my *pigua*." His second son (then age eleven) saw his sister cleaning the briefcase and for a few minutes thought that his father was dead. "He didn't know what had happened and was afraid to ask anybody. I've always had kind of a special relationship with him. And he became even a little bit closer afterwards, wanting to spend more time with me, but then he became a teenager and that sort of ended. I worry about him and wonder if he pulls back from attachments in a subconscious fear of losing the thing that he is most attached to."

BD's greater appreciation of life and focusing on what is important was a recurring theme and had an organizing effect on his life: "There are important things and there are trivial things. People, family, and spiritual things are more important than the fact that I have to call the banker and talk about the overdraft. For some months after the attack it helped me put everything into perspective. Trivial worries didn't seem very important in the face of knowing that my life had been spared. But I still have to work on that. I'll start to worry and I'll say, 'Now BD, remember that lonely night on the road when you were shot and you survived' and that kind of refocuses my thinking." Even six years later, "I sometimes do forcefully remind myself of those events in order to put some of life's more mundane events into some perspective. It helps me shape how I relate to things that are quite trivial in comparison. It's not that easy to do, but it's a goal and it reminds me that I've gone astray from where I was trying to refocus and that I need to get back into that space."

BD derives strength from the satisfaction of being in control and succeeding in challenges – overcoming both physical and psychological distress. He remembers the "challenges" of some previous events in his life – the murder of his girlfriend thirty years ago, the family trauma of his cousin's death in a mountain-climbing accident, and his own major back surgery confining him to a cast for six months when he was twenty-seven. After he was injured he took up his new physical challenge, saying, "I'm going to do that this time too. Instead of feeling sorry for myself that I have the cast on my arm, I'm going to try to work very, very hard so that I get back everything and I don't lose function.

And so when the occupational therapist gave me the exercises, boy was I going to do those exercises. When it was over, I think it paid off."

He feels like he was tested. "I had never been in that situation before and I got through it. I felt a certain amount of self-respect that I had handled the situation as best as anybody could handle it." But once again, he brings up the Israeli attitude – "You have to handle it that way. You have no choice. If I had been the driver and I lost control of the car, I would have felt like I blew it."

How BD deals with the aftermath is also very much influenced by his upbringing. His mother, a psychiatric social worker, and his grandmother taught him that "you have to be strong and if you are depressed you should work on yourself to get over it." He believes that "you can decide not to be depressed to some extent." Also because of his upbringing, "I really never like to be in a situation of needing help, except when I really, really, really need it. When the ambulance came and I was put on the stretcher that night, I really needed that help and I really appreciated it. I felt very good receiving it."

After the attack, BD felt this incredible outpouring of help and support from people who came to visit. He was tremendously impressed by the *chesed* that people showed him in the hospital – helping him put on *tefillin* (phylacteries worn during morning prayers) and providing meals for his wife who slept over in the hospital on Shabbat. "All those things made me feel wonderful. It was almost worth it just to experience this outpouring of *chesed*. And even the institutions – the organizations like Bituach Leumi (National Insurance) – they were so wonderful when they would come, and they kept coming. I didn't really feel like I needed to meet with the social worker, but I didn't say no because she felt so good about it." His neighbors and family were "just incredible. They gave me a tremendous ability to get through it with a smile to the extent that I could. So people were the thing – people and my family."

A few days before the attack, BD told a friend that "If I'm ever in a terrorist attack, I hope that I somehow will be worthy enough of having survived by being a better person, a more giving person, a more generous person, a more spiritual person." Reflecting on this hope,

BD says, "I can't say that I've done a good job of it, but at least I am conscious of it and it is a goal."

BD thinks back to that dark lonely night often. "I remember God's compassion and I still struggle to somehow be worthy of that compassion."

In the summer of 2012, eleven years after the attack, BD's two oldest children were married – his daughter who had been fourteen at the time of the terrorist attack and his oldest son who had been thirteen. "I was grateful that God and circumstance allowed me to survive that attack so that I could enjoy these two joyful occasions."

Egged bus no. 32 bombing, Patt Junction outside Gilo,
Jerusalem: June 18, 2002

Ronit Elchayani: Friendly Pain

"Writing...is the prize."

Ronit Tubul: You Will Never Be the Same Woman

"I will have children...like a regular person."

Ronit Elchayani's car was broken. "So after I dropped off the baby at the daycare center in Gilo, I took the Egged bus, the no. 32. The thought went through my mind that I should pick the least dangerous seat, so I sat down right behind the exit door in the back." Police superintendent Ronit Tubul also dropped off her nine-month-old baby daughter, Shira, at day care near her home in Gilo and caught the same bus to work.

At the stop near the friendly Arab village of Beit Safafa, Muhamed al-Ral, an Islamic law student at An-Najah National University in Nablus, boarded the bus and almost immediately exploded a bomb stuffed with ball bearings. The force of the blast destroyed the front half of the bus as it left Patt Junction, killing nineteen people and injuring seventy-four. Many of the passengers were students and office workers heading to downtown Jerusalem. According to Ronit E., "all those who sat in the seats before me died. All those behind me were less seriously injured than I was."

Both women were in a coma and hospitalized together in intensive care for brain injuries. They went through rehabilitation together and physical, occupational, speech, and psychological therapy at Hadassah University Hospital–Mount Scopus. Both are still suffering from physical and memory problems.

The two women did not know each other before the bombing, but because of their shared experience and similar injuries they became close friends and came to deeply understand one another. They even finish each other's sentences. Ronit E. says of her new friend, "I can talk more because she can understand what I feel. When we talk to others, we are too shy to say that we are forgetting." Likewise, Ronit T. "can't say to other friends what I can say to Ronit E. because she can understand me more than anyone else. And when we talk to each other – how do you feel about this and how do you feel about this – we are comparing our situations."

Though Ronit E. is older and has more children than Ronit T., they have many similarities. They were both born in Israel as Jews, lived in the same community, worked at responsible jobs, were happily married with little babies, and were stricken with very similar injuries in the same horrific bombing. Although Ronit E. predicted that "both of us will give the same answer," they responded differently to some questions. Ronit T. feels she has changed in small ways, making her a different person, yet is more accepting of her current situation. Ronit E. also is "not the same person" but she is more verbal about her neurological impairment and physical limitations and talks about the future as she confronts her fears and emotions. Both women describe having a greater appreciation of life and health, a stronger belief in God, and a desire for normalcy, and both derive strength from their husbands and children.

Both women appreciate the help they received from all kinds of organizations, especially when they came from another country "to show us that they care." They feel fortunate to have been invited to the United States to speak to Operation Embrace, an organization supporting terror victims, as well as Hadassah, the largest Zionist women's organization in the United States. Ronit T. speaks for both of them when she says that "I think the more that I talk about it, the more it helps me. After you talk about it, you feel a kind of relief. And it makes you feel good."

Ronit Elchayani

At the time of the attack, Ronit E. was thirty-seven years old and the mother of two boys and two girls – fifteen, twelve, eight, and eighteen months old – "who thought they had lost their mommy." It was painful when she came home from the hospital and her youngest child "did not know who I was and refused to talk to me or recognize me in any way."

She does not "remember the sound or the smell or the fear. My first memory is two weeks later, when I woke up in the Intensive Care Unit at Hadassah Hospital." She later learned what had happened to her. "My injuries were very serious. From the concussive force of the blast my eardrums were punctured and my lungs were damaged. That's called blast injury. The bomb was packed with ball bearings sent off at tremendous speed. One penetrated my lungs, another struck my ribs, another the back of my neck, and the worst passed through my cheek and lodged in my brain… When I woke up, one eye was closed because a muscle wasn't functioning. I had headaches of unbelievable strength. The trigeminal nerve in my face was damaged. My balance was off. The ball bearing in my neck caused paralysis and pain in my left arm. I was totally helpless. I had a breathing tube."

Ronit E. thinks "it's big miracle" that she is alive because another person with the same injury died from ball bearings inside him. Today, she suffers from physical and memory problems. She has double vision, gets terrible headaches, and sometimes has attacks of trembling and loss of balance. She has had multiple unsuccessful surgeries to fix the ringing in her ears. "If I were paralyzed, I think it would be easier because I would know that my leg wasn't working and I would know how to get better. But our heads and our hearts are the main things in our body. My handicap is in my mind and I'm not the same person anymore."

Many of the ball bearings are in very sensitive areas and have not been removed. "If the one in my brain moves, I will have to undergo brain surgery. But I know that whatever happens, the Hadassah staff will be there for me. Hadassah Hospital – where I was born, I was reborn."

While her love for her children is as strong as ever, it is a challenge to be the mother she wants to be. At first it was easier "because I was hospitalized and everyone took care of me – I was like a baby. Today, it's a struggle with life. It's more difficult to be a mother because I am very tired all the time and very weak. When the youngest comes from kindergarten, I have to be with him, play with him, and talk with him like any regular mother." Because of her memory loss, "I can go shopping with my little child and if he will not hold my hand tightly, I can forget about him. At home, I can't think about what to cook and at the same time talk on the phone or answer my child when he asks me 'Mommy, where is my sweater?' or to help with his homework." Also it is more difficult because her other children are older. "It's hard for me to understand them, especially at this age. When they are little, there are little problems. When they are bigger, the problems get bigger. I don't want them to see me as a weak mother. So I try all the time not to be like this. I try to look better and talk with them about school and their friends."

Since she now "looks as usual," her kids think that she can do everything like she did before. "And to me, of course, it's not easy because I am not the same person… It hurts a lot to feel this way… My husband, also, on the one hand acts like I'm the same normal person as before, but on the other hand he also sees me as very sick, very weak. He feels like I am his little girl, not his wife, because sometimes I react like a child. He is doing all he can, and I try not to make him sad with all my feelings, my thoughts, and I try all the time to say I'm fine, I'm good. But inside I'm not."

Six months after the attack Ronit E. went back to work at the Jewish National Fund, but had to change jobs. "Before, I was responsible for projects and ceremonies but today, it's too difficult for me. The doctors say that my sense of time is damaged. So I have a very big problem with arranging my time, and it's very difficult to plan things for tomorrow, or two weeks later, and to remember things that I've done before."

She focuses on the joy of her children, the little things, and the hope that someday she will stop suffering. She tries to stay positive and has a new appreciation of life. She is helped to move on with life by her own inner strength. "The things that are important to me are to take care of my children, to raise them, and to give them the right education so that they will have success in their future." She wants to be "like any regular mother" and is "trying to live as usual" even though "I am not the same.

I see life differently. I feel different... I'm trying to live as usual and to work and to be busy and not to think about all of these things. I am trying the best that I can."

She continues: "I draw a lot of power from within myself. If I see my little child laughing or when he's just yelling Mommy! – it's very exciting that I am a mother again... Getting up in the morning and seeing the sun shining outside is like a miracle. It's a new life, a new world; it's fantastic... I try not to think of the big problems, believing and hoping that someday all this will be better and life will be changed and I will stop suffering."

Her suffering is not just physical, but psychological and emotional as well. While she describes positive changes, at the same time she also experiences distress, living in fear that again she or someone in her family "will be injured or can lose their lives." She calls it "my private holocaust... After this *pigua*, I had nightmares and dream that I was in the Holocaust." She associates her trauma with the trauma of Holocaust victims that she learned about in school. "Of course it isn't the same, but some things are familiar."

Ronit E. does not want to surrender to these negative feelings nor does she like the feeling of being "out of control and not being able to take care of my life." She has learned "to let all the problems out of my body and to think of good things and to try to live better. I'm trying to live as usual. I tell my kids that there is no other way, there is no choice; if you have to get back home with the bus, then you should go by bus. I have to think positively all the time and that is good medicine. From the attack and all the suffering and pain, there are good things that you learn about yourself. You can follow these things and you will win; you get your life again and everything will be better."

Ronit E. confronts and talks about her fears and other feelings and thoughts to help others understand. "I try to explain what has changed inside me or what I am feeling and I'm trying to think logically. And I think that this has helped me struggle with all the change inside. I know what is right and what is wrong."

Ronit E. has a strong belief in God and hopes for a better world "because I was like a dead woman and it was a miracle that I was reborn.

My father, who is a rabbi, thinks he has some private angel in the skies that was taking care of me and helping me. Sometimes I say, 'Why is our God not doing anything? Or maybe He is doing something but we don't feel that anything has changed.' But I still believe that God's way is true and right and I hope that someday we will see that everything has changed and that we are in a better world."

Before the attack, Ronit E. wrote stories, poems, and blessings for the birthdays and anniversaries of her friends and family. Now her writing continues to be "like a present after all this effort." Her passion for writing "is my private world that gives me power and is like therapy." She believes her writing has improved after the attack to compensate for what she has lost. "Something became better in my writing – so that I should feel better, be happy, and not be sad." Through her writing she is trying to make sense of her experience.

She wrote *Friendly Pain* to inspire children and adults. It is based on her own struggle with constant pain. In the award-winning story,[1] she writes about how to deal with physical and emotional pains so as not to suffer, "to be friendly with the pain, not to treat it as the enemy. Then you feel good."

> This nice story talks about pains,
> With whom we'd like to live in peace.
> There's no need to be best of friends
> But, at least, to stop fighting them as enemies
> That's how our body is made to get rid of them.
> Let the young ones come to terms with them.
>
> Dear pain,
> Beloved pain,

---

1   Ronit Elchayani received an award in 2006 from the Inbar Fund, established in memory of Inbar Attiya, victim of the suicide terror attack on the Dizengoff Center (Tel Aviv) in March 1996. The fund encourages the study and research of terrorism, the courses of its occurrences, and ways to handle it strategically, psychologically, and physically. Inbar Fund, "Friendly Pain," http://www.keren -inbar.co.il/INB/front/Document.asp?ID=23017 (page now discontinued). Translated by Hadassah Fuchs from the Hebrew original.

Why suffer?
Fighting we'll stop,
Good friends we'll become,
Even if our ways will part,
We'll never be apart.

Let's stop now being enemies,
If only we have the desire and the courage,
All our pains will be friends,
And even our happiness will grow and intensify.

She says that "although I wrote for me, for my friends, for my family, my dream is to publish the story for children to laugh at this idea, not to cry." She does not know if people will understand the story, but, for her, "it's something that I feel, I know, I'm thinking."

For Ronit E. her physical pain is a metaphor for the situation in Israel and the world. She hopes for peace in both her inner and outer worlds. "The idea is like the whole situation here in the Middle East… that we are the enemy to the Palestinians and they are enemies to us; but we have to fight for peace, to make them not the enemy, to make them like a friend. If we do this, everything will be good. All of the world will be better and our lives will look better."

Five years after the attack, Ronit E. continues to work for the Jewish National Fund, organizing donor visits to JNF sites throughout the country. Then she comes home to the children, their homework, and the housework. She has a lot of friends, but no time for socializing because "I'm running all the time from work to home, from home to work, to doctors, to treatments." Her best form of relaxation is still writing. "If I have the time…to be sitting with myself and to write…to be with myself, for me that's the prize!"

In 2013, she still works, but her medical situation has gotten worse. She suffers from pain throughout her body from the shrapnel and takes many medications so that she can stand on her feet. Also, she has a very hard time emotionally.

Ronit Tubul

Like his wife, Ronit T.'s husband, Shlomo, is also with Jerusalem's police force and was part of the team conducting house-to-house searches in north Jerusalem when word came of the attack near Gilo on the southwestern outskirts of Jerusalem. "When my husband got to the area to do his job, he didn't have any idea that I might be there. But when he saw my jewelry and my watch, he said, 'This is my wife.'"

Thirty-year-old Ronit T. was in a coma for twelve days and underwent many surgical procedures to remove dozens of pieces of shrapnel from her head and body. The hardest part of the *pigua* for her was that she could not remember anything, a situation she shared with Ronit E. "Our families had to explain to us what had happened and what we were doing in the hospital. Everything that I am telling you about the event is from what people are telling me… The doctors say we're lucky that we don't remember because it's very traumatic to remember everything that happened. Both of us were unconscious. We didn't know what happened to us…and we didn't believe them. It was very difficult for us to realize what our situation was after this *pigua*. Until today, it's very difficult for me to believe that I was there."

The doctor explained to Ronit T. that because of her brain injury and resulting problems with memory and motion, "I would never be the same woman that I was – medically, physically, and emotionally. What I have gone through is going to be with me forever, making me different from a regular person." She was still nursing her infant daughter when she was injured. "It was very hard for Shira to suddenly be without Mommy for a long time. And when she saw me the first time, she turned her back to me, like *I don't want to talk to you*… My mother-in-law took care of her while I was in the hospital, and for two months she didn't sleep in her own home. Finally, when I came home from the hospital we moved her to her room. And of course I'm not nursing anymore. Such big changes, but they grow" – as demonstrated by the well-adjusted two-year-old girl happily playing in the living room as we talked.

After Ronit T. returned home from the hospital and rehabilitation, even with the help of a nanny, it was still very difficult to take care of her baby. But, as a mother, she understood her daughter's need for her mother's "warmth and touch more than anything. Although I was too weak to pick her up, I took her to bed and held her there because she wanted it so much."

When Ronit T. went back to work part-time in her job as a policewoman, people expected her to be back to her old self. She was frustrated that they didn't understand that this does not happen with a brain injury. "Maybe I look good – it's not that I don't have a hand or a leg – it's in my head. Unfortunately, no one can understand it and, as time passes, everyone expects that I will be more and more like a regular person." She expected consideration and knows it does not exist in her work. She worried that they might fire her. But despite these concerns about her job, she is grateful for the great support from the police for her, her husband, and her family. It showed her that they are "very special – like a family."

Two years after the attack, she was still working part-time, but "everything is slower, harder to do at work and at home." She was strengthened by her child and husband "because they need me." And she recognized "how life is valuable. You learn to live with what you have. You have to look at the good side, that you are living – that you are alive. It could have been very different – it could have been worse… The most important thing in life is your health and all other things are very small in comparison… After a few months, you get back into the routine of life and decide to do things like before. Maybe little things make you sad or nervous. You forget that you went through something bad. You forget that health and life are the most important things and that everything else is very small. But then I remind myself to forget these little things because they are nothing in comparison to what I had. When I overreact, what relaxes me is to think about what I went through and where I am now. Simply to be alive and feel healthy are the most important things."

Ronit T. accepts her situation and feels that she has changed in small ways. "At first, when I was in the hospital there were a few days when I asked myself why did it happen and why me, but it was only for a few days. I understood the situation and accepted it. I've changed, that's a fact, but not in any major way, nothing extreme…but little changes that make me a different person."

Although everything is as important as it was before – her family, friends, work, politics, and religion, Ronit T. now has a greater belief in God and thinks differently about the "importance of life. This is the one thing that I didn't think about before and now I know how important it is. I will never forget what happened for the rest of my life. I don't forget, not for a second, what a miracle I experienced. I got my life back and I believe that what God has done is a miracle. Actually I became Shabbat observant. I guess I understand the importance of what I went through. I will never, never, ever stop thanking God."

Ronit T. is on an anticoagulant medication for the rest of her life because of the remaining shrapnel in her body and her blood vessels were traumatized by her injuries. She was warned against another pregnancy, but the warning fell on deaf ears as she looked forward with hope and faith. "I will have children, even though I know it will be hard. But I am willing to suffer because I want brothers and sisters for my child."

And sure enough, almost three years after the fateful day she boarded the Jerusalem bus, Ronit T. gave birth to a healthy baby boy at Hadassah Hospital. "I'm not irresponsible. But I wanted another child and I was determined to have one. Shlomo and I know we took a risk in having this baby. We're so very, very grateful that things turned out as they have. And I want to do things like a regular person, more and more as I can."

Chapter 4

Judea, Samaria, and the Lower Galilee

riding in cars and buses... going to concerts
and shopping malls

Numerous attacks were also perpetrated in the areas of Karnei Shomron in western Samaria, Hebron in southern Judea, and Afula in the lower Galilee.

Karnei Shomron, literally "the Horns of Samaria," is a settlement in western Samaria established in 1977 which prides itself on its diversity. Its six thousand residents represent young families and senior citizens; new immigrants from North America, Europe, and the former Soviet Union, and native-born Israelis; religious and secular alike. Tragedy struck the community three times between May 2001 and February 2002. In May 2001 RH's car was shot at by terrorists as he was driving home; on August 5, 2001, forty-year-old Tehiya Bloomberg was killed and three other people were injured by shots from a passing Palestinian vehicle on the Azoun bypass road leading from Kfar Saba to Karnei Shomron; and on February 16, 2002, three teenagers were murdered and over thirty civilians injured by a suicide bombing on a Saturday night at a pizzeria in the Karnei Shomron shopping mall.

The West Bank city of Hebron, located in Judea thirty kilometers (19 mi.) south of Jerusalem, is the burial place of the patriarchs and matriarchs and a holy site to all three Abrahamic faiths – Judaism, Christianity, and Islam. Today it is home to some 166,000 Palestinians and five hundred Jews and has seen numerous acts of violence from both sides. The Hebron Jewish community has been subject to attacks by Palestinian militants since the Oslo agreement, with three fatal stabbings and nine fatal shootings in between the First and Second Intifadas and seventeen fatal shootings and two fatalities from a bombing during the Second Intifada. In addition, thousands of rounds have been fired from the hills above the Abu-Sneina and Harat al-Sheikh neighborhoods. Feige Fishman Glasomitsky was injured in one of these attacks while she was attending a Sukkot holiday concert in Hebron. From the other side, the Jewish settler compound of Beit Hadassah has been used as a firing point to shoot indiscriminately into Palestinian areas.

Just north of Samaria and located in the lower Galilee region of Israel, Afula is roughly halfway between Jenin and Nazareth. Because of its proximity to the West Bank, it also has been a target for terrorists during the Oslo peace process and the Second Intifada. As a hub for northern Israel, the Afula central bus station and the major junctions nearby were the sites of five suicide bombings between October 2001 and June 2002. Thirty four people were killed and over two hundred others were wounded in these attacks, including Avraham (Avi) Robinson, who was injured when a car packed with explosives struck his bus at Megiddo Junction near Afula. In another attack, Dr. SY was among seventy people wounded and three people killed by a suicide bombing at the entrance to the Amakim Mall in Afula. Avi and SY, as well as RH and Feige, describe their horrific experiences and how they moved beyond their serious injuries.

Shooting attack on the road from Petach Tikvah to Karnei Shomron: May 13, 2001

RH: Time to Think and to See

"I want to do things to change the world."

Although RH understood immediately that he was hurt, he continued driving away from where the terrorists were shooting because "they could continue and I could die." The dumdum bullets pierced the car door, striking his ankle, but he remained in control until he went into surgery. He recalls that "I did not lose consciousness and I remember everything." His three brothers traveling with him were not injured in the shooting. They were all returning to their parents' home in Karnei Shomron from their grandfather's funeral in Petach Tikvah, a suburb of Tel Aviv.

RH was twenty-six years old at the time of the attack. He was the oldest of eight brothers and sisters growing up in Karnei Shomron. Following his recovery at home, he moved to his late grandfather's apartment in Petach Tikvah to be close to Beilinson Hospital for physical therapy and to Bar-Ilan University, where he and his new wife were studying. After many surgeries and physical therapy, his injured leg is shorter than the other and still painful, but his attitude is "this is what we have, so we live with that." He cannot do a lot of things that he did before, like run and play basketball – "It bothers you. But when you think about what it could be... Even one bullet can kill you, and if you take twenty bullets from just fifteen meters and you're only hurt in your leg, you say *baruch Hashem* (thank God)." He ends philosophically with: "So you got what you got and you try to do your best. I don't think about the pain and I try to continue my life."

RH understands and appreciates the importance of life. He is an Orthodox Jew and has a strong belief in God. "If God tried me, it means that I can pass this trial; because if not, God would not try me." As a result he has become more religious. "It's not a dramatic change, but I believe that if I believe in God, I need to believe also that He made something like that. He tried me to see what I would do in this situation. So I say, okay, I'll go with that." In acknowledgment of his experience he named his first son Eliad, meaning "my God forever," and his daughter Oriah, meaning "the light of God."

RH quickly understood that hundreds of possible answers exist to the question "why did God do this to me?" – "but no way that I can know really if it's right. It doesn't help to think about why it happened; so I think the better attitude is to think about what the meaning of it is for me." He had a lot of time during his lengthy recovery to reflect on the meaning of the event, drawing on his prior religious beliefs and strengths. Rather than think about bad things, "I think about my life, what I want to change, what I want to do better, and how I want to help people. You see that you really have a meaningful life – a *tachlis* (purpose) – knowing exactly what you want to do. I haven't changed things, dramatic things, but my goals are now stronger and more specific. I really want to do things now. It's not because of what happened to me, but because I really have time to think and to see."

He seeks to be stronger and better than before – to grow from his traumatic experience. "You think about things in another way. You see that your life is very important. No one wants to fall down in the dumps. So I say, I don't want to descend to the level that I was at before. I have the option now to go up, for the better, from what I had before." RH takes his own advice not to waste time thinking about bad things, but instead to focus on doing good things. "I want to help people. I want to do things to change the world. So I say okay, it's easy to speak about that, but I need to begin practicing it now." While still in the hospital he had a positive attitude and spoke with people who were sad or afraid in order to help them through their ordeals "to give them moral support that you can make it. If I came to the hospital, I guess God sent me to this place, so I'll do a few things that I think maybe was my goal."

Although he does not know where it came from, he has a great deal of personal strength. "Maybe I was born with it, maybe it's something you work on, and maybe it's because I am religious." RH's recovery was helped by his optimism, hard work, and having a high goal: "I don't want to be disabled. I really want to walk. I need to think optimistically and also I need to work very hard to change because if I do nothing for myself – it's not going to happen." He was married exactly a year after he was wounded, by which time he was able to walk a few steps without crutches. He had achieved his secret goal, proclaiming "I really made it."

He was also helped by the loving people around him: his girlfriend – who is now his wife and stayed with him even though they had only known each other a month at the time of the *pigua*; his family – his brothers and his mother "who tried to do the best for me"; and his friends who decided that one of them should come and sleep with him every night and brought all of the schoolwork he missed. "In this situation you see who your friends really are. They came and they did everything that I needed and even things that I didn't need. It's a very important thing."

Five years after surviving the *pigua*, on August 12, 2006, RH's brother – IDF captain RB, age twenty-seven, was one of nineteen soldiers killed in fighting against Hezbollah terrorists in southern Lebanon. What Palestinian terrorists couldn't do, Hezbollah terrorists succeeded in doing with an anti-tank missile fired at the tank commanded by RB. RB's death further put things in perspective for RH – "Now no matter what happens to me, for me it is nothing. My brother's death changed everything. Before, being injured was the worst thing in the world, but now, it's not such a big deal. I know I have to continue my life. I know it is time to be happy, even with what happened. And sometimes you cry and sometimes you are happy. It's simple maybe to say it, but it's really hard to do."

After RH was injured he completed his BA and MA degrees in public management. He works as an economist with the Israeli police and is responsible for logistics and purchasing. He is proud that he "looks after the money like it is my money, saving the country a lot of money that can be spent on something else."

From his parents and from his religious education, RH learned the importance of good deeds – providing for others, especially the needy. "When you see something from the time when you were a child, you do the same – for bad or for good." He gives seminars about his experience because he likes teaching and "I very much like to work with people," especially youth. He uses his story to help other people heal. "First I speak about what happened to me and about the long process that I went through until today. Then I speak about what the meaning is for me and what I can learn from it. Finally, I speak about what they should know about friendship and about my girlfriend who became my wife during this process."

RH and his wife, a psychologist, and their young children continued to live in Petach Tikvah for several years, where RH volunteered to prepare Russian immigrants for their bar mitzvahs and his wife counseled couples before their weddings. Their dream was to move out of the city some day and back to another settlement, a very small, young one – "we want to build something new." They like the settlement life, where "everyone is religious and you live life more fully. It's better also for the children's education and they can go everywhere without a car and play anywhere they want."

Today, RH, his wife, and five children – Eliad, Oriah, Shachar, Aciya, and Noam – live in Alei Zahav (meaning Golden Leaves), another settlement in the Shomron, eleven kilometers (7 mi.) from his family in Karnei Shomron.

Shooting attack at a concert in Hebron: October 3, 2001

Feige Fishman Glasomitsky: Happy Ending

"Everything eventually went back to normal, except in my mind, which sees life a bit differently now."

It was Sukkot and Feige, an Orthodox Jew and a follower of the Lubavitcher Rebbe, decided to celebrate the holiday by attending a Hasidic music concert in the West Bank city of Hebron – the burial place of the patriarchs and matriarchs. "I went to hear music, and by the way, to give regards to our forefathers, whom I hadn't visited in years. As it turned out I required their prompt intervention." She managed to hear only a few chords from the orchestra before feeling the blast from Palestinian gunfire "like a baseball, or coconut, fired from a cannon." Feige was seriously injured and a nineteen-year-old woman was lightly wounded in the shooting incident. "Fortunately it was not so dramatic – I got shot, I got better. Unfortunately other people have got worse stories than mine. Now I can see that it was very much something to be thankful for. Everything eventually went back to normal, except in my mind, which sees life a bit differently now."

Feige was a thirty-eight-year-old, twice-divorced mother of five (ages six to seventeen) who had made *aliya* to Israel from the United States in 1979 with her family for religious reasons. "What are we doing in Israel if not for religion?" She has had several prior traumas and feels the hardships have made her stronger. "Getting shot in a terrorist attack was the tip of the iceberg. I've gone through worse things – two divorces, a terrorist attack, five kids, and coming to Israel."

For Feige, the attack lasted "the length of eternity, divided into many split seconds, each of which is etched into my being forever. In the first split second, a voice from deep within me said, in English, 'You're going to live.' In the next split second, I thought, 'Gosh, I ought to let someone know about this,' and besides, it's customary in such situations to fall on the floor, which I accomplished promptly; but when I tried to scream '*Niftzati!*' (I'm wounded!), it came out like a groan. In the next split seconds, I heard what sounded like popcorn popping and I thought, 'What a *shlemazel* (luckless person) – you're even missing the firework display.' Then, I heard an announcement over the loudspeaker that we're being fired upon and that the IDF (Israel Defense Forces) is returning fire."

Next thing she knew, "I'm surrounded by people with pitying looks on their faces and I wonder, 'Why are they looking at me like that and does all that blood over there belong to me, and I hope they get someone professional over here to take care of this, and I wish those people with the television cameras would go away because I don't think my *sheitel* (wig) is on straight.' I was greatly relieved to see the men in the orange vests, and pleased when they wrapped me up thoroughly, so that my insides would stop falling out."

As they rushed her to Hadassah Hospital thirty kilometers (19 mi.) north in Jerusalem, she explained to them that "everything is fine, it's just a bit difficult to breathe, so they should please drive slower if they can. They didn't even answer me. They just looked at each other and drove faster. They called base: 'We're bringing in a casualty, moderate to serious.' I thought, 'Who can they mean? The only one in here is me!' I asked them to call my sister-in-law, who was in my house with my two youngest daughters. The thought bothered me that maybe no one knew that I was wounded. Little did I know that everyone knew, and immediately."

Between the time that she was shot and they got her to the hospital, "my situation started clarifying itself. It seems that in the human body everything is interconnected. Getting one part hurt can get so complicated because it affects everything else. In a *pigua*, sometimes it seems like a tunnel without a light at the end. One situation in your body gets better and then another one is worse. And you just don't see the end of the tunnel and you and the doctor together don't always know what to decide."

The doctor told her: "Lady, you had a miracle. The bullet went in here, on your right side and stuck here" – just under the skin of her left breast. Bituach Leumi (National Insurance) considers Feige to be 11 percent disabled due to a hole in her liver that she can feel when she breathes deeply. "I like my scars. They remind me again that you aren't just here for nothing. But I was fortunate that I didn't see anything. I didn't hear anything. I just felt this bullet in my side. And so it's hard to be traumatized because I didn't really see anything." However, she – and her children – are still easily startled when they hear noises sounding like gunshot – or firecrackers from a nearby Arab celebration, as I witnessed while visiting them in their apartment in Ramot, one of Jerusalem's ring neighborhoods.

Feige feels that her experience mirrored others in similar life-threatening situations. She spoke of "a moment when their life is leaving them and – it sounds strange – whether or not to make an effort to keep their life in them, whether to drag themselves back and not give up on life. If they did give up on it, well, they're not around to tell about it… Getting shot didn't shake my faith in God. Just the opposite, I learned to appreciate even more God's divine providence over each person."

Feige appreciated the support she received. "One thing that was nice – if there are any nice parts to getting wounded – is finding out what everybody thinks of you, finding out that everyone likes you. It's one of these rare opportunities that most people don't get – like attending your own funeral and living to hear yourself eulogized. Everyone spoiled me after." The kind nurses tended to her personal and medical needs; her dedicated mother was torn between visiting her daughter at Hadassah Hospital and caring for her ninety-six-year-old mother; her brothers and sisters-in-law were called to help with the critical decisions; her community and neighbors took care of her, her kids, and her household; hundreds of people came to visit, worried, and prayed for her; people came from other countries in order to give healing treatments or donations; and various private organizations offered support – vegetable distribution, a trip, a camp for the children. And they all wanted to do everything for her. "I didn't have to worry about anything except getting better. The people were great!"

On the other hand, she admits that "I did not like needing others. I felt terrible when my mother had to accompany me to all of these tests. Then I had the opportunity to go with her for something simple, having a cataract removed. It felt much more natural, because it is natural to accompany your mother. It is not natural for a mother to be accompanying her daughter."

After the attack, Feige heard that the army had taken over the hilltop overlooking Hebron from where many others had been killed. "And I was happy about that. It made sense of my having gotten wounded. I went for a cause. I'm the last one and then it's going to be all better… But then they gave it up again." If she had any extra time or energy, Feige thinks she would like to work with politically oriented groups to save Israel, like VAT International (Victims of Arab Terror), founded by journalist and activist Shifra Hoffman "to publicize the crucial issue of Jewish victims in the Arab-Israeli conflict who are all too often ignored and forgotten."

Despite her personal hardships and living with the constant threat of terrorism, Feige remains a Zionist and wants to continue to live in Israel. Furthermore, she thinks every Jew has to come and make *aliya* because Israel is the safest place in the end, given all the anti-Semitism in the world which is "so close to what you hear about the Holocaust." Wherever one chooses or happens to live, Feige has come to the conclusion that "God makes it so people can live where they live; otherwise they wouldn't be able to live." She feels that Israel is the best place to raise children to be independent, healthy, and happy. She knows that she has to give her children their freedom, but "sometimes I feel as if having all my kids alive might be a temporary situation and I appreciate each day that I have them. You don't take it for granted that all your children went out and they all came back. You send them out in the morning and you bring them back and you feel like Little Bo-Peep counting her sheep when they come back."

Like other Israelis, Feige walks around with existential anxiety about living in Israel. "Today, the soldiers are fair prey and civilians are also targeted. Death becomes much more a way of life than it should be. I get even more upset than I used to whenever I hear of anyone else getting hurt. And I feel terribly helpless just going on with life after hearing of people wounded in terrorist attacks. I feel dysfunctional when I think of their suffering, which may be worse than mine was – a thought that is hard to bear, and vaguely guilty, as if I am not quite sure if I was wounded too badly or perhaps, somehow, not badly enough."

After recovering for six months, Feige went back to the same job she had before as a secretary for a company that imports medical equipment and chemicals. A few years later she left that job because she no longer wanted to work from nine to five. "The terror attack made me realize that not everything is work." She really likes to write, but is not writing a book about her own life because "it's too dangerous to really sink all your time and energy into remembering all the muck and mire that you went through and digging into it to write about it. It's too traumatizing."

Feige uses humor as a way to deflect attention away from her real fears and anxiety. A therapist helped her understand that her feeling of general anxiety is because "I am feeling inadequate. For the same price that it cost to think you are inadequate, you can also decide that you are adequate. It immediately drops a heck of a lot of the energy that you were wasting trying to cover up your supposed inadequacy. And it is nice to realize you are okay and you can use all that extra energy in making progress."

As she told her story to me, Feige discovered, much to her surprise and wonderment, that she is a survivor, not a victim. "That's the first time I have ever called myself a survivor and it rings with the same ring as a Holocaust survivor. Wow, it feels like Superman! It's nicer to say you are a survivor than a victim. I always call myself a terror victim. I didn't feel like a victim. Survivor is a good word – it gives a good psychological feeling." She realizes that "certainly I do have a lot in common with all the rest of them" and she recognizes that this might have been because she had been "denying to myself that it really happened – that it was bad." Maybe now she hopes "I'll do better things with my life."

In the summer of 2006 Feige and her *bashert* (destined) Asher Glasomitsky, a Russian immigrant and scribe of Torah scrolls and other religious writings, found each other. They married in September – the third marriage for each of them. They both like the image they have given themselves of "being an old, rather than a young, couple because it has the advantage of wisdom that develops with age." They joke about "where we've been all these years" without finding each other. They both bring to the marriage a lot of baggage – "with nine children, backgrounds, opinions, and habits" – as well as lively senses of humor and a mutual understanding that "had we met at any other time in our lives, it would not have worked. We both had to go through all of the terrible things that we went through and have our egos beaten out of us in order to appreciate normalcy. And to learn how to get along by overlooking things that are less important." They both have learned an important lesson from their hardships – not just from the *pigua*, but from all their life experiences – about how to find happiness and meaning in their lives.

On Sukkot of 2008, on the seventh anniversary of the attack, "the whole family – Asher's children and mine – went to a concert in Hebron – the same band playing at the same place. I was required to recite the blessing one makes upon returning to the spot where she was saved from danger: 'Blessed are You…Who made a miracle for me in this place.' I wondered how to say it so that those attending the concert could answer amen and the logical thing to do seemed to be to say it into the microphone. We approached the concert organizers, and before I knew it, I was introduced and my story recalled on stage. My blessing was broadcast to everyone attending the concert, on the radio, and over the internet! Asher saw that I was very emotional, and he's glad that God saved me for him. The Hebrew word *asher* means happy and we are still very happy together. He's a great guy and we are doing it together – repairing the trauma of being a trauma family… Happy ending!"

After seven years of marriage, Feige's and Asher's three oldest children are married, and their "babies" are eighteen and nineteen years old. They have struggled with and survived a few health problems, including Asher's recent bout with cancer. They are both survivors, surviving every day, he with his medical situation and she pulling him through. "It's all about surviving; is there a choice?"

Egged bus no. 830 bombing, Megiddo Junction near Afula: June 5, 2002

Avraham (Avi) Robinson: Half-Full Glass

"My philosophy is not to look to the past, but instead to look to the future."

Avi did not enjoy learning Talmud and was very bad at mathematics, so in high school he decided to study Arabic and linguistics. He studied for his first and second degrees and then went into the army where he spent ten years as an orientalist. He was a supervisor of Arabic studies in Jewish schools in the Ministry of Education for many years. After taking early retirement he continued to be involved in grading matriculation exams, marking notebooks for the written exams at home, and going to the schools for the oral exams. At the time of the attack, Avi was on a bus from Tel Aviv going to Bet Yerach High School by the Kinneret (Sea of Galilee) to administer the oral exams.

Avi was injured and seventeen people were killed when a booby-trapped car packed with a large quantity of explosives struck Egged bus no. 830 as they passed through Megiddo Junction near Afula. The early morning bus was packed with soldiers and a few civilians, including immigrants from Russia and Ethiopia. Avi "sat on the right side, two seats before the exit door, near the window. By me sat a female soldier." As they approached the junction, "the bus had to slow down for a traffic light. Suddenly I heard a huge explosion and saw fire. I was a little bit dizzy, but I understood immediately what had happened. I didn't know if it had happened inside the bus or outside the bus. Then I looked instinctively to the back and I saw a terrible fire and people being burned alive. I won't forget it my entire life. The fire was so big that they danced in the fire up and down, up and down. The fire shook them and they cried terribly. Afterwards the police told me it was 150 kilograms (330 lb.) of explosives, enough to raze a big mall."

During the attack, Avi remained in control. He told himself, "Avi, your life is not over. You have something to do in your life, save your life. Don't look back. You have to hurry. If you don't hurry, you will be dead or burned like them." Then he decided, "Avi, jump from the window. Maybe you'll break something, but you will stay alive! So my big fortune was that the bus inclined a little bit to the right side. I jumped and I fell, standing up. It was a miracle!" Avi grabbed the female soldier sitting next to him and jumped with her out of the bus, thus saving her life as well. Once safe, he had the presence of mind to borrow a cellular phone to contact his wife, his two sons, and his daughter. "I wanted to tell something to my family because I was sure they were watching the television."

A few hours later, he was on television, speaking from his hospital bed in a big hall full of wounded people at Emek Medical Center in Afula. "I think I was the only one who could speak English. And from the first moment media from all over the world came to me! I felt that I had to bring the words of Israel and the damages of terror to the world. If I could do it, I had to do it, even if I suffered and it was difficult for me. I saw it as a mission." Avi was in the hospital for four days. Later he spent fifteen days at Hadassah Hospital–Ein Kerem in Jerusalem for a skin graft.

Avi remembers and appreciates the goodness of many people who helped him through his ordeal and its aftermath: The driver of "a private pickup came and picked up all the wounded people who could stand or sit" and drove them directly to the hospital in Afula. Avi wasn't able to find him to say thank you. "That's a real mitzvah (meritorious or charitable deed) – to do a mitzvah without waiting for thanks." The x-ray technician calls every Rosh Hashanah, wishing Avi a "happy New Year, a better year than you had the last year. I can't forget you. I asked you to stand up because the x-ray would be better if you don't lie on the bed. I had doubted you could do it, but you did it very well. You suffered but you did it." Avi cannot forget "people we didn't know from Afula who saw that we were not from Afula and invited my family to their home," or members of a nearby kibbutz who "came to visit me and brought jam and everything that I liked and things that I needed."

The Hasidim from Chabad came with a band and danced and sang. And many VIPs visited, including Foreign Minister David Levi who came only "for the mitzvah of *bikkur cholim* (visiting the sick) and not for public relations. I appreciated it very much."

Avi was also supported by his friends and acquaintances outside the Jewish community. One friend, a political refugee from Egypt, didn't leave his bedside and helped a lot with services that were very difficult for his children and family to do "and did it very nicely and devotedly." Also one of the Arabs from a neighboorhood village, Dabourya, came and started to kiss him and hug him. Though Avi had met the Arab only once, at a conference, the man told Avi, "I'm so sorry about you. I am so sorry that it happened to you. You have to forgive us – the Arabs – for this." And finally, an Arab woman, who was afraid to identify herself "because there is a lot of prejudice against Arabs, especially after the terror attacks," left on each bed a package with a rose and chocolate and a greeting card in cellophane. On the unsigned card, she wrote, "Be healthy – if you will be with light you will win."

Avi freely describes his many physical and mental ailments resulting from the *pigua* and how he deals with them so they do not take over his life. According to the National Insurance, he has a 42 percent disability. In "good times" Avi is vital and full of life. In "bad times" he suffers from pains in his legs, especially the wounded leg where he was burned and had skin grafts; a recurrence of asthma that may have been caused by the smoke from the burning bus or from stress and anxiety; damage to his short-term memory but "my great fortune is that I have no damage to my long-term memory – all my knowledge is still there and I can work"; broken ribs "but I have no pain – a little pain, not so serious"; high blood pressure; fatigue, yet trouble sleeping; and more recently diabetes.

From time to time he becomes nervous and a little depressed and has "one or two days when I don't talk to anyone, only a few words. I also have problems with relationships inside the family because I have no patience for little things. I came to the conclusion after this *pigua* that the main thing in life is our life. And that quarreling about very tiny things – I can't do it anymore; so I go to my room and close the door. I enjoy the quiet – to watch television, to listen to music, or not to do anything. It's good for me." He cannot visit crowded places where a lot of people gather "unless it is entertainment or a concert." At first he was afraid to go by bus – "I went on buses sometimes and felt ill afterwards," but gradually he overcame his fears. Sometimes he sees "the fire, the explosion in front of my eyes." When something reminds him of what happened "I try to overcome it, but it's not in my control. I'm sorry it is not in my control. But I think that I am generally functioning quite well."

At a core level, Avi seems to have an innate sense of what he must do and initiates action in order to move himself forward in spite of his suffering. He actively took control of his recovery process and made healthy choices. Although many visitors came to visit when he came home, "I felt that I was alone – totally alone. I couldn't work. I couldn't even sit for ten minutes by the computer and work. I got terrible pains and I lost my concentration. I couldn't even watch television, which I usually really enjoy doing. The situation was terrible for me." Finally, the doctors told him that he had to go to physiotherapy and for daily walks by the sea with a friend or he would lose his ability to walk. "And it was good for me to get out. It made things a little bit better."

Finally he asked for psychological help despite the stigma. Avi believed that "in Israel, when you go to a shrink or psychiatrist you are a crazy man. You have to hide and not tell anyone. It's considered a shameful thing. I didn't think about this. I told myself, 'Avi, you have to get help to overcome all your problems, all of your mental problems. And you have an excuse. It would be abnormal if you don't.' They gave me a very nice shrink. I have someone to talk with, someone who will listen to me. Someone who will from time to time give me his advice. I think I learned something from him." Avi also participated in a few therapy groups with other survivors of terror attacks, but found that what helped him the most was "myself. I helped myself. I worked with myself on myself."

Avi draws strength from "my belief in the future and my work. I like my work very much, it keeps me busy." As part of the recovery process, he decided that he had to return to his part-time work teaching

Arabic. Again, "I told myself, 'Avi, you have to get out of your house. Don't stay at home. You will suffer. If it will be difficult for you, you will have to ask to go home early.' I informed the social worker at the National Insurance of my decision and she was astonished – it was the first time that someone had asked her not to use all of the sick days that the government allows and to go to work!" She even succeeded in getting him money for a special taxi to and from work for more than a year – an extraordinary accomplishment.

Avi also turned to good deeds and started to volunteer to help terror victims, sharing with them how he makes sense of the terror act and finds meaning in life. "If you need someone to comfort people or to try to help them, then you can send to me people to talk with, to encourage them. To show them that there is life after the terror act and that life is not finished. You can live after; with all of the burden that you carry, you can live. You can function. It's not the end of the story." He also studied all the laws and rights connected to terror victims and compiled the names of all of the volunteer organizations that deal with terror victims and the type of aid that each organization provides. "I am glad that I have these opportunities because I can help them a lot. I think it's because I have a special nature maybe, special characteristics, which enabled me to see myself as normal despite what happened. I have enough power to try to overcome my problems. And I talk and I hear a lot of stories. And I understand that my situation is not the worst one."

Avi has gained useful insights from observing terror victims he has worked with. "If you had personal or family troubles before you were wounded, then it becomes more and more intense after because you try to find a new focus for your personal disabilities, and hang everything on what happened to you and ignore your personal troubles that you had in the past. *Now I am not guilty. Now the government is guilty! Now the National Insurance is guilty!* Terror victims have a new address to blame others rather than themselves, and it's easy for them to look for help only from others, instead of doing it for themselves."

With this understanding, Avi tells every terror victim that "if you don't want to suffer, you have to be busy all the time – even to be tired – looking for new challenges. When you are busy you have no time to think about your suffering. Being at home and thinking about what happened makes you crazy. We have to be busy – at work, or going out to concerts, to music, to visit with friends. That is what keeps me going." But it is not just being busy that is important to him: "It was always the nature of what I've been doing – dealing with many sorts of work. Not routine work, but moving from place to place or doing many different things, many kinds of work."

Until his early twenties Avi was an Orthodox Jew, but he was secular before the attack and remains secular. He does not agree with his religious Jewish and Muslim friends who told him that "God kept an eye on you! God saved you! God loves you!" "I say if God loves me, why did He send me on this bus? He wanted to try you. I think it's nonsense! I don't know why it happened. I don't want to know. I don't bother myself. So it happened."

Now in his sixties, Avi has the wisdom of age – "It's not wisdom, it's my experience." He thinks about life a lot. "And I appreciate the times I am still living. All my life my philosophy has been to try not to look to the past, but instead to look to the future. I am sixty-five years old and I'm still searching for new ways or new directions for the future. I want to keep moving. I have a lot of trouble, but I try to exist. I think I could make some good things from this bad accident." Avi is hopeful, optimistic, and positive. "I try to see in everything the half-full glass, not the half-empty glass. I think I try to get some benefit from this wounding."

Five years after the attack, Avi is "working and functioning very well – more than in the past. I have more work, more jobs, and new projects." In addition to giving exams to high school students, he is lecturing at Bar-Ilan University, teaching Arabic to American government workers, translating for the Ministry of Foreign Affairs Arabic website, translating a book, teaching Arabic to health-care professionals, and providing guidance on the Arab culture to public institutions.

As an orientalist, Avi "still keeps very good relations with Arabs like before. I didn't change my opinions about it. My opinions about coexistence are not a supermarket to build with. My experience cannot change my opinions. My wife changed a little bit of her opinions. At the beginning she was not willing to visit Arab villages like we used to before, but good friends made us a party – Arab friends – and she went there in an Arab village. And we took part in some conferences and some of them I organized on coexistence of Jews and Arabs." He has started to organize tours for visitors from abroad and for Israelis to meet Arabs or Druze in their villages.

Telling his story "is like a catharsis for me." Avi has told his story numerous times, especially to non-Jewish Muslim and Christian audiences, both in Israel and abroad. He is an ardent advocate for peace. At a meeting with a Jordanian delegation, he told them that "'I work with Arabs – and by the way I gave a blood donation to the Israeli-Arab dispute.' 'What?! What happened?' 'Ah, you want to hear? I'll tell you what happened to me.' So I told them about terrorism and how bad terror is. I saw two women with tears in their eyes. And they were very, very interested – very, very."

On the eleventh anniversary of the attack, Avi writes that "it's like my second birthday. I have a lot of terrible memories. But let's start with good and happy things." He and his wife Sara are grandparents to four lovely grandchildren, three from their daughter Vardit, and one from their son Ziv. Their youngest son Paz left home a few months ago, so now they have empty rooms waiting for visits from the grandchildren.

Although most of his friends are retired and his wife works twice a week in an ulpan teaching Hebrew, "I'm working more than a full-time job because I love my work and I need it for economic reasons." For about two years, he has been freelancing for a high-tech company. "Imagine, I'm sixty-nine years old surrounded by youngsters." In addition, he has some other clients. "I need to work very hard, even if I don't feel well."

Avi still suffers from some symptoms of posttraumatic stress and is afraid to be in crowded and closed places and to use public transportation. His medical situation has deteriorated. He has serious damage to the nerves in his neck, which affects his feet and his balance. "I'm strong in my spirit. It's difficult for me to walk, but I'm walking with many limitations, because I have no other choice. My wife Sara helps me a lot and drives me everywhere I need." Although his physicians say that there is a direct connection between his injuries from the bombing and these later complications, the Israeli National Insurance doesn't acknowledge this connection. So he does a lot of sports and has various treatments to stabilize his balance, paying for them by himself.

Suicide bombing, Amakim Shopping Mall, Afula: May 19, 2003

SY: Living My Dream

"You have to survive for them."

S Y, a forty-eight-year-old Bolivian-born vascular surgeon, was living his dream. After completing his second residency at Soroka Hospital in Beer Sheva, he was invited to build a vascular surgery unit in Emek Medical Center in Afula – a hospital with a diverse staff in the middle of the Jezreel Valley, treating patients of all religious and cultural backgrounds. "I always had a dream to come back someday to our house here in Alon Hagalil, which is a green area and not like the desert. And from that moment I could not sleep. It came from excitement. And after one year of working in vascular surgery, everything was going so well I started to feel afraid. I started to worry. I said what's going on?"

He does not tell his story often. As he tells me his story over a freshly brewed cup of coffee, he is amazed "how things go one after the other to bring me to the exact moment." SY was supposed to return a movie to a video shop in the mall, but decided to go instead to a clinic in Kiryat Shmona near the Lebanon border to treat some patients. "So, I thought, I'll give the movie back tomorrow." The next day at the hospital, "I started to write a book. I remember making a good cup of coffee. I was in a good mood because I knew that I had to prepare three patients for a very big operation day on Tuesday. At ten to five, I wanted to go. I finished working and one of the nurses said to me, 'Listen, you worked too hard today. Sit here and drink one more coffee and then go home and drive carefully. Another ten minutes.'"

At 5:20 p.m., he walked into the Amakim Mall in Afula. "Nobody was at the entrance to the mall. I came in with the movie, and the security man started to check everything because he was new – his first hour and a half on the job. Politely, I said to him, 'Listen, you have to be more selective. You just questioned someone who speaks Hebrew and please, look what you've done.' By now, twenty people were in line… And then a woman came. I remember her face – not even hate in her eyes. She looked at me I'd say with cowy eyes, kind of looking at a distance, but not with hatred. She was sweaty and she had curly hair." The young woman was nineteen-year-old Palestinian suicide bomber Hiba Daraghmeh, an English literature student and a devout Muslim. She usually covered herself from head to toe in a traditional Islamic veil but she had removed it, disguising herself in the fashionable clothes of a modern Israeli woman, so nobody would suspect she had high-grade explosives strapped to her body.

SY continues his story: "As the security man said, 'Okay, you can take your phone,' there was a kind of noise. Afterwards I didn't see anymore, but I didn't feel yet the depth of what had happened. Because when you are near a bomb you don't hear it like you hear it when you are far. When you are far away, it moves air physically, and it sounds *boom*. When it is near you, it doesn't have time to move the air. So it sounds totally different. It sounds sharp and strong. And I knew that it was something that I had never heard before in my life – but I didn't grasp yet what it was. I stood still. I didn't see anything. I said to myself, 'Oh my God, something is happening here.'"

The security guard – Kiryl Shremko, twenty-two – was killed and his partner Hadar Gitlin was one of seventy people wounded in the blast. Kiryl had emigrated from Russia three years earlier and had recently completed his service in the IDF Armored Corps. By preventing the suicide bomber from entering the mall, filled with about twenty-five hundred people, the guards saved countless lives. Also killed were Avi Zerihan, thirty-six, of Beit Shean, who had gone to the mall to find a new job and had apparently been waiting in line for the security check, and Hassan Ismail Tawatha, forty-one, a devout Muslim from the Israeli Arab village of Jisr a-Zarqa, who was attending classes in electronics at the regional college located in the mall.

True to his profession, SY started to diagnose what was happening to him. He ruled out electrical shock and a short circuit. "'The third possibility is that you were hurt in your eyes. And if you were hurt in your eyes, first you have to let the hospital know to cancel the operation tomorrow. Now wait a moment, it may not be just tomorrow. It may be that also you won't see anymore. Maybe you won't see your children again. You won't play football. You won't dive again. You won't be able to run as you did before. If that's so, please sound one more sound like you did before.' I talked to God and asked Him to take me with Him. Then I said, 'Wait a moment. It's a good solution for you. But your oldest son is fifteen and the other ones are twelve and five. What would they do? So if it is a punishment of yours to receive what you just received, take it because you have to survive for them. So now that you cannot escape and cannot fight, pretend that you are dead. So lie down and wake up when the shooting finishes. And that is what I did.'"

He was confused, but still wasn't worried. "I didn't know how I looked. I didn't know what was hurt. I didn't know how serious it was. So I was still confident that I would get out of this quite well." At first, he didn't hear anything – his eardrums were blown. After a few minutes he woke up and asked, "'Is there anybody here?' And someone shouted, 'He's alive!' I said, 'Of course I'm alive. Do you think I'm a dead man talking?' It was a foolish feeling that I had survived something. So it was kind of a joke. But nobody dared to get close to me. Later on, I understood why. I looked terrible." He was burned and bleeding all over his body. His right eye was hanging out and the other was severely injured. His teeth were blown out. The terrorist, "she was made into butter on me because she stood near me. Only her leg was found about twenty meters (65 ft.) from the area."

SY started to feel desperate, but nobody would come close because they were scared...and shocked. Finally a young paramedic came and SY said to him, "Don't think I want to give you orders. I am asking – I am almost begging, please raise up my legs because I am going to faint. If you won't do it, I will lose consciousness." And then SY gave him his phone number and asked him to call his wife and tell her that "'I am blind, but I am still living.' And he said, 'I will raise your legs, but that sentence I will not say.' But he called her. He raised my legs and I felt a bit better."

The ambulance came and took him to Emek Medical Center's emergency room, where none of the attending staff recognized him due to his head injuries. They too felt shock and agitation when they learned that it was Dr. SY himself – not one of his patients – who had been injured. Finally, he told his colleague, the anesthesiologist, "'I've started to suffer. I'm starting to feel the pain and listen, I'm stable. No more stitches required. No more procedures are needed. I don't know what is going to be tomorrow. For today, please make me disappear. Give me something.' He said, 'Yes, he's right. I'm going to stop his suffering.' I thanked him and he gave me morphine. And the last thing I remember is my head falling down. And I said, 'Listen, I'll try to sleep because tomorrow probably when I wake up, I'll start thinking about what I'm going to have to go through. So let's live for today.'"

SY was transferred to Rambam Hospital in Haifa and spent a month undergoing multiple operations. His remaining eye improved, but "my torture was in parts." A few days before his son's bar mitzvah in November, he had a retinal detachment and was almost totally blind. "But I took a chance and I said I want the operation after the bar mitzvah in order to see what I can. Because I didn't know if that was the last time I would see him. So I had one more operation and then it got better." A year later he couldn't see anything. The cornea was dead. A month later, he received a cornea transplant.

When he first returned home from the hospital, "the dog wasn't sure. The family wasn't sure. I started with the dog because he was the first personality that I saw. He was so happy. He was a chow-chow dog. It takes years until he expresses love. By that time he had already started to love. To see a tough guy loving, it was something. I was waiting for it. And he came and he smelled me and he was in shock." After SY was injured, the dog lost his hair from depression. About a month later, he had a fight with another dog and died. Someone heard what happened and offered SY a new chow-chow dog. "And the children say that they think she was very, very important in the family recuperation."

"And here all of a sudden my life changed." SY's limited vision enables him to work here and there. "So it's okay." He has returned to vascular surgery, doing a bit of the diagnostic part, and working a lot. For a year he taught vascular surgery. He decided to try to practice psychiatry, but was discouraged when he was told that "you don't look sad enough and you're pretending that you're okay. You should be more sad because if you don't express your pain, the first wind that blows will knock you down. Someone going through what you have gone through should ask himself if he has the right to treat people." But he did know firsthand what it was like to experience depression, not only from the books. "I felt it. And it's not only a flash. It's not only in your muscles that you feel it. It is something that digs a soul, a brain, and gives a color to the world. Sometimes I woke up and didn't cry much, but I cried bitterly on my little woman's shoulder." He has not given up. He plans to study healing and hypnosis; then maybe he will study psychotherapy via an internet course.

SY has identified several phases that he has passed through since the trauma. "The first phase is the romantic phase – when everybody sympathizes with you and is afraid that something like this will happen to them. In the second phase, there are two possibilities: either you complain and ask for help and think you should take advantage of your injuries from the Bituach Leumi, from Social Security, from friends, and from everybody; or, you get back to the circle of life." And what he feels now in the last phase is that "the world goes on. Nobody has time to think about you. If you are not strong enough, and don't have the capacities and the will and the need, you are far behind. If you take advantage of your situation, then you can either choose something sweet or something bitter, and that's what I am doing." Once in a while, "I'm depressed, sad, or worried, and I ask why did it happen? And I still envy some of my colleagues who are operating. But on the other hand, I don't swim in that bitterness. I try to enjoy. I'm trying to live a far better life than people who were not injured or even how I was before the injury."

He finds that "now I have a bit more time. When I was busy – very, very busy, I always had the illusion that it's only today that I am working like this – tomorrow it will be over – it will be finished. Now I have the time to feel. If I am not lazy, maybe I will go for a walk outside with the dog."

As fate would have it, before the attack, Dr. SY had operated on wounded terrorists, saving the life of a suicide bomber wounded when his explosives detonated prematurely, and reattaching the hand of a bomb maker who only hours earlier had helped kill thirteen Israeli soldiers. SY remembers commenting during the surgery: "Tell the terrorists, when they make a bomb for me to make sure it's a small one because I have saved the lives of many of them... But I never for a moment thought it would come true."

Chapter 5

Tel Aviv

*high rises, high tech, and the high life... only
a few kilometers from the Green Line... frequent
stage for attack*

Tel Aviv, located on the coast of the Mediterranean Sea, is the
heart of the largest and most populous metropolitan area in Israel.
Greater Tel Aviv is Israel's economic and cultural capital with a vibrant,
cosmopolitan feel.

Early in the Second Intifada, on June 1, 2001, Tel Aviv was ravaged
by the massacre of twenty-one teenagers and the wounding of another
120 people – most of whom were new immigrants from the former
Soviet Union – when a suicide bomber blew himself up outside a
disco near Tel Aviv's Dolphinarium on the seafront promenade. It was
just before midnight on a Friday night and the area was packed with
youngsters waiting for admission to the disco and the adjacent "Pacha"
nightclub. Standing in line with the teenagers, the terrorist detonated
the explosives strapped to his body. The explosive charge contained a
large number of metal objects – including ball bearings and screws – to
increase the extent of injuries.

Despite international condemnations and negotiations, restaurants,
cafés, and clubs continued to be targeted, including the beachfront pub
Mike's Place on the Tel Aviv promenade, next door to the American
Embassy. Joshua Faudem, the pub's twenty-eight-year-old American-
born bartender and a filmmaker, captured the experience and its

aftermath in this chapter and in his award-winning film *Blues by the Beach*.

As in Jerusalem and throughout the country, buses and bus stops were also targeted. Thirty people were killed and two hundred were wounded in three attacks in and around Tel Aviv between September 2002 and January 2003. Aharon survived the bombing in the suburb of Ramat Gan across from Bar-Ilan University and shares his experience.

Tel Aviv and its neighboring communities were not the only targets. Traveling north along the coast are the cities of Herzliya and Netanya, whose beautiful beaches make them popular tourist resorts. Yet their proximity to the West Bank, only a few kilometers away, has made them frequent targets for terrorist attacks. Isaac Ashkenazy tells the story of how he and his eleven-year-old son Jonathan survived the bombing at the Jamil Shawarma Restaurant in downtown Herzliya.

In later chapters, we will hear from several other survivors of terrorist attacks in Netanya, where three deadly attacks occurred at the Hasharon Mall, another was in the market, and three more were in downtown Netanya, including the Park Hotel.

Son Jonathan injured, Jamil Shawarma Restaurant bombing, downtown Herzliya: June 11, 2002

Isaac Ashkenazy: Positive One

"If you are properly balanced, it's like a symphony"

Isaac was born in Calcutta, India, of Iraqi-Syrian Jewish heritage – a "Judeo-Arabic" heritage anglicized by the British colonial educational system, and was nurtured in the "soil of the Indian collage." Immigrating to Israel in his early twenties in 1977, he was forty-seven at the time of the attack. He runs his own freight-forwarding business. Once a professional musician, now it is "just a romance and a hobby" with occasional performances and music lessons. His wife Ester, originally from Buenos Aires, Argentina, is an assistant to the commercial attaché in the Mexican Embassy in Israel. They have two children – Jonathan, and a daughter Maayan. Maayan served in an army parachute regiment in Shechem (Nablus). "It's not the best of conditions there, even for a soldier. The traveling back and forth has an element of danger. Especially after what happened to Jonathan, you don't want a calamity happening to any other member of your family."

Although they were together, Isaac thinks of this as Jonathan's story "as he was sadly injured. My poor son is haunted daily by his physical scars, as well as the emotional trauma. It's really Jonathan's story – his *tikkun* (repairing or healing). I was there to nurse and offer moral support."

Isaac relates what happened: "It was just a coincidental evening. I left work early as I had to give a music lesson on the way home. But the pupil called me in my car to cancel the lesson, and I was thrilled to be arriving home early. I invited Jonathan to accompany me to the city center to buy some light bulbs. But, he wasn't keen on the idea. Literally I had one foot out of the door, when at the last minute he agreed to come with me. So we were happily walking hand in hand – a father and his beloved eleven-year-old son." They played the lottery for kicks, and then decided to step in somewhere for some fast food. It was a choice between a pizza and shawarma. Jonathan chose the shawarma. They walked into Jamil's Shawarma restaurant on the main street of Herzliya around 7:30 p.m. Shortly thereafter, "all hell broke loose."

Jonathan sat at a table inside the narrow restaurant. "I brought him his pita with two diet cokes and went back to pick up my order. I saw that Jonathan hadn't started on his pita and was waiting politely for me. I felt honored that he was such a gentleman. Turning back to the table, pita in hand, I was about to go around someone standing behind me, when there was an explosion… On a pleasant summer evening, orange skies of a setting sun – my life was cruelly plummeted into the bowels of hell."

"A loud *thud* – a powerful thump on my back – and I went sprawling on the floor; then the smell of gunpowder, black smoke, darkness, and the stunning seconds of silence. Throwing off to my left the person who was lying on my back, I noticed that he was of Arabic descent, and the entire front of his mid-lower body was gouged. Parts of his remains splattered on my back. I then grasped that this was a suicide bomb attack… Jumping to my feet, I rushed out of the restaurant. In the back of my mind I wondered, 'Why hasn't my son followed?' Before I could think any further, I heard his strong voice calling me in panic: '*Abba, Abba!*' (Father, Father!)."

"Gathering my legs, I charged back into the restaurant, skipping over the dead terrorist, jumping over his big black cloth bag that lay on the floor, and confronted a teenage girl – fifteen-year-old Hadar Hershkowitz – who sat on the floor, legs sprawled in an unnatural posture. She cried to me with panic-filled, young, innocent round-bespectacled eyes – 'What about me?' My mind rushed and fumbled for an answer. My heart and arms ached to reach out to her and offer her comfort, but I had to reach my son urgently. I knew that I had to offer hope and so I cried back, 'They're coming, they're coming!' and rushed to where my son was sitting frozen to his seat – panic-stricken! Hadar died later that evening; I was probably the last person she spoke to – the last soul that her earthly soul related to… I will forever remember."

Isaac shouted to Jonathan, "Come, let's get out!" But Jonathan cried back, "*Abba*, my eyes!" It was then that Isaac noticed that his son's left eye was bloody. "I rolled up his white T-shirt and held it to his eye in an attempt to bandage the bleeding. Holding him up under his armpits, I told him that we have to get out. Tripping over obstacles on the floor, I led us out of the restaurant and into the street. As I stood with his roughly bandaged head on my shoulders, I stroked his back, comforting him: 'Don't worry, don't worry, son.'"

It felt like an eternity until the paramedics arrived, but Isaac remained attuned to the environment. "Both of us were standing on the pavement – feeling a mess! – Jonathan half naked and bleeding all over his face. The front of my clothes was wet with my son's blood. From behind, I was bloodied with the terrorist's remains. The two of us clinging to each other, while around us, there was much turmoil. All around me was carnage; the injured lay bleeding, the cries, the panic, the police, the people, and traffic. But in that forced reality, all I could really feel was the thumping of my heart and the warmth of my son in my arms." The police were shouting at bystanders to stay away as there were still explosives in the black handbag. A passing friend asked if they needed assistance. "I told him to call my wife. I couldn't remember the number, but Jonathan somehow mumbled the number to him."

The paramedics arrived, and Isaac and Jonathan went to the hospital together. "All along I kept my son involved in conversation so that he would not lose consciousness. At the hospital I stayed by his side as we both went through a medical check-up. Holding one of my son's hands, I constantly reminded him that I was with him, informing him of what the doctors were doing." In about half an hour's time, Ester joined them, and together they accompanied Jonathan. "Henceforth began another stage in our lives – of hospitals, clinics, treatment, depression, emotional dysfunction at home and in society, financial setbacks, National Insurance, the list is long."

Isaac believes in the Jewish concept of *tikkun neshama* (repairing the soul) and that he was saved for some sort of purpose, and was meant to be there to give his injured son – his "soul brother" – his energies and help him heal and recover. "If you try and microfocus on that split second of life, I was so close! So close to my end! It just wasn't my time to go. Fate had ruled that it wasn't my time. I still hadn't done what I came to do in this life." And that purpose was to care for and comfort Jonathan throughout his recovery: "His love calms my spirit. Similarly I know that I offer him the same calm. Our souls are quite comforted with each other – our love, our energies."

Three weeks of intensive, grim, and excruciating hospital and medical treatment – all through which Jonathan didn't utter a word to anyone. "We will never forget the day when he finally had to remove his head bandages and view his new reality. After another three lengthy weeks of recuperation in hospice – our son finally returned home." He went back to school almost immediately; the educational system, the teachers, and his schoolmates helped him get back on his feet. "He's technically about 56 percent handicapped according to the National Insurance, but if I call him handicapped, he gets annoyed. He doesn't see himself as handicapped. Although Jonathan's facial scars are quite visible, he belittles it. His inner beauty is his *neshama* (soul). He has a lot of spirit and is full of life – he reminds us of our status in this tapestry of life and keeps us linked together."

At seventeen, Jonathan is tall, big, and strong. He loves music – playing piano, guitar, and singing. He studies theater at high school, and his physical handicap doesn't slow him down as he stands on stage facing rows of spectators. "In his mind he's just another normal person." Isaac believes that Jonathan's spirit and positive attitude comes from a higher source.

Isaac does not "look back, fortunately, and that's why I remain positive. I have to maintain strength for him. That's why he's turned out to be positive too." Although the attack happened to Isaac and Jonathan, his wife Ester suffered a mental and emotional breakdown and needed serious psychiatric treatment. Isaac cannot afford to allow himself to go backwards psychologically or emotionally. "With so much going on, I can't afford to be weak. I have to stand and stay strong – and make sure the family gets through the present storm – whatever the cost."

Isaac believes that his survival was a miracle and his life was offered to him as a second chance. "It was as if an angel smiled on me at the crucial second – just like the angel that spared the biblical Isaac's life from his father Abraham's sacrificial sword. Now that I live, I really feel that I have to fulfill my destiny – to move forward. That's the way I look at life. I have to remind myself to enjoy each day, every laughter, every song – and stay positive. My spiritual awareness gives me strength and purpose." When obstacles present themselves, "I have to go around them. My life was rewarded to me a second time around. I have to carry on. It's being human – a human being. Even from such horrific experiences, we learn something."

He describes his own "human-being defense mechanism": "You have two choices every morning when you wake up – to live the day positively, or negatively. When you are aware of sunshine and the brightness, you stay positive. So even my problems, I decide to accept positively. Maybe it's a form of rejection, but it's my way of getting over hard times. It's a matter of inner attitude – no time to look back."

Frustrated with government bureaucracy and the Bituach Leumi – the National Insurance, he decided that he couldn't wait for them to move forward. "So I decided to jump into the stormy water and open up my own company to try and cover our economic losses. At that time you don't think of what can happen. You just invest as much as you can, taking care of your son, taking care of your family." Isaac named his new global freight-forwarding company "Positive," reflecting his positive character and positive outlook on life – always taking positive action to move forward.

Isaac believes that if he as an individual is strong, it carries forward to his family, his neighbors, the neighborhood, the nation, the people, and the country. His personal strength comes from his beliefs and spiritual practices, including meditation, yoga, and studying the wisdom of Kabbalah. For him, spirituality is in every act you perform, your behavior, and your thoughts. He believes in inner beauty and inner peace and that everything is a matter of balance and harmony between the physical, intellectual, emotional, and spiritual dimensions. He has integrated all of these aspects in his own life and being, believing that "if you are properly balanced, it's like a symphony."

Ultimately, Isaac and Ester have learned how important it is to be with other people "who have been there" and not to be alone. Five years after the event, Isaac and Ester joined a Bituach Leumi support group of parents of children who were wounded in terror attacks – "to listen and to be listened to, and to help each other in a relaxing atmosphere of mutual respect and spiritual support." Their goal is to speak about their painful experiences and feelings, to legitimate their pain and difficult questions, and to work through what happened to themselves and their family.

Isaac is much more mindful about what he does, and what happens around him. "Now with a second chance to live, I ensure that I enjoy what I am doing, and don't idle on things that don't bring me pleasure. You learn to value each day and each moment, and live in it... I just value differently. I value with far more intensity and depth whatever I do. I don't do anything different from my past; I just value it with a higher awareness. The past is history. I am presently involved in this 'present' of life – and 'this' is the most valuable moment."

Eleven years "since our unfortunate brush with providence," including three years of trauma treatment on a one-on-one basis with a wonderful and experienced therapist and support groups, for Isaac "it is still painful and difficult to face the starkness of these emotional memories." However, "life goes on. We are all still loving and balanced individuals and a family. We are all still positive souls and '*am Yisrael* lives on...'"

Jonathan finished high school in 2009 and insisted on enlisting in the Israel Defense Forces for three years. Initially the IDF found it difficult to technically accept Jonathan into their ranks and on what status, as he is really exempt of his duties. But after continuous and stubborn pressure against the system, he succeeded in getting enlisted.

After his basic military training and a series of instructor courses, Jonathan charted his direction towards a position as an instructor at an army high school for youth from dysfunctional families. He enjoyed immense success, raising the percentage of students who finally completed their high school graduation and found themselves a technical profession within the framework of the army. He was complimented for his dedication, commitment, and love for his students and awarded the distinction of an outstanding soldier in a formal end-of-the-year ceremony in 2012. For his parents, "Pinning on his new rank and sharing photographs with the school staff and his superior army officers was a touching experience." He completed his service in September 2012 and in June 2013 again participated in the graduation of another year of students that he had guided and uplifted. Following his immense success in this sphere of life, Jonathan has decided to study at the university in Sderot to become a social worker.

Ester is still employed at the Embassy of Mexico in Israel. She still goes for weekly therapy for herself, but has also been through intensive training to volunteer her time to Natal – Israel's Trauma Center for Victims of Terror. From answering trauma victims over telephones, she has been requested to be available for home visits when necessary. She is also studying for "coaching" guidance at the Adler Institute. Maayan recently completed architectural studies at the Technion Haifa and lives in Tel Aviv with her boyfriend. Since 2010, Isaac has been blessed with a gratifying public relations position with the IJHC – Indian Jewish Heritage Center,[1] dedicated to preserving the united Indian Jewish heritage.

---

1   Indian Jewish Heritage Center, https://www.facebook.com/indianjews.

Dan bus no. 87 bombing, across from Bar-Ilan University:
October 10, 2002

Aharon: I Was in a Terrorist Attack

"Keep talking, telling the story."

It was shortly before 8:00 a.m. at a bus stop under the bridge across from Bar-Ilan University, in the Tel Aviv suburb of Ramat Gan. Aharon (a pseudonym) and his wife were on their way to their jobs at the university, where Aharon, forty-four, works as an audio-visual technician and his wife is a secretary. Dan bus no. 87 was just pulling up to the bus stop, which was crowded with rush-hour commuters. "The terrorist wanted to come to the rear door of the bus. The driver did not see him and closed the door. The terrorist fell down. Everyone thought it was an accident. When they opened his shirt to let him breathe, they saw the lines for the charge and let go of him."

"My wife and I were almost on the pedestrian bridge when people started shouting, 'Run away – it's a terrorist!' People say we did run. I don't remember; it was a matter of seconds. The minute people let go of him, he started walking around in circles. My wife cried, 'He's going to explode the bomb!' One second, two seconds, three seconds – on the ground – *boom!* I served in the army, I had a gun in the army, but this boom – it was not normal – between five and ten kilograms (10–20 lb.) – luckily it was an open space." The bomb was contained in an explosive belt strapped to the bomber's waist and was packed with bolts and ball bearings. Sa'ada Aharon, a seventy-one-year-old grandmother, was killed and about thirty people, mostly soldiers, were injured.

Despite an injured leg – "blood flew out like a sprinkler" – Aharon remained in control and took care of business. "I ran and got to the university gate. I sat and asked for some paper and I told my wife and the security people, 'Tell my office and the people I work with that I am hurt, and please open my office and do not forget to close it tonight.'

Only then I told him, 'Okay, get me an ambulance.'" Aharon also used his cellular phone to call his neighbor and to break the news to his daughter. "I told her a joke so that she'd relax."

Within moments of arriving at the hospital, he was surrounded by reporters and photographers. "It was hard to get away from them. Later on someone told me that immediately after the *pigua* they saw my name on the internet and then on the television. I refused to be interviewed because I didn't want my parents who are Holocaust survivors to know yet."

Aharon spent the weekend in the hospital following surgery to remove shrapnel from his leg. He recalls how wonderful people were in his religious community: "The word goes out and immediately someone takes care of you. The young ones were collected after kindergarten, fed, washed, and played with. Our neighbors even prepared the Shabbat food for us and I was told not to worry. At such minutes one realizes how good people can be. And when I came home from the hospital, my friends felt like family. It counts when you really need it."

In the hospital and later at home, "it's so quiet – you can read, sleep, and eat – but then the different thoughts take over and you see yourself as part of a chain of injured people – this one was injured, and this one, and this one, from settlements, from all over… Even though you want to see the kids, what you really want is this quiet. My thoughts drove me crazy. You try to sleep during the day, you sleep at night, and you keep seeing his face, the explosion, the blood coming out of my leg. You cry, 'I was injured!' You sit in the living room until you're tired, you fall asleep, and there it is again. You keep thinking, 'I was in a terrorist attack – what is to be?'

"In the first days you get annoyed by everything. I couldn't stand hearing kids bursting balloons. At first, I was left with two things – the strong smell of cordite (gunpowder) like you shoot in the army and this strong *boom-bum-bum* that you don't hear with weapons. This boom stays with you for a while, but slowly this too leaves and you return to yourself… And another thing – you see that everyone is watching you – it's a horrible feeling. It's not that you're different, but suddenly you're in the center of events – a terrorist attack!"

The advice from his Bituach Leumi (National Insurance) social workers and his doctors was very helpful: "'Relax, you are not the first one unable to get back to sleep; in time it will be over. Don't be stressed by it; let time take its course. Don't feel as if you're complaining; don't keep things inside; try to unburden. Keep talking, telling the story.' Really, you pour things out and you get to the point when it's natural, you won't weep; you talk and get it out, and it helped. Now I don't feel I need to talk about it."

For Aharon, "it's not the physical but the mental coping – the day-by-day coping – that is the most difficult, because the *pigua* actually creeps into your personality. Serving in the army is different: you have your comrades, and your weapon, and you're sort of ready; you carry a gun when you're in uniform. But here you feel like a martyr..." After a month at home, the social worker saw that Aharon was coping and told him "to get back to the routine of your life, get back to work – first because they needed me at work, and then for the coping – it's better to get back to work. I also kept myself busy teaching youngsters for their bar mitzvah; for me it's a kind of therapy, so that the head is less busy with what happened. I admit that in those weeks it was very difficult to concentrate. I listened, but it was not like now that I enjoy doing it. Then I had to fight with myself because I had to both separate myself from my feelings and listen to what others were saying."

The doctors also warned Aharon that "every terror event will always carry you back to the one you experienced." Now when an attack occurs, he is angry and nervous, but does not experience it as something personal. "Time does have an effect, but you're still more anxious... You are always carried back – sometimes to a greater degree, sometimes less, but you never get out of it altogether. But you learn how to get on with it, keep on living, there's nothing one can do. You have mixed feelings. You both remember how horrible it was and you're angry because it's happening again. How is it that people don't mind blowing themselves up?"

Aharon's parents are Holocaust survivors, and he learned from them about resilience. "Of course you are anxious, but you have the drive to go on. Thank God, my injury wasn't serious... It's just a particle of what they went through. It does have its impact, but one must keep going – that's the whole idea. The terrorist's goal is to interrupt the mental balance, so that people won't go to work, won't go to the theater, to youth movements – terrorists aim to disrupt the normal course of life. We go on, have weddings, bar mitzvahs, educate the kids, work as usual, but there's more fear, it's not the same."

Aharon also learned about coping and going on from other losses in his life – comrades from his army reserve unit and students at the university. "All of a sudden this one doesn't come back, and then another one." It was harder to cope with losing a friend who was a commander in Hebron or seeing the injured husband of a good friend than with the terrorist attack. "It shows that there are all kinds of difficult coping situations. But personally – I learned to go on, because there is no other way."

Aharon is an Orthodox Jew. His practice of religion has changed in at least one respect: "The relation to the words of the prayer has more meaning. Obviously, like everyone, there are highs and lows. Before and right after my operation, it was the peak of devotion; you feel like in seconds you won't be here. Now, I pay more attention to the words of the prayers, to really mean them."

Since the attack, Aharon understands what is and is not important and has "a more positive conception of life. You appreciate life more – how good it is, not how bad it is. After you're disabled, you value much more the fact that you're alive; you don't take it for granted. Thank God, the family is all right, the kids are all right. We study, we work, you go on living – there's no price tag for that." He also noticed something more – the family's reaction. "It united us, brought us closer together. Everyone has arguments with the kids, like homework issues, but since the event you feel the caring."

Mike's Place bombing, Tel Aviv promenade: April 30, 2003

Joshua Faudem: Rebuild and Continue On with Life[1]

"Life here in Israel – it's beautiful... This is what life should be about."

❝ I'm working at Mike's Place on the beachfront like a month and a half. About a hundred people were in the bar. And unfortunately, on April 30, the bomb went off at two minutes to one in the morning about eight meters (26 ft.) away from me… All I remember was seeing Gal Ganzman, the owner of the bar, behind the bar with his gun out; and he just hopped over the bar. I knew exactly what it was at the time and the first thing for me was to make sure my girlfriend, Pavla Fleischer, was okay. She had only been in Israel for two weeks. Everybody told her not to come. I was like, 'Whatever. What are the chances?' I jump on her, I take her, and I throw her in the kitchen in the back. And I come back out and I see all the debris in front of me. The first person that I got to was the security guard, Avi Tabib. He was a good friend of ours. Later we found out he stopped the terrorist from coming in. I got to him and I checked his pulse on his leg and there was barely a pulse. So this other guy came and said he was a doctor. He told me to go get a towel; so I ran and I got him a towel… And I'm just looking and I'm seeing the whole thing. Like the terrorist cut in half on the sidewalk – the whole thing – everything."

When the police and the medics arrived, "there was really nothing more for me to do. I would just get in the way. So I went back into the bar and it's empty, except for one customer, Yariv. He's standing in the bar with his cigarette and his glass of whiskey. He's like frozen – just looking at everything. I slapped him in the face and took him and my girlfriend out of there. We were the last people in there. From the

---

1   Joshua's mother, Arlene Faudem, contributed to this story. She moved to Israel from the United States in 1983 with her husband Burt and their four children, Michele, Jeffrey, Emily, and Joshua – ages fifteen through eight.

minute the bomb went off until the police got there, it was silent, scary silent. The minute the police came – *balagan* (confusion)."

"I saw dead bodies in front of me. At the same time I was giving CPR and looking around and making sure that I knew exactly who was hurt and where. I paid attention." Joshua reacted the way that he had thought he would. His army experience taught him to be very calm. "Not to freak out, to be relaxed and try to be in control and help others stay in control, and to be calm. If you're calm, you can help; if you're not calm, you're useless." He also was grateful for his father's inspiration, noting that his father would often say, "Relax, Joshua. Think out what you have to do. It's okay. Don't worry."

Fortunately, no nails were in the bombs. "If there were nails in that explosive, there would have been a lot more casualties, including myself probably. It was the first time that they used this chemical in the bomb that makes everybody dry and their heartbeat goes *bbb-bbb-bbb*." About sixty people were wounded and three people died. "One of them I knew very well. Dominique Hass was a waitress and she worked with me. She was a good enough friend for me to know about her love life and what she wanted to do with her future. Yanay Weiss was forty-six and came to the bar every Tuesday night for the jam session – it was a ritual. He would never drink a beer; he would have mineral water. He would play and then he would go home to his family. I didn't know the other guy who died, Ran Baron."

The next morning, when he heard that the security guard's condition had stabilized, "I couldn't believe it because I saw that he got it internally; on the other hand, because he was so close to the bomber, he was saved. The bomber had the bombs on his back – everybody who was in back of him or outside got it." Joshua and his girlfriend went to the hospital. "Our ears were shattered for about a week. And I don't remember this, but my girlfriend told me that for a month after the bombing, we would go to sleep and I would start shaking for a minute or two before I would fall asleep. I don't really remember having any dreams."

Nighttimes were the hardest for Joshua. "The night brings it all back. During the day, I'm busy as hell and I don't have time to think. Thank God." In the middle of the night, he drank whiskey and rode his bike at breakneck speed through the empty streets of Tel Aviv until he dropped.

Joshua, twenty-eight, was born in the United States and has lived in Israel since he was eight. When he was ten, his friend was killed in Sinai. "That was the day that I lost my innocence – my virginity. I love my religion. I love who I am. But I am just not a religious person. I never was and I'm still not." However, he believes in "some kind of energy, some kind of spirit, in reincarnation, in any religion that doesn't preach persecution and fundamentalism, that never hurt anybody – like Buddhism or Zen or whatever…or Judaism."

While serving in the army, he "experienced some sort of trauma. I was in a lot of places and I saw bodies. I saw detonations. I was shot at. I had Molotov cocktails thrown at me. But a terrorist attack is totally different. And I thought that I was immune. When I got out of the army, I thought that's it; but it's not like that at all. I needed a big breather; I needed to get out of here in order to come back." So Joshua lived abroad in New York, Prague, and Toronto for five years before returning to Israel. "I'm very much connected to Israel. It's the lifestyle. It's the habits. It's the culture. It's the freedom to go anywhere whenever I want."

Joshua does not worry about another attack. He knows that they happen and they are going to happen but he doesn't think about it. "And I don't say to myself, 'Oh, you're okay now. You don't have a chance, because you were already in one.'" He would rather think about a lot of other things "like my future, my future with my girlfriend, my family, my nephews, how to make myself a better person, how to help people who need my help… It comes back to friendships and stuff like that."

Following the attack at Mike's Place, Joshua and his friends immediately moved to action with purpose – rebuilding and reopening the bar within a week. His mother Arlene explains: "It was a week until Yom Hazikaron (National Memorial Day) and then that night was Yom Haatzmaut (National Independence Day). The kids were very busy because they wanted to have a memorial service on Yom Hazikaron in the early evening. And then they wanted to go into Yom Haatzmaut and celebrate, because that's what we do here. It had to be done and everyone worked hard doing it. I was surprised that after it happened they didn't collapse, emotionally. I mean I think they did, but it was a normal amount of collapsing. I thought for sure they were all going to be carried away, but it didn't happen and it's kind of who we are. I don't know where it comes from, because people do fall apart, but people go on."

Joshua is also a documentary filmmaker and, at the time of the bombing, he was in the process of shooting a film about the bar with American producer Jack Baxter. "The bomb goes off, everything changes. One of my main characters is gone. All of a sudden, Jack is injured and my girlfriend Pavla and I were in front of the camera instead of behind it." He continued with the documentary, finding it therapeutic, and completed it as a tribute to his friends and a lesson for the future.

His award-winning film, *Blues by the Beach*,[2] is a metaphor for how Joshua lives and appreciates life. Before the bombing, his purpose was to show the world the beautiful side of life in Israel, while living in the shadow of terrorism "because people in America don't know about this side of the life here in Israel and I think it's beautiful. And when I mean it's beautiful, this is what life should be about – blues and jazz and beautiful women and it's on the beach – a lot of people, Israelis, foreigners, Australians, English people." After the bombing, the focus of the film changed to show the world how people continue on with life in the aftermath of a terrorist attack. "It's about the reopening of the bar a week after the *shiva* (mourning period) – people just continuing on with life. Basically, it's very simple."

Joshua hopes that people will see the documentary and understand its powerful message. "The film is not political at all. And it so easily could have been political. Any person off the street knows what's happening in Israel. What people don't know are these little stories. It's just a human story and it's on a level that anybody who goes to a bar around the world will identify with, because it's about people – just a bar. You don't hear one word of incitement from anybody or anger or revenge – nothing. It's just that you've got to rebuild. You know we've got to keep on going. And that's the power of it."

---

2   *Blues by the Beach*, http://www.bluesbythebeachfilm.com/.

Pavla had come to Israel with him from Prague to try to find herself. After the attack their relationship completely nose-dived and she went back home. "She didn't understand the way I reacted. I didn't understand the way that she reacted. She needed to be with people who were not connected to the bombing, so she found her own whatever."

Joshua's parents thought he needed to speak to a psychologist because "something can set someone like that off and they could really be in a lot of trouble." At first he didn't go, feeling that there was a limit to what he could tell a stranger. "I can't talk to people that I don't know and I won't. It might be good. It might be bad. I choose to speak to people who know me and if someone who knows me gives me advice, I'll take it. If someone who doesn't know me gives me advice, why would I take his advice? He doesn't know who I am. He doesn't know my past."

Instead, he turned to his family and friends who have always been very important to him. He believes that part of being a friend is being the caretaker when needed. His mother vividly remembers going to see all of the people who worked in the bar – the "Mike's Place Family" – a couple of days after the *pigua*. "They were all in this apartment and it was like they were all sitting *shiva*. They were all in mourning. And that's where they needed to be – together. Because they all knew what had happened. They were all there." Joshua speaks with his friends about the bombing not to get answers, but just to get it out. He helped his friends and they helped him to heal in the aftermath of the trauma "by finding in each other something that they are good at and sharing the missing piece."

A year after the attack Joshua was still working in the bar around three times a week. He had a new girlfriend. He received a grant from a foundation in Israel that supports documentary films. And he was finishing another documentary that he had started before the bombing. A year later, "it all went to crap. My post-trauma disorder was at its height. I felt things closing in and I just lost it. My girlfriend Christina couldn't deal with it. She left and went back to the States. I scared the hell out of her. I scared the hell out of myself. It really broke my heart because she wouldn't deal with me. It was really hard for me because I was always told that you don't leave somebody when they are in the middle of a crisis. You don't jump ship on somebody who you love. That's what I was taught by my parents, in the army, in Israel society, growing up here. It was one of the most devastating things and it made me sink more into a slump and not open up and not trust a lot of people, except for really close friends. And still today I sometimes have these outbursts… I know that it is not going to be like it was before the bombing."

Finally, he went into therapy with a psychiatrist and found out that he had posttraumatic stress disorder, short-term memory issues, outbursts, and alcohol binges as a result of what he had witnessed. "Socially, I am not as open as I used to be, especially with women and relationships. I'm a little bit more reserved – but very loving, very affectionate, very physical. I think a lot of it has to do not only with my two girlfriends being scared and leaving, but also Dominique dying in front of my eyes. It's about not having control over the situation. I could only help my friends so little."

His therapist encouraged him to get out of the bar. "It was the best thing I did since the bombing, because I was very miserable. It was very good for me to be there right after the bombing. Now I don't go back to Mike's Place that much. I don't watch the movie at all. Why be somewhere where you are not happy? When people say, 'Well, if this hadn't happened, there would never have been a film,' I am absolutely willing to live with that, and without the prizes that we have won, or the festivals that I have been to, or having it help my career. I would take it back in a second."

It took him about a half a year to get himself together, get another job, and start working more as a freelancer, shooting and producing films. "I'm happier. I'm dating somebody who lives in Russia. Anastasia is a great, great woman. Unfortunately, I need to be pushed about personal things, about relationships, about our future. And I hate it because I was never like that." He is almost ready to settle down. "I picked a tough career; it's not a nine-to-five job. The girl that I am with is going to have to understand that – just like I'm going to have to understand."

According to Joshua's mother four years after the attack, "he has pretty much moved on. I don't think the experience will ever leave him, but I definitely believe that it is not in front of him anymore; it's right here on the side. It's always going to be there, but it's not stopping him from living. He's not afraid to do anything… I don't think he's really changed; but I think maybe he's matured a little." Living in Israel, she adds, "I'm sure that it is difficult for Joshua when something happens. It's difficult for me when something happens. But then again, it was always difficult even before Joshua was in a terror attack. It's just a way of life here. It's something that we all carry with us… We came to Israel because we believe in a Jewish state and I guess we still do. And I guess that is what keeps us here – that we believe in that."

In 2012 Joshua decided that he needed a break from Israel and moved to Brooklyn, New York, where he is trying to reboost his career. At the same time, he is seeking closure, hopefully through the publication of his graphic novel, *Mike's Place*, and the intertwining love stories of three couples at the bar – Gal and Dominique, Jack Baxter and his wife Fran, and Joshua and Pavla.

Chapter 6

Haifa

the sea, the mountains, and terraced landscapes...
peaceful coexistence... shattered lives and trust of
families of all faiths

Haifa is the largest city in northern Israel and the third largest city in the country. It is a seaport, located below and on Mount Carmel, and lies on the Mediterranean coast. Haifa and its environs are home to significant populations of Jews, Muslim and Christian Arabs, Druze, and others, and have often been characterized as a mosaic of peaceful coexistence between the communities.

Thirty-seven people were killed and one hundred people were wounded, both Arabs and Jews, in attacks on two popular Haifa restaurants. March 31, 2002, fell during the Passover holiday and the Matza Restaurant was crowded with families having lunch, including Bat-sheva Schaul and her family. Despite the Passover massacre which occurred just four days earlier in Netanya, and the tense atmosphere following it, the restaurant was an unlikely choice for a terrorist attack. Matza is owned by a Jew but managed by a family of Israeli Arabs. It sits next to a hillside on a block that includes a gas station and a car wash, in a neighborhood where Jews, Muslims, and Christians say they get along just fine. One of the five Arab employees wounded in the explosion told reporters from his hospital bed, "I never believed this would happen. The restaurant just exploded. They didn't differentiate between Jews and Arabs."

Then, on October 4, 2003, a suicide bomber blew herself up in the middle of Maxim Restaurant, devastating the seaside restaurant owned jointly by Jews and Arabs. It was packed with regular customers, among them Ola Korol and Gil Carmely.

As in other urban and rural areas, Haifa buses also were the targets of suicide bombings, killing and maiming countless people, including passersby Ismini (Maria) Soyvadzogloy, Molly Shwisha, and Sharon Stav, who were injured on March 5, 2003, when a suicide bomber exploded on a bus traveling along Moriah Boulevard in the Carmel section of Haifa.

In addition to the suicide bombings, the north of Israel was hit hard by rocket attacks from Lebanon during the 2006 Israel-Hezbollah/ Lebanon War. Residents of Haifa and outlying villages were affected – Jews, Christians, Muslims, and Druze. Unbelievably, Sharon Stav was involved in another attack when her apartment building was hit by a Katyusha rocket. A few weeks later, a rocket struck and collapsed a residential building and set it ablaze, as rescue workers and civilians scrambled to help those trapped inside – Nabila Khouri and her parents, Mounir and Fahima.

These survivors, reflecting the diversity of Haifa's residents, share their experiences: the Christian Arab Khouri family; Ola, who had chosen to move to Israel from Moldova in the former Soviet Union three years earlier; Maria, a Greek woman who is "not Jewish, but I feel more than Jewish" and her friend Molly, the Israeli Jewish daughter of Greek parents; American-born Sharon, the survivor of two attacks; Israeli born Bat-sheva and Gil; as well as Ethiopian-born Elad Wassa, injured in an attack at the Netanya market.

Matza Restaurant bombing, near Grand Canyon Mall, Haifa: March 31, 2002

Bat-sheva Schaul: Premonition

"I like the life and I'm happy the life likes me."

B at-sheva Schaul, forty-three, had a premonition of the suicide bombing and requested a table next to the window of the crowded Matza Restaurant even though it wasn't clean "because the day before there was a terror attack in a Tel Aviv restaurant and all the people who were sitting near the window were saved." She and her three children – sons Dar, nine, and Idan, twelve, and fifteen-year-old daughter Inbar – were eating lunch with her sister's children who were visiting from Tel Aviv. Her husband, Ramy, the owner of a chain of optical stores, had just come over from his store at the nearby Grand Canyon Shopping Mall and sat down at their table when twenty-three-year-old Shadi Toubasi – a Palestinian Hamas suicide bomber from nearby Jenin in the West Bank – detonated his bomb, killing fourteen people and injuring over forty. The Schauls were the only family not physically injured – and the only family that "didn't eat pita and asked for matzah (unleavened bread) because it was Passover."

When she saw the flash and heard the explosion, Bat-sheva did not immediately realize what had happened, but her husband thought it was "a *pigua* and told us to go under the table. I saw there was a window and I went out alone from the window." Thinking back, she can't understand how she could have left her children. "Afterwards, I felt very upset about this. In that moment I didn't behave like a mother. I ran away. Only after my husband asked me to come back to take the kids did I come back. I saw only my two boys. I came back inside and took them outside with me through the window and into the adjacent valley. It was good for us because we didn't see all of the horrible sights. We didn't see a lot of the people or the dead man. I saw two or three people lying on the floor and only afterwards did I understand that they were dead." Meanwhile, her daughter and niece went out through the front door.

The family met with a psychologist for three months, but Idan continued for a longer time because "he didn't speak – he kept everything inside." Dar is a little more frightened than before, but he doesn't want any help from a psychologist or from anybody. "Sometimes he wants to sleep with us and he won't stay alone when we're not there. I know that he is afraid. He takes our wallet and keys when we try to go out. And before he goes to sleep, he says, 'Good night, nothing should happen to father, to mother, to grandfather, to grandmother, to the children' – every night, with a kiss."

Two years after the attack, Inbar finally told Bat-sheva that she had seen everything as she went out of the restaurant. Several months later, Inbar happened to meet another girl who had survived the attack at Matza, but her father had been killed. "They went to a restaurant and talked about it for four hours and she came home and cried all night. It was the first time that I saw her crying a lot. It helped Inbar and her friend to talk about it. But they agreed that this was the only conversation they would have about the attack." For Inbar, it was too difficult to see the girl again, because it made her think about what would happen if her father were dead. Coincidentally, years later, both girls married on the same day!

Nor do Bat-sheva and her family "speak about it or the feeling" to each other. They keep everything inside although they fear another attack. "I feel that it's better not to tell it over." As we progress in the interview, however, Bat-sheva begins to realize that "maybe it's good for me to talk about it" and requests that her story be told because it will show others that something happened in Israel. "It keeps happening again and again over the years. We're always caught in a conflict with somebody."

For Bat-sheva, the shared experience with her husband and family was very important "so we can know each other's feelings. If my husband hadn't been there, I couldn't describe to him what I saw and what I feel. But he was there. And it's good that we were all together at the same place and felt the same thing and saw the same thing." Her family – immediate and extended – was very important "because a lot of people who don't have good help from the family break down." Bat-sheva is grateful that she and her family are alive and "that is enough for now."

She is more aware of the importance of her family. When she hears about another attack, "it makes me cry. I think about what would happen to me if something would happen to one of my family. I think about how I was so lucky, but I don't understand why I was so lucky. It makes me a little bit happy, but it makes me a little bit afraid. Maybe something will happen, not from a *pigua*, but from something else."

As a result, she is more protective of her kids, not wanting them to leave and wanting "them near me. I am frightened all the time and I worry that maybe it will happen another time. In the newspaper you read that at least 10 percent of terror victims will be in a terror attack again, not in the same place, but in terrorism, and I am very, very frightened to encounter this situation again... So sometimes when I shout at my children, I say, 'Why are you shouting at them?' And when I think about it, it's a red light for me."

Bat-sheva appreciates life. "I like the life and I'm happy the life likes me. I love life because nobody destroyed my life. If somebody would have been hurt, of course, my life would have changed." She is frightened to think too much. "I continue with my life. I don't think about it." Her family made a big party for their son Dar's bar mitzvah and to celebrate the first year after the attack. She enjoys travel – most recently to Burma, Bangkok, and Paris "to feel good" and perhaps to escape her constant fear in Israel. Yet at home, she goes out to restaurants, just not Arab restaurants, and especially not back to the Matza Restaurant.

When Bat-sheva first returned to her part-time job as a midwife in a hospital, she could not stand to see blood because she imagined the blood from the suicide bombing. "If a woman was bleeding more than normal, I couldn't be in the room. Although I don't remember seeing blood at the restaurant, I used the blood that I saw at work to reconstruct the images that I knew I had been exposed to. I was frightened to see the woman bleeding." The first time she worked with Arab patients after the *pigua*, "I didn't touch them or help them, but now it changed. I see them as a patient and that's all…but I do acknowledge to myself that it disturbs me that another martyr is born."

She continued working as a midwife because she believed that "I bring life and if you bring life to others, no one can take life away from you." Since the attack, she feels more relaxed and nicer to her patients "maybe because somebody gave me the power to give power to the women who are coming to me for help. The women all tell me that they want me to be their midwife and that makes me feel good. It makes me say that this is my job and I can't change my job because maybe this job was given to me to do."

Since the attack, Bat-sheva is also less attracted to advancing herself professionally and wants to live more in the moment and not think about her career. "For my family now I want more than before to be at home and not take another job in my work." She is happy with her life as it is and does not think that she will change. Although she is not religious, she now feels closer to her religion and has changed some of her religious practice. On Friday night, Bat-sheva lights candles and prays "that nothing will happen, that our lives will continue like this because I don't want more than what my life is like right now. I feel good with this situation, with my husband, with the children, with everything until now." If she has a dream, "it will be like it was – the same. My daughter will get married and my son will finish the army."

Inbar did marry in 2013 and is completing her university studies in special education and communication, after finishing the army and traveling in the United States, Thailand, and Laos. The army did not want her to serve because she had been traumatized by the attack, but at her insistence she was recruited and "had a hard time, but an amazing experience!" Idan also finished the army, where he served as a fighter; then spent six months in South America before beginning his studies in accountancy. Her youngest son, Dar, is finishing the army, also as a fighter.

In 2006 Bat-sheva faced another traumatic challenge – she was diagnosed with cancer of the uterus and underwent a hysterectomy. "It was harder than the *pigua* for me." With it behind her she feels well and is back to work in the labor room. While she was recovering physically and emotionally, she worked in another department. "But I saw that it wasn't for me. I saw that the labor room is the department for me. I help women in their labor. This is my job and I do it very well. I chose a good job for me."

Friend Nir Regev killed, Maxim Restaurant bombing, Haifa seashore: October 4, 2003

Ola Korol: Journey to Emotional Healing

"Every year on October fourth...I celebrate my second birthday."

❝ It was a sunny day, so my friend Nir and I decided to go to the sea to have some fun. It was the weekend so we had nothing to do. We had finished our exams, so why not? I slept at his place. We went out to the discotheque and the next day we decided to go to the beach and, before that, to a restaurant. Nir decided to go to Maxim's – it had good food." Suddenly, the suicide bomber, Hanadi Jaradat, a twenty-nine-year-old female lawyer from Jenin, managed to get past Maxim's security guard before blowing herself up in the middle of the restaurant, killing Nir Regev and shattering the life of Ola Korol, a young woman and university student, who had moved to Israel from Moldova in the former Soviet Union three years earlier. Twenty-one people, including Nir, three children, a baby girl, the security guard, and three Israeli Arab employees were killed and sixty people were wounded.

For Ola, "it was really messy when you sit down to eat and after five seconds you hear nothing, see nothing, and understand nothing. It was really difficult for me because my really good friend is the first person in my life who has died. Just like that. He was twenty-five years old. He was the funniest man in the world for me and it was really difficult."

Ola was hospitalized for twenty days with injuries to her arm, back, and legs, and was operated on three times. She had a complex fracture of her arm and could not breathe because of damage to her lungs but says "it is really *mazal* (luck) that I am alive."

Her first thoughts were about the impact on her divorced parents and then she worried about her appearance. "I went out from the restaurant and called my mom and said that I had been in a *pigua* and had lost my hand. She was in Tel Aviv and had an hour and a half ride to come to see me. I think it was really more difficult for her and for my daddy than it was for me because I didn't see myself. I just knew that it's pain, it's how can I do anything, I just wanted to breathe. When they saw me I had blood all over my body. But the first question that I asked was 'How do I look?' and then I asked them for a mirror." It took her time to understand that "it was you. Yes, it was your friend. Yes, it happened. It's not fatal. It's not news. It's not somebody from your work. It's you. It's your family. It's my mom. It's me."

Ola just wanted to survive, breathe, and, for the first time in her life, have a future. When she was a little girl somebody told her that she would have some very difficult and painful event in her life. "So when it came and I realized that I had been there, I wasn't surprised. I just wanted to survive." She no longer has to live with the ominous prediction that something bad would happen to her. "Now I believe more. Now I understand more things. I always thought that all the things that happen to us – to me – are because of something we did. Either we did the wrong things or our parents did the wrong things or because that's why it had to be. When it happened, I didn't ask myself or God why it happened to me. Maybe because I knew that it would happen. Thank you, God, that I'm alive and everybody is happy."

Ola is on a journey to emotional healing and is trying to find the meaning in what happened. She quickly sought the help of a psychologist, not because she had symptoms of distress, but because she had a lot of questions and no answers. She realizes that it will take time and that "it's a story. It's really a story that hasn't ended yet. It's still developing." She also learned she can do things with her life and is proud of her accomplishments since the attack, although she does not know if her accomplishments are a natural result of her "growing up or if they're because of the *pigua*."

Her parents supported her growth in this difficult time. "They believed in me. They helped me." She understands the importance of real relationships with her parents and with others. She wants love and to give to others. "It's changed my life and what I'm doing. It's like to be born. You learn to talk, to sit, to eat, to have a shower, to talk with your friends, to see yourself anew, to love yourself. The relationships with my family and friends are turned upside down; not with my mom, because my mom was always with me, and we understand each other; but with my daddy, because he had changed and so had I. But the *pigua* – that's what changed my relationship with him."

A year after the *pigua*, she still has a need to talk about it. "I don't want to forget it. I won't forget it! It is something that I want to live with and I want my friends and family to understand me – not to tell me forget about it." Her mom understands that "if I talk about it, she shouldn't say, 'Oh, let's talk about something else. It's not something I want to hear.' If I want to cry, that's fine. I just come to my mom and look at her and she says, 'Oh, my baby, come to me,' and I start to cry just like a little girl, because I still need to."

Ola is also helped by talking to people who understand – other people who were in a terror attack or lost something, and people from various helping organizations. "I don't know how it happens that I take a taxi and the driver understands me because he was in a *pigua* or in the army and lost something. Most of my new friends are from a *pigua* and they understand me. All of them were there. You don't have to explain everything – they just understand it… And the best thing is that I realized that I emerged not unscathed but, relative to others, with a minor price to be paid."

She met a man via an internet meeting service, who coincidentally worked with the helping organization OneFamily. He had lost his leg in a *pigua* "and he just knew when to call me. I don't know why he called me that day and that hour and I just began to cry. He said, 'It's okay. It will be okay.' He told me how he comes to the hospital and helps people. He can do it. He lost his leg. It's amazing. And I just understood it – that man gives me so much energy. I feel stronger when I talk to him."

Ola has grown and her life has changed in every respect, starting from the inside and working outwards. She has developed a healthy understanding of her self. Early on she was "focused on myself. I was really injured physically. I felt really bad. So I decided to focus on my body – the most important thing for the first two months was my body – on health, on beauty – it was really important to me. And after that I decided okay, I'm okay, I love myself, I can breathe, I can do something with this arm. I focused on what was inside. Because I have to understand myself, I talk a lot with myself."

She has come to recognize that, with time, she will understand more about her external world. "Now, all the things that I've done were for me. Later I will think about things connected to the outside world and I will understand other things. It's come to me that you need time, just time."

After five months, she was able to realize that she had lost her friend and his spirit had "calmed down" because at first "he continued to come to me and to his family. I'm sure that he was there to check if everything was okay with me, his parents, his brother and sister. Now I think that he thinks that I will be okay and I think too that he will be okay. He's gone from my room. He's still in my head. He's still in my heart. I have a big place in my heart that always will be for him."

A year after the attack, she finally went to the cemetery and met Nir's family. She thought that they would think of her only as "a reminder of Nir. They would look at me and just think of Nir. They would not be thinking of Ola." She went back to their house. "It's an amazing house – a house of love and pictures and smiling people – and people are happy there. Their lives are continuing and his friends are still laughing. It really was helpful because I understood that they understand me – they love me. They want me to continue my life."

Every year on October fourth "I celebrate New Year's eve, my birthday – my second birthday. On the one hand it is a bad day because my friend was killed. But on the other hand it is my New Year. I became a new person; I was given a second chance." She also learned how strong she is and how well she can do things with her life. After graduation she took her mother to Barcelona "to spend an amazing eight days there. Something I did. Something I said I would do. I am proud of myself, very proud of myself."

As to her future: "Until the *pigua*, the terror attack, I had no wishes. I didn't see my future. I didn't think about my future. I just lived day by day, hour by hour. And after the *pigua*, I just opened my eyes and understood how beautiful life is. I want to marry and I want to have children and I want to have my future. I have the feeling that now it's a beginning of something."

Ola continued her studies and graduated with a degree in statistics. She thinks about studying philosophy or of becoming a social worker "to help people – to give, not to receive back. I want to do the things that everybody does. I want to be happy in the moment."

Four years after the *pigua*, Ola knows that "I'm growing up" and that it is not just because she is getting older. "The *pigua* came just at the age when I needed to change. So like many things in my life, it came and helped me to change. But I think the *pigua* changed me much more than everything else. Because I know people at my age and they don't see life like I do. They are not interested in things that I am. I don't know what to talk about with them because it is different. I'm still growing; I'm still going up higher. It was always important for me, but now it's even more important."

Sometimes it still is really hard for Ola, but "most of the fears, they pass away. Everything that I felt before, now I can feel it less. Like it was very tough for me to take a bus and I was really scared when I was entering places; I was really looking to see who was sitting around me. Or I was startled all the time. Now I still am, but less. Maybe it's also because the situation is different in Israel than it was a few years ago. But I feel good. Sometimes I am more nervous than I want to be. Sometimes I cannot control my anger. I would love to, but I cannot. But I am working on it all the time. I worry about it, but in a good way, like don't do this, don't be nervous, it isn't worth it. Think positive. Before, I took a lot of things really personally, and now I just don't. I am more confident, stronger, and quieter."

The Israel-Hezbollah/Lebanon War stirred up traumatic memories. "My friends were *in* Lebanon – *in* the fight – and I knew everything. So it was really hard for me. I couldn't stop looking at the television and watching news. Because of what had happened to me, I couldn't think about anything else but the war and the soldiers and what they were going through and the hospitals and the pain for the parents – and if they would come back. It was really hard for me." Her therapist helped her "talk about my place in this and what I feel and what's happened to me." She also taught her to look at herself in different ways – "to look in your eyes and look inside."

She understands that she is still very breakable now and is continuing to work on herself – to overcome the many different small troublesome problems in her life – to become stronger. But, overall, Ola is healthier, taking care of her body, mind, and soul. Four years after the *pigua*, she plays ping-pong "for fun, but not professionally." She goes to the gym, swims, dances, exercises, reads books, and meditates "to get to know myself better… I don't need much to enjoy the day – the moment. I think this is also what the *pigua* gave me.

"I was in a hospital for two weeks and I underwent three surgeries and I have four pieces of shrapnel in my body and it's nothing. I have all the pieces of my body. Thank you very much. And I am very lucky – physically and emotionally… And I recently caught the bouquet at a friend's wedding – unbelievable – with one arm."

In 2011 Ola married a "very nice guy" who she met at work and a year later she gave birth to a baby girl. After six years of nonstop work, she took a year off and spent an amazing year with her baby.

She still visits Nir's family in Nahariya once a year. "While everything has changed – all of his friends are married and have children and his parents became grandparents for a fourth time – it's also all the same… Our Nir is gone and never will come back, and everyone learned to live without him."

Ola continues to "have a very positive view on life. My goals are to move on, to be happy from very small things, to remember the good things, and to look forward and hope for a healthy and happy future for my family and me. I'm very grateful for the support and love from my family, I move on and feel very happy, but I am not healed yet… I'm not sure if I ever will be." She still shivers from every loud sound, tries to escape crowded places, and wakes up once in a while terrified and in tears. "The most difficult day for me is Yom Hazikaron, and every time there's a siren in Israel. I stay at home on Purim, the most joyful holiday in Israel, because I am very afraid of firecrackers. And every time I see a woman in a burqa, I try to cross the street to get as far away as I can." She vividly demonstrates that personal growth and distress coexist.

Maxim Restaurant bombing, Haifa seashore: October 4, 2003

Gil Carmely: An Opportunity to Change My Life

"If they discover the power inside themselves, they can do everything."

G il has four children – three sons and the Triathlon Project for Ethiopian Youth at Risk in Kiryat Yam. This special project rose from the ashes of a horrific suicide bombing and from his understanding, as a triathlete, of the power inside the human body to overcome adversity.

Gil, his pregnant wife Michal, and their fifteen-year-old son Guy were waiting to be seated at a table in Maxim Restaurant. Their older son Amir, an air force mechanic, was not with them. Gil immediately knew it was a *pigua*. His wife thought it was a gas explosion, but soon realized it was a terrorist attack and "she took the fifteen-year-old and closed his eyes and led him out of the restaurant so he didn't see a lot of blood." The blast injured Guy's eardrum, which required subsequent surgery.

Gil was not prepared for the bombing. Usually he is afraid of danger in buses or crowds, "but on this holy Sabbath, in the restaurant, it caught me unprepared. When you are a soldier and you are going to fight, to war, you prepare yourself. You take up your rifle and you wait for someone to come at you. But when you are in your bathing suit on your way to a swim – it was not in my mind and it caught me very, very much by surprise."

Gil was ten meters (32 ft.) from his wife and son when the bomb exploded. Like Bat-sheva at the Matza Restaurant bombing, "I found myself alone – I didn't remember that someone was with me. The fact that I didn't remember my family and cared only about myself was the most difficult part of the event for me. I was injured and bleeding. I felt that I was going to die. And the first instinct that I had was to look at what was wrong in my body. And the next thing was to run away from the area. Afterwards it was difficult for me to deal with my reaction. I needed a good therapist to help me understand because it was very hard for me that I didn't think about my wife and my child." Gil was injured by shrapnel, which broke his jaw and cut his tongue. His twin brother, a physical therapist, arrived on the scene five minutes after the attack and found him outside the restaurant dazed and unable to speak.

Gil's social worker gave him tools to deal with his self-blame, explaining the three *F*'s – Fight, Flight, and Freeze – and why people in a sudden catastrophe behave like he did. He also met with the social worker and people from other *piguim*. They spoke about "how to cope and how to face traumatic events, how to know yourself, and how to handle posttraumatic feelings." Except for his guilt over abandoning his family and his physical disabilities, "my mood was very good. I didn't lose much of my confidence or my powers or my ambitions of doing good. I didn't lose hope." From his experience, he learned that "sometimes we may need help, but we can cope with everything."

For Gil, "the *pigua* was something that made me think about my life and gave me an opportunity to change my life. I took the chance to change it." Although he does not consider himself to be religious, "the event was an opportunity from heaven. Maybe someone loves me up there. Maybe I have some people that I lost who are up there – and maybe they spoke about me with God. The fortune was that I was so close to death and so far away from death, because I could have lost everything by moving one centimeter." He is "sure the *pigua* took me and got me some place that I wanted to get to and I couldn't have done it without this event." Although the terror attack gave him the financial ability and time to become what he wanted to be, his personal strength and power from within allowed him to do everything in the outside world. He knows his own abilities and is "not afraid to deal with challenges in work and in sports." He believes that "I can do everything in life if I want to do it; I have the power. And that is something I have inside of me."

Previously Gil was a self-employed carpenter and retired army officer and then briefly drove a taxi, but his passion and hobby was being a triathlete. "And I love to do it. I love to compete. I try to be the best." Through his sports background, he learned from his own body to see things more clearly and in proper perspective and tries to explain this to others. "Triathlon is a very hard sport and you have to be very strong inside to make yourself do it every day. I try to convince people that they have a lot of power inside their bodies, but they don't know it because they don't know how to use that power or the chemicals in the brain to make the body move. They don't know how to connect it. And if they discover the power inside themselves, they can do everything. They can do it in sports. They can do it in life."

Gil had a bachelor's degree in history and went back to Haifa University for a degree in social work because "I think it was a natural result of my maturing. I care about people. I believe that now I can understand their problems much more because of my own experience. It gives me more when I give to someone else. I am much kinder than I was before. Maybe it is because of the event. I think I can help everyone. I can feel it from inside after working with social workers, meeting with people who were injured in other *piguim*, and seeing how they react to me, and to my beliefs after the *piguim*." He understands that to help people you need to show them how to "go forward step by step; it can't be going back."

He has turned his own life around, living life more fully and understanding what is important. "I'm close to fifty and going back to university to begin another life. I feel very strong and enjoy every moment. Now I learn with more joy and I feel much fuller inside." He counts his age backwards: he is now forty-nine, next year he will be forty-eight. "I feel young. I act young. I am a young-old. I am more optimistic and I believe in myself and I hope for everything. It will not be easy, but I don't see everything in only black and white; I can see other colors. My whole life – I can see much more clearly what is important and what is not important. I can see what is serious and what is not serious. I enjoy life better than I enjoyed it before." He and his wife named their new son Alon – oak tree, famous for its strength and resilience – because "I think that is my story."

Gil helps others learn by modeling his own positive actions and deeds. He speaks freely about the event because "I hope it will help other people in Israel and in the world to face traumatic events... I show them my view of life and what you can bring from your own body. How you can enjoy life with family, how you can make sense from the event, and how you can take the event from the darkness by seeing it as full of opportunities and maybe using it to move to places that you were afraid to go. And the strength that I give them, I can see it, I can feel it, I can contribute to them. I saw that there were people who had lost their strength, lost their belief in human beings, lost their power, have problems at home. They became nervous. They are not relaxed. And I try to show them the beauty of life. I try to show them the beautiful things that they forgot – that they are alive after all and they must enjoy life now more than they did before. And they must see it more beautifully now than before the *pigua*."

Four years after the attack, Gil has realized his dreams. As part of the field work for his degree in social work, he took his ideas to the town of Kiryat Yam – home to many immigrants from the former Soviet Union, North Africa, and Ethiopia – and put them into action in a special community project – "The Sky Is the Limit" – a triathlon project for Ethiopian children at risk. Many Ethiopian immigrants have difficulty adjusting to the education system, the language, and the values of Israeli society. From the numerous accomplishments of Ethiopian athletes worldwide, Gil knew the great sports potential yet to be discovered in Israel. He also recognized that sports are a way of keeping the youngsters off the streets, reducing violence, and directing their energies in a normative and productive direction.

So he designed a program to help the youth improve their self-esteem and self-confidence, develop personal and group skills, and learn ethical behavior. "I took ten high-risk Ethiopian teenagers and I thought about how I could make them believe in themselves. I was a triathlete before and I know that a triathlon gives you self-confidence and makes you strong. It makes you believe that for you the sky is the limit." He decided to teach these teenagers triathlon – swimming, biking, and running.

Gil raised all of the funds for the project from a friend in Geneva, from Elem – a nonprofit organization for children at risk – and from Nike Israel. "After four months, I took the children to the first competition and the next day we took another fifteen boys. And then we made a mixed group, *sabra*s – native Israelis – and Ethiopians together and it was a wonderful team. And now we are doing the third group. Luckily this was a great project. No one ever thought it would be so impressive, so big, and so emotional." And then he repeated his success by building – from nothing – and managing a club for teenage boys in Kiryat Yam.

Gil received a scholarship from Operation Embrace, a nonprofit organization from Maryland, to continue his studies and received a second degree in community mental health at Haifa University – "one big dream come true." Another nonprofit organization in the United States – CAF (Challenged Athletes Foundation) also gave him a scholarship to pursue his other dream "to go back to triathlon and to get into shape again. They gave me all that I needed and I participated in two triathlon competitions. Now I'm training every day, two hours a day, running and biking and swimming. And I enjoy every minute."

The process has been very emotional for Gil. "It is very touching when you know that people believe in you and they want to help you. And all the things that I get for myself, I also want to give to the children – to give them the same feeling and the same experience." Gil made a CD of his classroom project and titled it *A Story of Rehabilitation* – "not only for me, but for the children. I mixed my rehabilitation process with theirs. So the rehab project was not only for the Ethiopians, it was for me as well. It gives me back my self-confidence about what I can do. It was a very significant event for me, a very emotional event for me. I brought to this project all of my knowledge from the university and what I did in my life and what I suffered in the *pigua* and all of my emotions and all of my efforts."

For the past four years, Gil has been a social worker, first working with the elderly in a nursing home, then as director of housing operations for autistic people. He came to realize that he was bothered at work by rescue fantasies – posttraumatic symptoms that made him confront his employees on behalf of his clients. Today, he has mastered this problem and is successful in his new workplace.

Suicide bombing, Netanya market: May 19, 2002

Andalau (Elad) Wassa: Ethiopian Israeli

"Smile first – then go forward."

If Gil Carmely needs another role model for his children at risk, then Ethiopian-born Elad would be a great choice. His full name, Andalau, means *leader* and it fits him well. Wheeling around his apartment or the basketball court in his wheelchair, flashing his broad smile and looking younger than his thirty years, Elad's demeanor and attitude exude optimism and hope. Paralyzed from the waist down, he has come to realize that "not everything depends on the legs."

After walking with his family almost one thousand kilometers (600 mi.) from his village to a refugee camp in Sudan, eight-year-old Elad and his family were brought to Israel in 1984 in the first Ethiopian airlift – Operation Moshe. His parents raised him and his nine sisters and brothers in Netanya on the Mediterranean coast. He went to a religious high school and competed in long-distance races. Then he entered the army where he learned survival skills and coping mechanisms. "It's everlasting. He who doesn't serve in the army doesn't get the meaning. One learns a lot in the army; it's better than school."

On May 19, 2002, Elad was working, selling vegetables at the open-air *shuk* (market) in Netanya – a job he enjoyed and that fed his passion for working with and helping people. "It was on a Sunday. About four in the afternoon I went to have lunch. When I came back, I saw potatoes on the pavement. I don't like food to be on the ground, so I bent down to pick it up." While he was getting up, a Palestinian suicide bomber disguised as an Israeli soldier blew up his bomb, killing himself and three others and wounding at least fifty-nine Israelis, including Elad.

Elad says the explosion was "like a volcano… I was like a sheet of paper, on the pavement. I don't remember anything. My arm hurt. I was picked up. They took me to Hillel Yaffe Hospital in Hadera – intensive care. They took out some of the nails that were inside my body. Since that day life changed." Elad suffered very severe burns and his spine was severed by shrapnel from the bomb, resulting in the paralysis of his lower body.

He was transferred to Sheba Medical Center at Tel Hashomer in Tel Aviv for rehabilitation. "I started working on my balance, how to move. At the beginning it was very hard. I was mad, very angry. I sat with my mother and cried, 'Why, why?' Now I regret my crying. Everything went very slowly. I stayed there four and a half months. When released, I stayed in a hotel for almost a year." Now he rents a small house. "I have a cleaning lady and my family lives here in Netanya and when I need them they come."

"At the beginning people would say, 'Hi, how are you?' They would see me and cry. I felt bad about that, so I tried to cheer them up. Then I started to work on my body. I took classes for a year to pass the matriculation exams. I have so many things on my mind, but slowly everything will fall into place. I'm still young. There are so many things to do, and since I left the hospital I'm working hard, and, thank God, it's getting better… To undergo such a disaster isn't easy, it takes hard work, psychologically, and one needs a lot of patience."

He believes that "everything is God's will. To whom should I complain? I have no complaints. As long as I'm alive, I thank God. Others may ask, 'Why me? Why not him?' I don't blame anyone. It happened. Everything is from above. It's lucky that I'm strong mentally. I received a big blow physically, and I struggle. Sometimes there are crises. I sit here and wait a while until it's better. Nothing is going to stop me. It all depends on the individual himself… People told me: 'Had you still been in Ethiopia it wouldn't have happened.' But I said that I blame no one, it makes no difference – here, there, no matter where one is, people are being blown up – one never knows. If I was spared there, I thank God, every day."

Elad describes the differences in his life now. "Before the attack, I would run from place to place. I wouldn't take notice of anything around me. I was under a lot of pressure. But now I'm not in a hurry – I have time – that's how I look at life now. If you're in a hurry, you won't know where you'll wind up. That's why I now say you only have one life to live."[1] He is trying to build something different. "Now I am searching for solutions, realizing not everything depends on my legs. I have my hands, head, eyes. Most importantly, my mind works, and one should think positively. I don't sit and complain that everything is hard – if I did, then everyone would run away. This way many people are willing to help and I'm not ashamed. I ask for help and I always get it."

Elad understands the importance of having a healthy body. Like Gil Carmely, he works his body "so that it will be easier to think. It has to be a combination of mind and body, to work both simultaneously, that's the principle." His optimistic and energetic personality made him popular and he quickly found his way back to sports through physiotherapy, swimming, playing basketball, and horse riding. "I have lots of hope – if I work really hard, maybe I'll run one day."

Elad's idol was Christopher Reeve, the actor who played Superman and was paralyzed from the neck down in a 1995 horse-riding accident. A year before he died in 2004, Reeve visited Israel, which he considered to be the world center for research on paralysis treatment. Reeve had received a letter from Wassa and said that "the letter left a deep impression. I wanted to meet him." For Elad, it was a dream come true. "This visit will bring hope to a lot of people who, like me, are confined to a wheelchair." Elad told Reeve that "for me he is a role model. He brings encouragement to people who feel as if their whole world has been destroyed. I'm one of them."[2]

Elad also brings encouragement to others. At the beginning, he frequently visited with other people who were in the attack. "Now, when my help is needed, I go and sit with people and talk; those who are willing, I help. But sometimes it's difficult, so I ask others." He also tries to cheer up his parents. "It's hard on them and a mother is always

---

1   Quoted in Mike Fishbein and Loren Brindze, *My Friend Elad* (a film documenting the effects of the attack), 2005, http://labs.triggerstreet.com/short-film/my-friend-elad.

2   Joel Leyden, "Israel Mourns Death of 'Superman' Christopher Reeve," October 11, 2004, http://www.israelnewsagency.com/israelreevesuperman588690.html (accessed May 6, 2008; site now discontinued).

a mother. She always worries that I should get married and have kids. Both my mother and father will always care and want to know how I feel." But he does not yet have a girlfriend, believing that "when she comes, she comes. There are many girls, but none that I really like. Some are nice; some others aren't clever. They want to know about the wheelchair; it seems a problem. I don't take it to heart. One doesn't need to get acquainted with the chair, but with the person, what he says, what he thinks, what he feels. If that was the way it went, the world would be in order. But I know people think differently."

Elad faces life with a positive outlook. "I always think about better days. If it's a difficult day, I go outside, leave my troubles behind, play, enjoy. When I get back I think things over: what I did wrong today, how to put it right tomorrow. That's the way I am. And I can see the results, thank God." And most importantly, "I always smile, even when it's difficult, I smile. A smile is comforting and then I go forward and move to action."

Elad remains cheerful eleven years after the attack, but has resigned himself to no longer being able to volunteer, play sports, or study.

Egged bus no. 37 bombing, Moriah Boulevard, Haifa:
March 5, 2003

Sharon Stav: Two Attacks

"You did it once, you'll do it again – but not always did that work."

Ismini (Maria) Soyvadzogloy and Molly Shwisha: My Life, My Memories, My Autobus

"Love is power for people after the terrorist attack."

After work Maria was standing under a tree next to the crowded bus shelter on Haifa's main Moriah Boulevard near the Carmel Center, waiting for her girlfriend Molly to go home with her. "I looked along the street. The day was very nice, the sun was very, very nice, the sky was blue." Egged bus no. 37 was traveling one of Haifa's central routes, picking up passengers from various Jewish and Arab neighborhoods on Mount Carmel, passing schools and commercial centers, and climbing toward Haifa University. "The bus comes slowly, slowly, slowly and *boom!*" The suicide bomb – strapped to the body of Mahmoud Amadan Salim Kawasme, twenty, a computer student – was laden with metal shrapnel to maximize the number of injuries. The blast turned the bus into a charred wreck and scattered bodies along the road. Victims were Jewish, Muslim, Druze, and Christian. Seventeen people were killed, including nine children on their way home from school, and fifty-three were wounded.

Maria continues: "After, I didn't understand anything. I didn't hear anything. *Mmmmm*, it sounded like that. My head seemed like a watermelon. There was smoke, darkness, blood, burning flesh, fire, heat from the explosion. It's a picture I won't forget my entire life. This picture is always in my eyes and in my mind. Haifa is a small town, like one family. Many people from this bus were my friends, neighbors, their children, their mothers. I didn't know what I could do. I went to the bus and helped the people because all the people standing around were saying, 'Oh my God, oh my God, oh my God' – the panic – the shock – the war."

Molly arrived ten minutes after the *pigua* and desperately searched for Maria. "I screamed, 'My friend, my friend!' Everyone was out of the bus. She couldn't be on the bus. Everything was closed. I ran looking for her. Finally I found her in the clinic where the people of Magen David Adom were talking to her." Maria adds: "She thought I was injured because of all the blood from the other people, not from me."

Meanwhile, Sharon was sitting in her car at a nearby stoplight when the bus exploded. "The impact was so great that my car flew up in the air and then dropped down with a bang. The whole bus was on fire and you could see the flames coming from it and things flying in the air that you realize afterwards could have been arms, legs, or God knows what. And then smoke filled the whole street, so you couldn't even see two meters in front of you. I figured that I didn't know enough about things like this, so I had just better get away from here and leave room for professional help to arrive. I knew I had to get home because when you don't feel good, you want to go home."

 She doesn't remember getting into her house. "Sometimes you can erase big dangers so you don't have to think about it. I was shaking and crying and very, very unsettled. And I looked down and my pants were all torn and my feet were all scratched and bleeding. And I realized that I had crawled up all forty-three stairs to get into the house. Automatically, the first thing I did was push the button to turn on the television. I don't know why, but I had this drive pulling me to see more and more of it on the television, to understand what was going on. Every time it took me back, but I felt like a magnet was pulling me to it."

All three women are overwhelmed by physical, psychological, and financial issues that they attribute to the attack. Both Maria and Sharon suffered from ruptured eardrums and permanent hearing loss. In addition, Maria injured her neck falling off the bus when a policeman, fearing another bomb, forced her off the bus. Sharon also had a concussion and problems keeping her balance, but "I am alive, thank you."

Ismini (Maria) Soyvadzogloy and Molly Shwisha

Maria was fifty-three years old at the time of the attack. She was born in Salonika, Greece, and moved to Israel fifteen years before the attack. "I'm not Jewish, but I feel more than Jewish. Maybe my mother is Jewish, I don't know. I love Israel very much. I love the Jewish people. It's something in my feelings, in my body." She studied medicine in Greece for three years but the political unrest interfered with her studies. She then became a singer, performing all over the world. "I had so much money – every night, three places – two hours here, two hours there. Good life. Good clothes. Molly and I traveled to Eilat, Beer Sheva, Tiberias, Greece, and London. Everything was okay. I had a future." Before the attack she was working as a nursemaid, but since the *pigua* she no longer has the strength.

Maria shares an apartment in Haifa with Molly, the Israeli Jewish daughter of Greek parents, and Molly's eighteen-year-old daughter. Molly suffers from thalassemia, a hereditary blood disease common to the Mediterranean region, and does not work. Maria and Molly met in Greece, where Molly and her late husband were visiting and Maria was performing. A few years later, Maria came to Israel to sing and ran into the newly widowed Molly and her one-year-old daughter. She stayed in Israel and they lived together. Until the *pigua*, "this was a good life."

The day after the attack, Maria went back to the site, where she found, and still has, a melted CD-ROM, a disc from a child's Walkman, a charred wooden spatula and fork, and the bright red question-mark-shaped key for breaking into the fire-extinguisher case – all covered with ash and still having the stench of burned skin and metal more than a year later. In the weeks following the attack, she collected newspaper articles and pictures of the bloody carnage and stories of the victims, survivors, and rescuers. Maria does not want to forget. She wants to make sure that everyone understands and knows what the people here in Israel suffer. "You must know the truth." She vividly recalls the sights, sounds, and emotions of the *pigua* – "This is my life. These are my memories." Maria lights memorial candles at the cemetery, at the rebuilt bus stop, and at the adjacent memorial wall, where small young flowers push up through the cracks – symbolizing rebirth and new growth.

Since the *pigua*, Maria's life is focused on the attack. She blames it for the loss of her beauty, voice, hearing, health, relationships, and mental and economic stability. "After the explosion, I am alone in life. I hide behind a mask – inside I'm broken. I don't understand anything. I stay alone in my home. I cry alone in my home. I make theater to express my pain. No one listens to me because no one understands our problems and we are fighting alone. This is not life. This is slowly, slowly, slowly – slowly inside death. This is a documentary – the situation here in Israel – my autobus." She sees herself and others who experience an attack as "terror victims" who suffer – "not from the wound, but inside from post-trauma." She has trouble sleeping, is afraid of the dark, and takes pills. She attempted suicide. Before another *pigua* occurs, she says she "has a feeling that something will happen. I can't sleep, I have dreams – bad dreams. I'm crazy – fuelled. After the *pigua*, I relax again." She sees a psychologist and "talks, emotes, and gets it out."

After a year of listening to Maria, Molly "couldn't listen any more. It was too hard for me. At home all day, everything is about the *pigua*. She is afraid and it passes on to me. And then I pass it on to my daughter." Maria and Molly both energize and deplete one another. Molly describes the situation: "I gave her my strength for almost two years and now I have fallen and I don't have strength." She continues to remind Maria: "If you help yourself, I will help you and others will help you." Maria feels that her strength comes "half from Molly – half from nationality. I am from Greece – a very strong country. I am a very, very strong woman. Molly is my power. She is my hope. She is my life, and love is power for people after the terrorist attack. No terrorist attack, or anything else, can end this love."

Following the attack Maria and Molly received assistance from support organizations for terror victims, including OneFamily – an organization that provides financial, legal, and emotional assistance to victims of terrorism. OneFamily took them on a three-day vacation where they met with other terror survivors and families of terror victims.

"We played. We cried. We now have a community of terror victims who survived. It's good for them. Now this is my life. I help these people. I sing for these people. I live with my hope. This is my dream."

Maria hopes that "things will be normal – without nervousness. I want to write a book about the situation in Israel – as my situation slowly gets better. I want to take my girlfriend on a vacation to Hawaii, the Fiji Islands, and the Bahamas."

Four and a half years after the attack, she is consumed by her financial problems. Bituach Leumi gives her only one thousand shekels a month for her 35 percent disability and she cannot work. "There is no future because I don't know what will be tomorrow. If we have a war with Iran, I'll stay in my house, in my bed, in my home. I won't leave. I won't go back to Greece. I won't leave Israel. I love Israel and I love my girlfriend."

Ten years later, Maria still has not recovered and is still in treatment. She and Molly have lost their joie de vivre, stopped working, and cannot afford many things, like travel which they would love to do. They are grateful to OneFamily, Operation Embrace, and Rambam Hospital for their ongoing services and support.

Sharon Stav

Sharon was sixty-two years old, a native Detroiter, a mother and grandmother. She is divorced from an Israeli *kibbutznik* and has lived in Israel for forty-four years. "Israel is my country now – because I am a majority here and not a minority."

For Sharon, "since the *pigua*, I do nothing but run from one doctor to another and it drives me insane. I am just a mess. I wasn't like that before. It all started rolling downhill right after the incident. I have a lot of expenses because of this *pigua*. And to this day I still haven't gotten a penny back from Bituach Leumi (National Insurance). I went into debt and I'm retired and I have no way to pay my debts back, so I had to cut down." She moved to a smaller apartment and sold her car – she now gets around by taxi. Without regular transportation and suffering from cataracts and hearing loss, she no longer goes out to concerts and rarely gets together with her friends. She continues to keep in touch by phone. Her daughter manages her finances. "It has taken away my independence, and that is very hard for me to accept. I'm a very independent woman, and now somebody else is doing everything. I have no idea what's going on. It's a different way of life – very different from what I was living, but I'm not going to cry about it." She acknowledges that "it is both age and the *pigua*."

Sharon had been through traumas before – her son's fall from a three-story building and his recovery, a nasty divorce, wars, riots, and her father's leukemia. "I keep saying, 'Why do they pick me all the time?' Today I laugh, but then it was not so funny." She has learned to "always be ready. You never know what's waiting for you around the corner." And she knows from experience that "if you did it once, you'll do it again – but not always did that work."

She has learned that she is stronger than she thought she was and credits her parents for her strength. She says she inherited her optimism from her mother; and her sense of humor and frequent laughter from her father. She is coping with her situation and tries to overcome these problems, using her past survival experiences and her fighting spirit.

Sharon is grateful to be alive and now looks differently at life. "If you want to live, you've got to fight and you've got to stand up and know what you want and move in the right direction to get it." Her aunt, a Holocaust survivor from Poland, told her that "you are a survivor more than I." She always valued her self-reliance. "I have to count on myself more than anybody else. As we say in Hebrew, *im ein ani li, mi li*, if I am not for me, who else is there? You have to learn to be on your own." Although she finds it very difficult to ask for help, she is learning that sometimes you have to do it. "I know how to help other people, but I don't know how to ask for help myself."

Sharon received some help from her family and friends in Israel and abroad. "It made me feel that I was not alone. I didn't keep it inside myself. I am the type of person that if anything very difficult happens, I have to talk it out. And that helps a great deal." Volunteers from organizations like OneFamily and Natal "would talk to me and calm me down on the phone – at least three times a week for almost a year. One volunteer was very patient, very warm. Finally I said to her, 'I think I'm okay. So maybe you should spend more time with somebody who is more needy of it than I am right now.'"

Sharon still gets easily startled and cringes when she hears unexpected loud noises and anything that sounds like an explosion or shooting – firecrackers, airplanes flying overhead, or even doors slamming. While not afraid, she is "uneasy" going out on her own at night. The memories reappear with each new trauma. "But it comes back in different situations or on a different level or whatever. Some little thing, whatever it might be – some stupid part even will trigger it. No psychiatrist is going to help you get rid of the memories. You have to learn to go around them and keep on."

Sharon thinks that she is "too old to start making goals at this age for myself – although to wake up in the morning and to have as good health as can be expected are goals. Oh, and to win the lottery!" Or possibly to meet someone who would be willing to live half their life in Israel and half their life in the United States. "But Prince Charming hasn't shown up yet."

Unbelievably, Sharon had "to do it again" on July 17, 2006. A Katyusha rocket – one of hundreds of rockets fired by Hezbollah from southern Lebanon during the 2006 Israel-Hezbollah/Lebanon War – hit another part of her building on Leon Blum Street in Haifa, completely destroying a vacant apartment. Although a lot of people left their homes for safety, she had decided to stay in her apartment "because we were under the impression that it would be over in a day or two. So why make all this *schlep* (tedious journey) to America?"

The entrance to her house is next to the entrance to the air-raid shelter and she kept the telephone nearby and the television turned on to the breaking news reports. "I was in contact with everyone by telephone; everybody was calling – people from all over," especially after a Detroit television station showed her standing outside the demolished building. "I don't know why I stayed; I just felt something kept me where I was." A Russian lady and her three young daughters shared the shelter. "I remember saying to myself, 'If I go that whole family will be on their own. I've got to help them.' I was very stupid." But her grandma instincts won out and she stayed.

The rocket attack did not upset her as much as the *pigua*. "I wasn't alone in this war and plenty of other people were with me. But the *pigua* – I was all on my own then."

Sadly, Sharon passed away on September 20, 2010, at age sixty-nine – six years after our first meeting. Before we met, I had intended to interview people ages twenty-five to fifty; after meeting Sharon, I immediately raised the age limit to seventy because she so vividly demonstrated that growth and positive change were possible well after age fifty.

Rocket attack, Wadi Nisnas, Haifa: August 6, 2006

Nabila, Mounir, and Fahima Khouri: Believers

"For me, the *azaka* (warning siren) is the end of the world."

The deadliest barrage of Hezbollah rocket attacks in nearly a month of fighting hit northern Israel on Sunday, August 6, 2006, killing twelve army reservists resting at Kfar Giladi near the Lebanon border. Hours later, around dusk, Hezbollah rockets hit Haifa, the normally bustling Israeli port that had been largely paralyzed by the daily attacks. Three people were killed and more than forty others were wounded when rockets fired from the Lebanese village of Qana struck at seven residential locations in Haifa.

Thirty-eight-year-old Nabila and her parents, Mounir and Fahima, are Christian Arabs. They were all born in Israel – Mounir in the village of Peki'in in the Galilee – Fahima, daughters Nabila and Jameela, and son Elias in Haifa. At the time of the attack Fahima was still recovering from a broken hip suffered ten months before. She and her family were in their apartment on Caesarea Street in the mostly Arab neighborhood of Wadi Nisnas in Haifa when a rocket hit their building – a one-story, three-room house above a storage room attached to another house. Before the attack they had thought they were safe. "When you are in your home, you think it is a protected place where nothing can harm you. And surprisingly it occurred in our home, so now home is the more dangerous place for me."

Nabila describes the attack, made even more vivid by photographs of her being taken from the rubble. "It was seven in the evening. A half hour earlier, we heard an *azaka* (warning siren), but it was very far away." After it stopped, she had the feeling that "if there would be another *azaka*, the next rocket would fall here in my house. I was crying. I felt that something would happen. Ten minutes later we heard another *azaka*. There were many rockets, and they were very close to us. One fell in the port of Haifa, another in our neighborhood, and another close to the house. When it fell in Wadi Nisnas, I yelled. My mother and I succeeded in getting to the safe room. We heard a boom. I was flying. The entire house was falling down, nothing remained. All of a sudden it was dark, then light, then dark again. There was a gas smell. Later I learned there had been a fire. They tried to put out the fire, but from the burning fire we started to have problems breathing. I had fallen on my mother. I didn't know where my father was. He was holding my mother's leg, but I didn't see or feel him at all. I heard only his voice, sounding very faint and distant."

Mounir recalls his actions upon hearing the *azaka*: "Usually, I don't wake up. But in the middle room I have a radio and I went to turn it on and heard a boom from afar. *Boom*, the home collapsed. We remained under the destruction until people came to take us out. They took out my wife and Nabila, and they didn't know where I was."

Nabila continues. "Then we started to yell for help. Many people were outside. No one could hear us, but we heard them. So I asked my mother if she thought we were going to die. She said, 'No, we are believers.' When I asked her if Jesus the prophet would leave us, she told me that he would not leave us for sure. Then we even lost this hope because we couldn't take a breath. We said that is it, if we stayed there another minute we would die."

Nabila was standing, wedged between her mother on one side and a clothes storage cabinet on the other side. "There was a small window. I tried to get out one hand but didn't succeed, because the storage cabinet was falling and clothes were flying. It was dark. I found a T-shirt and put it out the window and started to signal so people would know that we were inside the house. The people outside shouted to each other that we were still inside and started moving the stones and the storage cabinet until they reached us and then the firefighters also reached us." She does not know how she found the strength to shout that "my father is under here – you have to help him. In the end they succeeded in saving my mother and me, but I didn't agree to go out until I saw that my father was whole and everything was okay. He moved and was breathing. Then they took me outside and I fell down. I had no strength to speak or to stand on my legs – nothing."

Nabila and Fahima were taken to Bnai Zion Hospital, while Mounir went to Rambam Hospital. Fortunately for Mounir, somebody else from the attack was also in the hospital with him. "He told me that my wife and my daughter were in Bnai Zion Hospital. So, I knew. After that my son came; also my sister and her husband, my son-in-law, and other relatives." Nabila was in the other hospital for four or five hours and didn't know where her father was. "I didn't want people to touch me until I knew about my father, but nobody knew what had happened to him. I was nervous. The staff asked me to lie down – I sat – to drink – I wouldn't drink. I didn't agree until my sister came and told me that my father was okay, that he was in the other hospital. I asked her twenty thousand times if everything was okay. She told me yes; then I could relax."

Family is of utmost importance to Nabila. She acknowledges that "I am who I am because of my parents." Her sister Jameela lives nearby – a few houses away with her husband and three children. "Jameela suffered more than me," thinking her parents and her sister had died. When the rocket fell, she was in her home. The windows were closed and she didn't hear the boom at all. Her neighbor knocked on her door and told her that her parents' house was gone. "When my sister heard what happened, she was certain that we were dead and contacted my brother in Acre. As he drove to Haifa he was thinking about how he would arrange the funeral for his family. When I met my sister, it was very emotional – the most emotional part of this story. When I knew that she and her sons were okay, I felt very good."

The house was completely destroyed. "The roof fell in – and the room we were in fell into the storage room. It was really a miracle." The attached house was not destroyed, but their neighbors' son Mohammed (Don) Saloum, forty-one, ran into the burning house to save his mother and sister, who were not at home. The fire caused a gas tank to explode as Saloum entered the house, burning him severely. After a year fighting for his life in a Haifa hospital, Saloum succumbed to his wounds.

Fahima and Nabila were released from the hospital the next day and went to stay with family. Mounir was in the hospital for eight days and was treated for burns on his feet, head, and neck. For three months he could not lift his injured leg. Finally, friends found them an apartment with a safe room and the government paid their rent while it had their house rebuilt.

The Khouris talk a lot "about the tragedy that happened to us. When they ask us about what happened – how we feel – it brings it back. Always it's hard." But Nabila does not have a problem talking about it, despite the pain, and is an inspiration to others. "Talking about it feels comfortable and helps me a lot. When other people talk about something little that they lost – and cry about it – I tell them, 'You are alive, and what you lost is nothing.' I give my case as an example: 'I was almost killed. We left our home without anything. We started from zero. We got our life again as a gift and you shouldn't cry about belongings. You should say thanks that you are still alive.' Even with all the pain I have, I tell my story to everybody even though it hurts every time I think about it. I lost my clothes, my bed, and other things. It hurts me – it is childhood, memories. Even though I live here with many new things, it's not the same."

Mounir adds: "It hurts a lot that I lost everything. I saved my pension in order to be comfortable in these days. I was a carpenter. The house was full – thank God. Suddenly, I haven't anything – no clothes, no shoes, no food, no plates, nothing." For Mounir, it's not just the money, but losing family heirlooms and photos that hurts. He enjoyed creating art from stone and wood pieces and spent hundreds of hours on his projects. "Now everything is gone and I can't replace the lost stones and olive-wood pieces… Forty years I saved to do what I like. I can still do it but I don't know if I have enough strength."

Even before they were almost killed, the rockets terrorized Nabila. "When I heard an *azaka*, I was afraid. I went to the prepared room. I remember a few weeks before the war started that a rocket fell in the Hadar area, very close – about twenty-one meters (70 ft.) from here. We felt the boom in our whole house. I fell. I couldn't stand on my legs. It took me a few days before I could walk well. I didn't go to work. When I went back to work, a rocket fell on Rambam Hospital close by. And the same thing happened to me. I started to cry. I was so panicked.

I wanted to call my parents, my sister, my brother to see if they were okay. My coworkers lifted me up and after the booms stopped they took me to the office because I couldn't walk home. I was terrified every time I heard or saw an attack. I started to panic – to cry. I always needed support to relax. I had to close my ears in order not to hear the noise. It was the most difficult week – the last one in the war."

The fear remains. "Always I hear a boom, and I am afraid. When the *azaka* of remembrance was sounded on Memorial Day, it wasn't really an *azaka* from the war, but it was an *azaka* for me. I was at work. I couldn't speak. I ran. I cried. I was sweating. I didn't feel anything. Half of the day I was in a panic." She saw a psychotherapist who tried to treat her fear of hearing an *azaka*. Although, "he is my angel…I couldn't do it. I'm ready for everything, but I can't hear an *azaka*. For me, it's the end of the world."

Yet Nabila does not think about leaving Haifa or Israel. "No, this is my house and my family." Even if there is another war, "if I stay here, my situation will be more difficult, but this is the only thing that I can do… How can I leave Haifa, the nicest place in the world? I can't replace Haifa for any other place. And if I go, I leave my family – my parents, my sister, my brother. It would be harder for me to leave them than to be in a war. If something would happen I prefer that it happen when we are together." Mounir adds: "If we were going to leave we would have left a long time ago, when we were younger. Then, it would have been easier to move to another place. Even if a war begins now, I won't leave. Whatever happens from God, will be."

The Khouris are not religious, but they are believers. "It helps us very much to believe in something. We were always like this. It did not start with the war. And my belief is more than those who are religious. You don't have to be religious to believe." When their house was destroyed, nothing remained, everything fell, yet the pictures of Jesus and the Holy Mary weren't harmed. "We were thrown to all the corners of the room, but the pictures didn't fall. They stayed in place. When the police came, one of them called my sister and said, 'Let me show you something – this is what saved your parents.'" Also the pictures of the Holy Mary and Elijah the Prophet that Mounir always carried in his shirt pocket survived the explosion. Although his clothes were all torn, the pictures were somehow tossed out and were found hanging on a tree outside. "You asked how I believe?"

They are also helped by their network of friends. "It is a very good feeling that in difficult times you can know who really stands with you and who pretends they are your friends." Nabila, a well-known manager at an automotive garage, was comforted by the many friends and acquaintances who reached out to her "and asked, and worried, and tried to help as much as they could. Good people and friends don't leave."

Mounir also tells the story of good friends – a brother and sister and the sister's son – that he met when he lived in Tel Aviv. "Twelve years we were together, we are not just friends. Friends like that are difficult to find. They knew I was not Jewish and helped me more than if I had been family." When the attack occurred, the brother was in Germany. "He saw me on the news. He called his sister in Tel Aviv to get my phone number. Then he called me from Germany and from France. He came to Tel Aviv and visited me. His sister kept in touch almost daily and asked me if I would send my family to Tel Aviv. After the war ended, her son called with greetings for me from – guess who – the policeman who saved me. He was the son's neighbor."

Mounir tells another story about unexpected friendship and coincidence. When the first rocket fell in Haifa, he was cleaning a synagogue. "Someone took pictures of us and said he would bring them to my house. When the rocket fell on my house, he saw my picture in the newspaper, found me in the hospital, and brought the newspaper to me. He said, 'I promised you your picture but not like this.' Two days later he came back and brought the pictures of me in the synagogue. There are not many people like that; it is more important than any money. You can't compare the love of people with any value."

Nabila was strengthened by her experiences and had to remain strong for her family. "All the pain and the fear I would put on one side. On the other side, I met many people I hadn't met before. I have double the strength and courage that I had before. Because after what happened, I was the one who was responsible for everything – this one to an appointment with Bituach Leumi, that one to a doctor, and that one at home. I did everything. It gave me more strength." At the same time, it has taken a toll: "I am very tired. I can't go on more. I worked hard. I gave a lot. I had to show everyone that I am strong and happy. But now, I really can't. I have no more strength. I am very sad. I can't laugh. I can't continue when I am sad inside and tired. People tell me, 'Stop, a year has passed. What happened to you? Nothing.' But they can't feel my pain. It is what I feel. This is starting to kill me from the inside."

After the war, for Nabila "everything changed, it is not the same. Before, I was normal, like everyone. I never thought about anything. And then suddenly all the time we hear about war; but we didn't understand it until we experienced it. Now I think about the possibility of another war – with all the anxiety, fear, depression, sleeplessness, and flashbacks. I used to live like everyone without the confusion. Now my thoughts are not just about my life, but about the war – how to cope and continue. I am afraid all the time, it is totally different." She also sees people differently now. "There are bad people and good people, but most people are a combination. As human beings, we have the negative and the positive in our hearts. So why do we use the negative? It's nicer to use the positive."

Her psychologist has helped her cope with her situation and shown her how to relax. "He told me that whenever I think about bad things, instead try to think about nice things – like my brother's sons, my life… He also told me that 'you can't know what will happen, you aren't a magician. If you were a magician, the whole world would be white, people would love each other, there would be peace, and there would be no differences at all between Arabs and Jews and Christians.' I know it won't happen but this is what I hope – a white world. This war was so difficult, and in this war there was no difference between people – Arabs, Jews, Christians – the blood of all was involved together. So, we should stop focusing on differences and live together in Israel, the nicest place in the world. In a war it doesn't matter who you are; in the end, a mother is at home concerned about her son."

On July 20, 2013, Nabila celebrated her marriage to Ramzi Arram.

Part 2

From Grief to Meaning
and Healing

Many lives have been lost as a result of politically motivated violence and many lives have been changed forever. More than twelve hundred people have been killed in Israel since the start of the Second Intifada in September 2000. Left behind is the "family of the bereaved," as described by Possick et al.:

> The term "family of the bereaved" has existed in Israel since the founding of the State, referring to the group of families whose loved ones fell on the battlefield. Although Israel has a long history of civilian deaths in terror attacks, it is only since the Second Intifada that the term has expanded to include those families who have lost loved ones in this sudden and violent way.
>
> The term is a cultural construct that emerged to help Israelis cope with the trauma of continual loss. Its meaning now includes the surviving family's need for connection and communion following the death of their loved ones. For Jewish families, a week of *shiva* following the funeral is a time for consolation visits that take place in the home of the bereaved. It is often the time for the first meeting of the newest members of the family of the bereaved with the veteran members. While *shiva* may be the first contact, the bonding also can take place in organizational activities and support groups arranged by nonprofit organizations.
>
> In addition to being a cultural symbol of bereavement, being part of the family of the bereaved affords a special status, including taking part in national commemoration ceremonies and being entitled to publicly funded social services.[1]

---

1   Chaya Possick, Ruth Ann Sadeh, and Michal Shamai, "Parents' Experience and Meaning Construction of the Loss of a Child in a National Terror Attack," *American Journal of Orthopsychiatry* 78, no. 1 (2008): 97–98.

The stories in the following chapters are told by several members of the "family of the bereaved," who provide each other with the kind of support that only someone who also has experienced such loss and grief can provide. They turn to or even establish their own helping organizations to provide loving care, services, and support to the bereaved, as well as to survivors.

A family member's search for meaning often leads to creative expression. Some demonstrate their commitment to a loved one after his or her death through commemoration activities or by creating memorials to recognize and honor them. Others create meaning through altruism – selflessly helping others, contributing to society, and turning tragedy into action or activism. In these stories the bereaved share how they channeled their grief, pain, anger, and helplessness into life-affirming activities of remembrance, education, good deeds, and activism, making a difference in their lives and the lives of others. Through these acts of *tikkun olam* – repairing the world – they repair their own hearts and souls (*tikkun halev* and *tikkun haneshama*) and those of future generations (*tikkun hador*).

Chapter 7

Personal Injury and Profound Traumatic Loss

creating memories

W e cope with the loss of a loved one and go through the bereavement and mourning process in many ways, as influenced by our cultural and religious backgrounds, coping skills, mental history, support systems, and social and financial status.[1]

Commemoration, the creation of memorials, can be a significant part of the bereavement process as it continues the commitment to a loved one after his or her death in a world that has been challenged by loss. By doing so, the survivor can reconstruct the personal meaning of the lost relationship and establish his identity as a survivor and his place within the family and community.[2]

In Israel, the commemoration process is known as *hantzacha*, which means perpetuation or immortalization, and has been described as remembering:

> It is one way in which the bereaved create a new presence of the deceased so that a continuing bond can be maintained

---

1   Roxanne Dryden-Edwards, MD, "Loss, Grief, and Bereavement," http://www .onhealth.com/loss_grief_and_bereavement/article.htm.
2   R. A. Neimeyer and A. Anderson, "Meaning Reconstruction Theory," in *Loss and Grief: A Guide for Human Services Practitioners*, ed. N. Thompson (London: Palgrave, 2002), 45–64.

with him/her. It is a conscious attempt to preserve the
memory and eternalize the essence of the deceased in both
the personal and the collective contexts.[3]

There are different types of commemoration. It may be spontaneous,
as in the placing of flowers, pictures, and memorial candles at the site
of an attack, or in the handwritten messages of love and remembrance
painted on nearby stone walls. Later, the family and friends of the
person who died may design and fund private commemoration at the
place of the attack, in schools or playgrounds, on the internet, in the
synagogues, and elsewhere, allowing people who never met the fallen
to know something about them and, more importantly, to remember
them. Finally, public municipal and state commemoration allows the
society as a whole to mourn and remember, for example at the national
cemetery at Mount Herzl in Jerusalem on Yom Hazikaron (Israel's
national memorial day for the fallen soldiers and the victims of terror).

The bereaved families in this chapter suffered profound and traumatic
loss in addition to personally experiencing the attack. They are coping
with their losses, willing themselves to live for their surviving families
and moving forward, one step at a time. Each discovers his or her own
creative way to meaningfully recognize and memorialize a loved one:
Corinne Hamami designed a memorial wall in memory of her husband
Amiram, who was fatally injured in the Park Hotel Massacre; Arnaud
Harenstein and Chana Nathansen worked on writing books about their
experiences after the shooting of Arnaud's wife Yafit at their home and
the death of Chana's daughter in the suicide bombing of the Children's
Bus; and Iris Yihichya, Yafit's mother, paints and teaches art-therapy
classes to get the pain out from deep inside.

---

3   Chaya Possick, Ruth Ann Sadeh, and Michal Shamai, "Parents' Experience
and Meaning Construction of the Loss of a Child in a National Terror Attack,"
American Journal of Orthopsychiatry 78, no. 1 (2008): 99. See also Possick et
al., "Reconstructing the Loss: Hantzacha Commemoration Following the Death
of a Spouse in a Terror Attack," *Journal of Loss and Trauma* 12, no. 2 (2007):
111–112.

All of these families, as well as Ora Cohen and her family who were injured in the attack on the Children's Bus, continue to live with the repercussions of the attacks and tell their stories of personal injury and profound traumatic loss, describing how they keep alive the memories of their loved ones.

Husband Amiram killed, Park Hotel (Passover Massacre)
bombing, Netanya: March 27, 2002

Corinne Hamami: Fight to Survive

"Do what you believe in... If you don't believe, don't do it."

On the eve of Passover 2002 a terrorist walked past a security guard at the entrance to the Park Hotel in the coastal city of Netanya and into the dining room, where 250 guests had just sat down to begin the Seder (the Passover ceremonial dinner). The suicide bomber, Abdel-Basset Odeh, twenty-five, was on Israel's list of wanted terrorists and was from the West Bank city of Tulkarem, which is just ten kilometers (6 mi.) east of Netanya. He detonated an explosive device carried in a suitcase, killing thirty people and injuring 140 in what became known as the "Passover Massacre." Most of the victims were elderly Jews who did not have families and relatives; many of them were Holocaust survivors who perished in the very homeland that was supposed to keep them safe. Amiram Hamami, forty-four, the Park Hotel manager and security officer, was fatally injured and died thirty-six hours later without regaining consciousness.

Amiram and his wife Corinne, the hotel owners' daughter, had six sons, who were ages six to twenty at the time of the attack. The oldest, Itai, was in the army and the other five were at the hotel. The second oldest, Gilad, was standing behind a pillar in the hotel entrance when the explosion occurred. Yair, thirteen, and Yotam, sixteen, were saved because they were on the second floor of the hotel playing backgammon. Michael, nine, and Netanel, seven, were playing in the lobby; Netanel was slightly wounded in the knee and Michael was frozen into inaction.

For Corinne, who arrived five minutes after the bombing, "it was a little bit different than when you see the fire or when you see the explosion. I did not have time to feel. I was only worried about what was happening with my family. I just was looking for my husband

and my children. Two of my children were outside and were crying hysterically. I went to look for the other children. I couldn't find them. I was also looking for Ami, my husband, but I couldn't find him."

Corinne was forty-three and a religious Jew who had moved to Israel from France with her parents and four sisters and brothers when she was thirteen. She worked as the economist at the hotel. She shares "only the facts" about the bombing because she does not want to "involve my feelings now. I don't want to cry. I don't want to remember all the things. It's too difficult to speak about it." Since the attack, her entire life has changed. "I have to be strong enough to be alone at home and to educate the younger children. The two oldest are in the army, so they can't come home every day. Until now it has not been easy."

Her priorities have changed and, in little ways, so has she. She focuses on what is important and not on the small details. "Before, I would make a big deal about everything. Now I look at it and I say, 'okay, it's okay.' Before, if a child didn't go to school, it was a big thing. But now if he doesn't want to go, 'okay, don't go.' If he doesn't want to do his homework, I try to get him to do the homework. But if he really doesn't want to do it, so 'okay, don't do it, it's all right.' If he doesn't want to pray, 'okay, it's between you and God.' These things are not so important and it is more important that you feel good with yourself – that you are happy – that you do what you really believe in. If you don't believe, don't do it." As a result, "I'm moving on in life."

"This experience is very difficult. In the beginning I thought I would die – even if I have six children and I am a mother with small children. But the children want a life. So they pushed me a lot. I saw the negative reaction of the children when I was sad or crying or I was in bed and didn't want to go to work. Very quickly I understood that I can't stay down and I have to do something. They give me a lot of strength to fight."

Her relationship with her children has changed. "Before I was with my husband, and the children were living their lives and were with their friends. Now they are closer to me and I am closer to them. Sometimes, especially with the teenagers, it's very difficult because I am a mother first of all and not a father." Her oldest son Itai was very close to his father. "And most of the time I couldn't understand either of them. Like many men, they had a very deep and beautiful relationship without speaking too much, but they could understand each other. Itai was a fighter in the army in a special unit. I expected him to stop being in the army, but he wanted to be there. He didn't understand that I couldn't suffer anymore, but I didn't say anything about it and now we are closer."

Corinne's goals for the future are "to be a very good mother and to give my children the best education. I want them to be happy. So I think it is important for me also to be happy. If they are happy, I am happy. If I were mourning or very sad all the time, they would also be sad and they might run away from home. I have to find a way for us all to be together and feeling good."

She does not worry more than she used to. "I'm not hysterical and I never was hysterical. This hasn't changed. If the children want to go somewhere, I let them go." She believes that "our souls are just in this body temporarily; the most important is after this world." Yet if a terrorist is on the news, "I may be more careful. I tell the children not to go to public places where there are too many people. But that's all. I don't want the children at home with me all the time. It's impossible to live like that."

After the *pigua* happened, Corinne read a lot of books about child development. "Each one was in another stage. So it was very important to know what a child of seven years feels, what a child of thirteen feels. And I came to understand it through the researchers. It gives me a lot of courage. Somebody also wrote a book about an attack and I read it to my children so they would know what other children feel."

Yotam spent the Chanukah holiday after the attack in Eilat at Camp Koby, a camp meant specifically for children struck by terror. "My friends at home can talk with me and try and understand, but they never will, because they have never been there. The other guys at camp – they know. They feel the same." Yotam says being with these friends gives him strength to deal with his loss. "Mostly in the evenings, when we are alone in our rooms, we talk, one to each other. And we tell all the troubles we have. And it helps to solve those problems."[1]

---

1   John Yang, "Coping at Camp," December 9, 2002, kobymandell.site.aplus.net /news1p.htm.

Corinne also has learned the value of seeking out and connecting with others who have had similar experiences. She was helped most by very good friends "who can understand me, who I can speak with, I can go with them where I want to go. If I need something, I can phone them in the middle of the night and tell them I need help." Although her sisters support her, "they can't understand what we've been through. They can't understand that after three months you are still mourning." She spends a lot of time with another woman who also lost her husband in the Park Hotel bombing. "We have a very, very good relationship. I help her and she helps me. We talk about everything – the *pigua* and our husbands. And our children are together. That is the greatest help."

She also belongs to a group from Bituach Leumi and has gone on retreats with other widows through organizations like OneFamily and the Koby Mandell Foundation, which runs Camp Koby. "It's nice that we are together. We can speak together, we can understand each other, and we build good relationships with other women that have the same situation." She was also helped by her psychologist and her social worker – "She's an angel for me. She is really something special. She has a lot of experience – not with terrorists, but with widows. So she can see what we see and she helped me a lot.

"The support of people – family, extended family, coworkers, neighbors, people from the municipality – most of the people who come to help are the best. I learned how wonderful people are." But there are also disappointments. Echoing the experiences of other bereaved family members, she relates: "Some people see me in the street and go to the other side. And this is the biggest humiliation that you can get. They don't know how to behave or how to make contact. I think in a country like Israel that has seen so many *piguim* and so much pain and with soldiers in the army, people have to know how to react." She hopes to educate people on how to behave with survivors and bereaved family members. She also advocates for people to know their rights in the event of a *pigua*.

At first Corinne spoke a lot about her experience "because people asked me what happened. I was in the newspaper and on television. I told them what I feel. A lot of people don't know what we are feeling and what happened to Israelis here. So I give them good information and tell them my side of this story. But sometimes in the press, they change things." Living in Israel, "every day is a fight. Also in my private life, I have to fight. I have to fight to survive."

Corinne has created several truly meaningful memorials to her husband. As we sat in the lobby of the renovated Park Hotel, she pointed to the beautiful memorial wall that she had designed. It was made of stones for strength, some with seashells embedded because Ami loved the sun. In one part a stone is missing, reflecting the void Ami's death has created. Also displayed is a photo album inscribed with *v'ahavta l're'acha kamocha* (you should love your friends as yourself) and **AMI** – *Al Matzot u'merorim Yochluhu* (you shall eat [the Paschal Lamb] with matzos and bitter herbs) in memory of Amiram Hamami, Pesach 1958–Pesach 2002.

For the fifth anniversary of Ami's death, Corinne made a movie with the family about him. "First of all, we did it because some of the children were so young they don't know their father. And I want them to know him. So everybody spoke about him – his parents, my mother who worked with him, a good friend of ours, his brother and sister, and his children. Even the small one shared what he remembers. We tried to do it in an optimistic way, so we spoke only about the good memories, and the good things that we did together."

Five and a half years after the attack, Corinne continued to work at the hotel part time, because "I prefer to put all my energy in the family and less in a career. After what happened, I don't have as much energy as I had before. And I am only one person; before we were two."

She does not think about the *pigua*. "I just think about my husband. I still think about him a lot. It was nice to be together. I have a lot of memories. He was an optimistic man and he knew what he wanted. He had a presence. He was a very good man also. He liked to help a lot of people – that was one of the special things about him." Because of that, "Itai and Gilad created a nonprofit association to help the needy buy food. They received a prize from the mayor of Netanya as excellent volunteers because of what they do for society."

Eleven years after the attack, her sons have grown and are moving on with their lives. The four oldest boys are all married and have given Corinne six grandchildren – four girls and two boys. Itai is a mechanical engineer, Gilad is an architect, Yotam learns in a yeshiva, and Yair is studying to be an electrical engineer. The two youngest boys have struggled since the attack. Netanel "made me crazy and had so many problems, but now it's exactly the opposite. He made all this effort alone" and is now volunteering with at-risk children for a year before beginning his army service. Michael was the most affected and responded by retreating into himself, playing imaginary games on his computer. He finally went to a psychologist and, after a few years of treatment, is a little better and is beginning his army service.

In March 2008 Corinne married Ramy Chalaf, a retired police trainer and father of three children, but "I still live with Ami in my heart, missing him very much; the past is very strong."

Wife and daughter Yafit killed, Moshav Mechora shooting,
Jordan Valley: August 10, 2002

Arnaud Harenstein (Husband): Life Is a Puzzle

"There is death, there is love, there is hope."

Iris Yihichya (Mother): *Tzemicha v'Pericha* (Growing and Blossoming)

"Together with the pain and hardships that we carry with us the whole time, there is a light at the end of the tunnel."

Iris Yihichya remembers her daughter Yafit Harenstein as "a stunning young woman. She was always smiling; everything was good, even if things weren't okay. She was very intelligent, very well groomed. She took things very seriously and used to say that someday a terrorist would enter the moshav. She didn't leave a thing undone, as if she felt that she wouldn't always be here. She kept her house clean and paid off the debts. And, at the end, Yafit was a heroine. I'm proud that my daughter saved her daughters, her husband, and the whole moshav. She fought and gave her life so that her family and all of us will live. How many more would have been killed had she not shouted and by her scream woken everyone up?"

Yafit, her husband Arnaud, and their two young daughters – two-year-old Shai and four-month-old Chen – were at home in Moshav Mechora, a farming village in the Jordan Valley established in 1973 and home to about thirty families, including Iris and her husband Shlomi, a school bus driver, who were founding members of the moshav. The Yihichyas came "because we wanted a better life for our kids. We didn't worry about terrorists, we just came. We were idealistic. We wanted to help settle *Eretz Yisrael* (the Land of Israel), our state, and so we said,

'Let's go!' We wanted our own house, we wanted quality of life, and here we found it – until that fateful evening in August 2002."

On that night a high alert was sounded, warning that terrorists were in the area. Arnaud, who headed the village civilian defense committee, realized he'd left his walkie-talkie at his in-laws' house nearby and rushed by car to get it. The round trip took only a few minutes. When he pulled back into his driveway, the terrorist, a member of the Fatah al-Aqsa Brigade from a nearby village, was waiting.

Arnaud Harenstein

Arnaud describes the attack: "It was Saturday night, at almost ten in the evening. I had just come back by car. At the moment I pulled the handbrake, I saw the Palestinian terrorist in my private garden, between the main entrance of my house and the car. I immediately understood that he was a terrorist and that in a few seconds I would die. I was unarmed and I couldn't drive around him. So I decided to put the car in reverse, just to take him away a little bit from the main entrance of the house, because my two daughters were there with my wife Yafit. I hoped that he would run after the car and then shoot at me and maybe forget about the house. Immediately, he shot three bullets at me and then he yelled in Arabic, '*Allahu Akhbar*' (God is great). I remember thinking, 'Why are you talking about God? You are shooting at me now – where is God?' He continued to run in the direction of the car and shot four more bullets."

The terrorist came to the passenger side. "There was no window because it was blown out by the shooting – and he put his hand with the weapon into the car and wanted to shoot me in the head. My wife came out of the house with my weapon – an M-16. She saved my life because, at the moment she pulled the trigger, the terrorist heard her and turned his whole body and his arm moved with the weapon. Instead of hitting my head, it hit my leg. I was hit by seven bullets. The terrorist proceeded to wrest the weapon from my wife's hands and he shot her with his automatic weapon – twenty bullets. She died immediately."

Then the terrorist went inside the house to the children's room, "where my wife had put them together in the same bed with pillows about them; he shot a few bullets into the pillows and the bed. It's a miracle, nothing happened to them." Later, the girls were safely taken from the home by their grandfather Shlomi and uncle Noam who witnessed the attack from their nearby home. They had been sitting outside chatting and laughing with Yafit's older sister and their friends when they heard the gunshots.

The army arrived and killed the terrorist as he came out shooting at the soldiers. "The soldiers were sure that I was dead because the whole car was bloody, with no windows, and I wasn't able to move. I was still conscious but I wasn't able to speak or yell. Thinking that maybe there was another terrorist, the soldiers began to search the moshav. They searched for twenty-five minutes and then they came to take the dead body from the car. Only then did they realize that I was still alive. And only then did they call the helicopter. I arrived at the hospital exactly two hours after the attack, still conscious, and gave them my ID number, my address, and my phone number. Then I was in a coma for ten days and in the ICU for twenty-one days. I lost five liters of blood, which is everything in a normal human being. I had two bullets in the left leg, two in the left shoulder, three in the right arm and shoulder, and one that made it through the lung – just one millimeter from the heart. That was close! I was on the critical list three times. The doctors said that I was a medical miracle."

But Arnaud does not believe that his recovery was a miracle. "Fortunately, we have terrific doctors in Israel, especially in Hadassah–Ein Kerem, and they have a lot of experience. And I wanted to survive. I didn't know that my wife was killed. I didn't know what had happened to my daughters, but I was sure that they were okay and for them I really wanted to live. That is the reason that I am now alive – to take care of the next generation of the family. So between great doctors and a patient who didn't want to die, there was a good likelihood that I would survive."

Six months after he left the hospital and went to rehab, he met Inbal. "That was the biggest help, because Shai, my older daughter, began to call her mom." They married a few years later and have two sons, Yuval and Yoav. "Now that my two sons were born, there is only one family. There are no differences with the children."

Looking back, for Arnaud, as for other survivors of terrorist attacks, "the terrorist attack was almost like a holocaust." He compares himself to other terrorism survivors whom he has met at rehabilitation or seen on television. "A lot of people need help after such an attack, especially those who are the sole survivors of a terrorist attack and lost their entire family." As he understands it, "In Israel, most of the terror survivors and terror victims still live the act of terrorism. They are stuck there. As far as I can see, almost everybody continues to live, but like dead live people. They lose something and they don't find a way to continue life, to enjoy life."

He believes that "everyone has to find his own reason to live and to enjoy life." In his case, "I now enjoy life much more than I enjoyed my life before." Even though he has a 92 percent handicap and suffers a lot of pain, "I can do almost everything, except play basketball or karate. I don't let my handicap prevent me from doing anything that I want to do." He believes that "the best help is you. I don't believe in external help. If you find reasons to live – the wife, the children, maybe the dog, and maybe your parents – it's more than 90 percent of the rehab – only 10 percent is occupational therapy, physical therapy, and psychotherapy."

Since the attack, Arnaud feels more focused and calmer. "When you know what is important and what is not important, you are calmer." He accepts the way life is now. "This is my life now and this is the way life is. I don't ask any questions – 'why me, why my wife, why our family, what would happen if I weren't handicapped?' Life continues. I don't worry about it, I just look forward. It's not that you forget what happened, but you have no time to be there." Before the attack, "I thought like that but I didn't act like that. I always wanted more – to be more important at work or to get more money or a better salary – every time more, more, and more. Not that I now love my children more than I loved them before or that I love anyone more than before, but now I know what is very important in life and what is not important. The most important thing is that I have two daughters and I think the only thing that I have to do is to be a good parent and take care of them. That is the real thing in life."

Sitting in his living room with his children afoot and the television blaring with cartoons, I was able to personally observe what a wonderful, loving father he was and the important role his children have played in helping him recover and move forward in life.

In addition to receiving strength from his daughters, Arnaud was strengthened by his past experiences – making *aliya* with his family from France when he was ten years old, nearly losing his mother in a car accident at age fifteen, and fighting in the army at age eighteen and losing some friends or seeing others become handicapped. He does not find any answers in religion, nor does he find solace in being told that his loved one's untimely death made her a saint, that her death in some way played a part in repairing the world (*tikkun*), or that God kept him alive to prove to him how strong he was. "I would prefer to be very weak and that my wife would still be here for my daughters and I would be in better condition. So I can't understand religious people, who say that it happened because it is written in the Torah or because God says so. He never talked to me. Maybe if I meet Him I will feel differently."

Arnaud learned that life is full of surprises, both good and bad. "The surprise for me wasn't the attack or the situation. The surprise for me is that I am still alive, because I saw the terrorist and he shot me and I was bleeding to death and I understood everything. For me the surprise is a good one. Also I am lucky that I understand at a young age what is important in life. Everything that happened to me is luck. And now to wake up in the morning is enough. I wish that everybody would understand this, that everyone would enjoy the sunshine in the morning. Maybe then it would be a better world."

Arnaud started speaking about his experience as "a way to say thank you to Hadassah Hospital for saving my life, for giving my daughters back their father. I can't give them money, so I do anything that gives me the opportunity to say thank you." He has spoken on many occasions after seeing that he had no trouble talking about it and realizing that people were interested in his story. "Even though it is my life, the story is an interesting story. It has everything in it. There is death, there is love, and there is hope."

He has tried to write a book about the night at the moshav and his hospitalization, including about being paranoid and hallucinating that the doctors were terrorists coming to kill him. "It was like I was in a movie. I didn't know what was true and what wasn't true." But he had to give it up "because when you speak about something, you are not going deep inside; you talk about facts and it is very clear. But when you are writing and reflecting on it, you are more inside, more into the feelings. So then I understood that it's too painful and I am not there anymore. I prefer to be present in my day, in my house, taking care of my family."

Arnaud had worked as a security agent for the Israeli Embassy in Moscow and as a duty manager at the Allenby Bridge, the main crossing point between Jordan and Israel. He had hoped to become a general in the army. After the attack, he was financially secure due to his and his wife's insurance and additional money he received as a French citizen from a terrorism fund in France; however, "it's very hard to accept that the country – the people – are taking care of you."

Immediately after the attack, Arnaud decided that "when my daughters are at home, I am at home. They are in kindergarten from eight in the morning to four in the afternoon. So those are the hours that I can work. Before and after, it doesn't matter what happens, I am at home. I am a fulltime parent. It's me! It is what I do now and I hope that I will do that until the day that they say, '*Abba*, enough.' And I hope that day isn't tomorrow. I understand that I am much more protective than other parents. I try to let go because maybe it's not the best thing for my children. So, you learn every day from your mistakes… I think I am a good father, which is not always easy in normal life. After a very, very traumatic event, if you have the right proportion, you are a much better parent because you understand what is important and what is less important."

Now he wants to do something to contribute. "I don't want to work for somebody else. And I am very afraid of mistakes with money. I think a lot about what to do, but I haven't found the right idea yet. And it is disturbing that I still feel a little bit like a parasite. It's not easy. I feel I am missing something. I am not fulfilled. I don't want to be seventy or eighty years old and tell my grandchildren that, looking back, I didn't do anything." Before the attack, Arnaud wanted to be a politician; now he is considering becoming a lawyer. "I think the most important thing is to have some direction, even if it is not immediately acted upon."

During the 2006 Israel-Hezbollah/Lebanon War, when Katyusha rockets hit in the north close to their home, Arnaud and his family went to stay with some friends in Ra'anana further south. "I learned that when someone is shooting at you, run away. Don't stay. I am not a fighter any more. I have to think of my family. They shoot, I leave. I already paid a price. I don't want my children to pay any more than they already have."

On the other hand, he remains in Israel because of his children. Having been born in France, he knows that "to be a Jew out of Israel is bad, especially in Europe, especially in France with potential anti-Semitism. I prefer to die as an Israeli in Israel than as a Jew in France and I think that the best place for my daughters to grow up and to make a life is in Israel."

Arnaud describes his life as a puzzle. "The terrorist came and broke my puzzle completely. And when I woke up in the hospital, I didn't know how to put the pieces together again. But now the image is the same as it was, although some pieces are still not exactly in the same place. I changed some pieces and some pieces might be cut, but the image as a whole is normal."

Iris Yihichya

When the shooting happened, Yafit's mother, Iris, was on a Caribbean cruise with her friend Mazal as a fiftieth birthday present from her husband. She had a feeling "that something was happening at home – that something was wrong." She had just started taking a shower, when "I looked up and suddenly saw my mother, who had passed away four months earlier. I saw her weeping as if something had happened."

The Israeli Consul informed the captain of the ship of what had happened. "The captain took me to his office and asked me to sit and calm down and dialed my home number. I talked with Shlomi, my husband, and he told me to get back home. He told me a catastrophe had occurred. I have two sons, one of them in the army in Shechem

(Nablus), the other with the security forces of the Knesset. So I said immediately, 'What happened? Ilan? Noam?' You don't think it's at home; the first thing that comes to mind is that it's those serving in the defense or security forces. And he says to me, 'No, it's Yafit. A terrorist entered the house.' He couldn't talk and he gave the phone to the social worker who told me Yafit was very, very seriously wounded, although they knew that she was already gone. Then I asked, 'What's with the children, the house?' And she says, 'Everything is all right, don't worry' – while there everything was a *balagan*."

The flight from Nassau through London to Israel was a logistical and emotional nightmare. "You're on a plane – sitting, weeping the whole time, thinking maybe it's not true, maybe it's just a dream, maybe you'll get there and they'll tell you it's not true, and all of a sudden you get frightened, your whole body starts shaking. You think about the whole world, about what happened to you throughout your life, what for, why, what you've done, had you done something wrong? It's like a film running in front of your eyes from the time you were little until this very minute; from the time your kids were born to this day. How can it be? Maybe it's not true."

On her way home, Iris decided that she had to be stronger for her family. "I have a family to look after and if I fell, everyone else would fall too. I have three other kids, and a husband, and granddaughters, and if they saw me falling, it would be the end of the world. Looking back, I think it was a mistake because I think we too are allowed to fall down because we are human too. I don't think we have to be the strongest, or to uphold the whole world on our shoulders. Nevertheless, when I saw my family I said, 'I am not falling, there is nothing to do but take hold of myself.' I won't say that I didn't have tough days, when I wanted to stay in bed or I didn't know what to do with myself. I was on the verge of falling to pieces. The whole week of the *shiva*, a lot of people kept coming, but I felt all alone – alone and without anyone. I had my family, but I was all alone."

At first, Yafit's daughters moved in with Iris and Shlomi. "That's what kept me from falling, being busy the whole time with the girls, the housekeeping, my own family, and the people who came in to help and talk, sit with us, get something for us. It's impossible to describe how much the moshav and all its members helped; but for myself I had no time left – not to sit, think, nothing. For a long period of time, I didn't go into mourning; I didn't let myself."

When Arnaud recovered and left the moshav with his girls, Iris broke down. "Yafit's daughters were what connected the two of us, me and her, what bound us together, and now I was denied this too. I felt that I was losing another dear one and it was very, very difficult." Iris became ill and was hospitalized. "That's when the big *balagan* began; the questions arose: 'Who are you; what are you doing with your life; how do you build your life around it?' Either you sink down or you soar upward. And how does one soar up? It's difficult. It's easiest to sink and say, 'I don't want to go on living, I want to leave, I want to die; it's over, it's the end.'"

Fortuitously, Iris was invited to a Koby Mandell Foundation women's workshop with ten other bereaved mothers. "Those were a very tough two days, because there you don't differ from the other members, although each has her own story. You listen to all of them, and you have to tell your own story which is difficult as well. There was a moment when we all wanted to get up and leave – it was so heavy. But the retreat was about telling and listening and reacting and remembering; about seeing your friend weeping and shouting; about listening to yourself telling your story and crying, on the verge of fainting. It was very hard. But we decided we're staying on, and in the evening we sat together after getting all those things off our chests. We all had something in common – our child who was taken away. And now we had a place where we were listened to and understood, and we knew how we felt. With all the hardships, it is very important."

On the second day, the participants were given various materials and told to create a piece of artwork from them. "I sat there, doing nothing, for about an hour and a half. All of a sudden, I took a paintbrush, paints, and pictures from magazines and out came a stunning picture. I created what I felt inside – where I was coming from, where I had arrived at, and where she went to." For the first time, Iris expressed her feelings through art, something she had never done before.

From that minute, something amazing happened to Iris. "I came home – it was winter, rainy, there was nothing to do – and I looked at Yafit's picture on the wall. I sat opposite it, took a pencil with paper, and drew Yafit. I drew her down to the nose, eyes and all. Suddenly I realized I could draw. I got scared and stopped; and then, late at night, I couldn't sleep, so I took the pencil again and went on drawing. In the drawing, she had very long hair, not straight but beautifully curled, and from the curls I brought out people and there were terrorists among them. The more I brought out, the more difficult the drawing became. The next day, I took another piece of paper and drew a mother that resembles Yafit with a baby who's sucking on her breast. I was sitting and painting and drawing the whole time, on and on and on. It was like a painting obsession. That's when I started getting out things from deep inside onto the paper, and today that's what I do."

At the suggestion of her rehabilitation worker, Iris applied for and was accepted to a two-year program at the Center for Arts in Jerusalem. "It helped me enormously, and still helps, because during the eight hours of studying, it's not that I forget, but I'm busy. In the beginning, I used to do very heavy stuff dealing with what happened to me, like a sculptured piece that is a scream of parents shouting at God; it represented my feeling guilty because I had not been there during the attack."

Iris became an art instructor, working with dyslexic children and cancer patients and instructing other bereaved mothers in the Koby Mandell program. She had them make a night-light out of wax, surrounding a candle. "I started the lesson with a story to show them that, together with the pain and hardships that we carry with us the whole time, there is a light at the end of the tunnel. There is a candle; and whenever you see it, you will know that there is still a light at the end of the tunnel and that our kids wouldn't want to see us collapsing. It was very successful, very beautiful."

She also has been writing her thoughts in a diary for her granddaughters about what happened since their mother was killed. "I'm writing these things down like I'm talking to them. I've written about a hundred pages and it's very difficult because I wrote down all the tough things, the beautiful ones and the ugly ones, so they'll know.

When they grow up, not now, I'll ask them if they want to read it; and if they don't want to read it, I'll put it in a safe place so that no one will read it. I feel that I want to write many things, but when I read it, it's hard and I start crying. Had I not written, I wouldn't have remembered; it helps me think how I would have done things differently. The writing helps, but not as much as the painting."

Five years after the attack, Iris thinks of herself as growing and blossoming like a flower, and she named her recent art exhibition *Tzemicha v'Pericha* – Growing and Blossoming. "My daughter was murdered, but I am in *tzemicha* (growing). Every day I do things. I draw. I sculpt. I'm an artist. I had an art exhibition at the Jerusalem Theater. In the beginning, it was all inside and I wanted to let it all out. It was very hard." One painting from that time pictured her daughter entwined with terrorists. "Today I won't do that. Today I'll do things that are more beautiful. I study; I also teach children. I am always doing; I don't want to stop. The pain, of course, is here. It is like a hole that cannot close. It's like a wound that nothing can cure. But you learn to *live next to it*. It is together with you all the time."

Today Iris is finally in mourning, "because today I understand that my daughter is not coming back. I can open a window and I will not see her coming. Before it was like maybe, maybe she'll come back, maybe it's not true, maybe she traveled and she'll come back. Everything is maybe, maybe, maybe, maybe. Inside you don't want to believe it's true. Today, it is what it is." She describes this change as *hashlama* – acceptance.

She believes time is not a healer for a parent. "It isn't time. It's always there. It's not a thing that goes away and that's it. I'm talking about a mom and dad; I'm not talking about others. A husband gets married and has two more kids; brothers continue their lives. It hurts them, but it's not like a mother and a father. Finally something happens in the head. You decide that you either die, or if you want to live, then you live. It's impossible to be in the middle. I decided I didn't want to die. It's the easiest solution to die, to go to sleep, and that's it. But no, you have to learn to live."

She recognized that she was confused. She wanted to move forward but wasn't sure how. A psychologist helped. "I didn't do it alone. I knew what I wanted. I needed order, to organize my thoughts. I told him, I am choosing to move on. I want to move forward and do things – drawing and continuing my artwork, thinking and letting those thoughts go out. And that's what I'm doing."

She also learned important lessons from another bereaved mother about how to act and how to be a human being. "It was something special. I said, 'If from her I took, why shouldn't I give to others?' And that's what I do, even though it's difficult and it hurts." As a result, Iris gives others strength to move forward. At a three-day retreat with fifteen mothers who lost sons in the Israel-Hezbollah/Lebanon War, "I was the only mother who was a 'veteran' – meaning that I had lost a child more than five years before, while for everyone else it had only been a year. It was hard. Everything came back. Poor things, what they went through. I know; I was there. I was like a cow that gives milk, and they were like a baby that wants milk. They always asked me questions, 'How will it be? Then what? You did the same? Are we allowed to laugh? Are we allowed to sing?' Everything is allowed. You have to do this. I know because I was there before and now I'm here. You're there and I'm already here. And they asked me, 'And you don't forget?' I said, 'No, never. You have to learn to live with it; to go with it together.' They were miserable, but I gave them strength to move forward. There are those who wanted to die, and they will not die because they saw me. They saw that it is possible to live."

Sadly, Shlomi Yihichya passed away in June 2013 of a broken heart following a brief illness. A week after his death and eleven years after the murder of his daughter, the Israeli Ministry of Defense finally admitted that the moshav had not been properly guarded on the day of the attack. "But for Shlomi, it was too late."

And then, shortly before Rosh Hashanah 2013, Iris's car was shot at by terrorists on the road between Jerusalem and Moshav Mechora. The army, police, and security forces searched for the attackers, but did not find them. Iris's ear was grazed by a bullet and she is in pain, "but it will be okay. What can I do? Thank God that it was not worse."

Daughter Tehilla Nathansen killed, Egged bus no. 2
(the Children's Bus) bombing, Jerusalem: August 19, 2003

Chana Nathansen: *Tehilla* – Praise to God

"What happened to me today can happen to you tomorrow."

Ora Cohen: Religion Saved Us

"My life changed; it never goes back to what I had before."

It was vacation time and the eve of Rosh Chodesh Elul, the beginning of the month preceding Rosh Hashanah. The Nathansen and Cohen families spent the evening at the Kotel, the Western Wall, in the Old City of Jerusalem. They were on their way home on the crowded Egged bus no. 2, which was making its way to several religious neighborhoods. As the bus drove through Jerusalem's Shmuel Hanavi neighborhood, a Palestinian suicide bomber disguised as a religious Jew detonated a five-kilogram (11 lb.) device packed with ball bearings, killing 23 people and wounding over 130. Seven children, ages three months to sixteen years, were killed on the "Children's Bus"; one-third of those wounded were youngsters, children whose parents, brothers, or sisters were also wounded or killed.

Chana Nathansen

The Nathansens of Zichron Yaacov – parents Matanya (27) and American-born Chana (26), with their children Yehudit (6), Tehilla (3), Shoshana (six months), and Matanya's youngest sister Sara – were visiting family in Jerusalem and had begun their evening with prayers at the Kotel. Chana was holding Tehilla on her left knee next to her baby sister Shoshana on the right and Matanya, Yehudit, and Sara were standing in the aisle behind them when the bus exploded. Tehilla died instantly and Chana was severely injured, with a broken thigh and ribs, shattered hip, torn spleen, and shrapnel in her right eye and face. She had many metal pellets in her body. "I must have lost consciousness. I remember thinking it can't be happening; it must be a dream. I remember myself crying again and again, 'My thigh, my thigh!' but I have no memory of pain. I wasn't really there. I guess I knew something was going on and I remember telling myself it's impossible that I was in a *pigua*. So thank heaven for that. I didn't have to deal with the fears and worries and whatever…at the beginning."

Matanya flew through the doors when the bus exploded and landed a long distance away, breaking his shoulder and foot and tearing the cornea in his eye. Yehudit was lightly wounded in the neck by shrapnel – millimeters away from her jugular vein. Shoshana was almost not recognizable; she suffered second degree burns to her face and was hit by two small ball bearings. In the hospital, Chana pumped milk to breast-feed her baby and resumed breast feeding from her damaged breast when she was released from the hospital two weeks later. "I think it helped it heal."

Fifteen months after the attack, Chana and her family were still recovering, and words could not describe their pain. "We don't have to describe what it feels like to lose a child. Words aren't sufficient enough… Obviously, we are not back to normal. We are still not back to ourselves physically. We are busy with treatments and surgery." What helped her most was "*emuna*, my belief, the knowledge that everything is from above. We know that nothing happens without a reason. Everything has a reason." She believes the saying in Hebrew, "*l'kol kadur yesh ketovet* – each bullet has its address. So my daughter had one of these in her head. She was suddenly like an angel. We were hurt more than she was. So we know everything is planned. Nothing just happens by chance." She believes that "my whole life before – all of my experiences put together – is what makes me a person and helps me deal with crisis."

Chana is grateful to Hashem for the "miracle" of their survival. "In the beginning, we were very, very grateful for all the miracles. But then the more that time passes, the more you become busy with yourself and where you've been. Because we had suffered our loss, it put everything in proportion so it made the physical changes easier. On the one hand, we didn't have the energy to deal with all the technicalities. On the other hand, it caused us to see things for what they really were."

She also is very grateful about life. "I was always very grateful and I'm a very appreciative type of person. Every morning I would wake up and thank God for everything that He gave us. Now I pray more than I did. It's not like I have a stronger belief, because I had a strong belief. But I did feel the difference in the small things of life. I never took for granted that I have three beautiful daughters and I always thank Hashem for it. I did, however, take for granted that I can use the facilities alone, without help. I can just go ahead and walk to wherever I can. So those things have changed." And she is grateful for the physical pain from her severe injury "because if not for the pain that I was in – I was so busy with myself – the emotional pain of my daughter's death would have really been unbearable." While suffering unbearable pain – physically and emotionally – she was helped by recalling a sentence from the latest Harry Potter book: "Pain makes us human; it gave meaning to my pain."

It was a relief to Chana that, because of her wounds, people did not expect her to make a complete recovery. "People that aren't wounded are expected to return back to life as if nothing happened. After the loss of a child, you just can't be back to what you were. And many times those around you don't understand and it is very difficult. But because I was wounded and I'm not as capable as I was before, it's very obvious that I can't be what I was. So I don't have to deal so much with this. Unfortunately, it is a plus, even though I would rather be healthy. Each thing has its advantages."

During Chana's recovery, her husband's support was "amazing and helped me through," as did her mother who lives nearby, her small but "very, very understanding" Orthodox community, and an informal support group of mothers who had lost children. The support of everyone meant a lot. "We really felt the meaning of nation and unity. People came from all over the country, people who I knew and people who I didn't know. Visitors from the United States also came to give their support. During those first overwhelming moments, the support was really very important. Of course, we needed it all along the way

– but then people forget. But that's natural, and there's nothing to do about it." She still needs help and has "those few friends who are still understanding of my need."

Although Chana went back to her job as a high school teacher for a short time, she stopped because "it was just too much. I was just so busy running – doing errands, going for therapies and treatments – I didn't have time for the things that I had to do." Exercising, an activity that had been important to Chana before the bombing, also became difficult. She does not think much about the future, preferring to "take one step at a time. I am very happy I am like this. It makes things easier."

Chana likes to write and, with her family, published a memorial booklet about Tehilla on the first anniversary of her death. She is also working on a book about her family's struggle with the traumatic experience – as a memorial for her daughter and "because it is important for people to know." The book is titled *Nesaper Tehillotecha* (we will tell Your praises), which is both a play on Tehilla's name and an expression of thanksgiving to God for saving them. The book is also a memorial to other victims of terror. "I always took very much to heart all the *piguim* and had a plan to interview families and put together a book of stories and remembrance. Unfortunately there are so many tragedies and we forget the next day, but we do have to remember because what happened to me today can happen to you tomorrow. I really had this plan… Unfortunately it became my story." Chana also hopes to increase awareness so that people will be more sensitive after a crisis. "People don't know how to speak, how to act. Many times they say the wrong things. They don't understand it makes you feel bad. And I think it is very important for people to read the book."

At first Chana was very motivated and was writing a lot. "In the beginning it was more like therapy for me. Because as the events were taking place, I was writing." Even though she has more time now, her pace has slowed significantly now that she is rewriting "to be more professional. It's more difficult because it brings me back to where I was a year ago" – to the horrors of the event and the terrible loss that might provoke feelings of anxiety and grief. Four years after the event, she once again has started working with another author. She hopes this author will give her deadlines – "the push I need" – as well as generally helping her organize her work: "I must have order, not only in writing, but in the many realms of my life." As with others, storytelling provides her with order, structure, and purpose.

Chana has shared her love for writing and her understanding of its power with her six-year-old daughter, Yehudit, to help her deal with the loss of her sister. "Yehudit writes a lot. She is very expressive and it is very good for her too."

Chana believes that good things should come out of the bad experience. In spite of the disorder and distress in her life, she recognizes that she experienced growth "in the deeper inner spiritual meaning. Of course our aim is to be better people and when you face death face to face, you want to make life more meaningful." People helped her so much at first that it made her want to give to others. "I felt like I owed the world because everyone was so nice to me. I felt like I had to pay a debt – to be on the giving end." As a result, she turned to charitable deeds to help others and in memory of Tehilla.

She started a fund, through the larger organization Ezer Mizion, to provide physiotherapy and other paramedical treatments for needy children with Down syndrome. She also founded and runs a community organization called Ner l'Tehilla (A candle, or memorial, for Tehilla), which supports women after childbirth. "We want good things to come out of this experience – positive growth. We don't want such tragedies to happen, but if nothing good is going to happen as a result of these tragedies, then, to a certain extent, I would feel like all these people died for nothing."

For Chana, four years after the attack, the reality of her situation has set in. "It is impossible in the beginning to feel how it affects your life. It takes a while before you grasp the full meaning and the full consequences of what really happened." Although the biggest struggle for Chana was emotional, "I feel that we did a very good job of dealing with the loss. Of course, it is a painful issue. But I am proud of the way I'm dealing with it. I've put a lot of strength into that issue."

In addition to coming to terms with the loss of her daughter, Chana had to face her physical problems. "In the beginning, my struggle was to get back more of life, to get back to myself physically. I was struggling to walk well and then things started deteriorating. I was pregnant at the time, and then I found out that something was wrong with my leg. I couldn't do anything about it. I just had to wait and it is difficult to wait. I had a chance to really practice and strengthen my *bitachon* (trust in God) and my *emuna* in Hashem (belief in God). Physically, I was in a very bad state. I guess when we are physically down, our emotions fall. I re-experienced all the emotions of my daughter's death. And I was very full of fear. I couldn't even believe I was going to have a baby."

Two months after her son Yehuda was born in 2005, Chana went through a very complicated surgery on her leg. "I was even worse than I had been two years earlier. I was not able to use my foot at all. I wasn't able to bend my foot. I wasn't able to put on my shoes and socks by myself. I wasn't able to hold my baby standing – only sitting. I wasn't able to walk. I found myself back with crutches. It was very depressing and I was tired after struggling for so long. In the beginning I had thought that at least on a physical level everything would basically return to how it had been before the *pigua*."

Thigh surgery was only the first stage toward hip-replacement surgery. "I wasn't happy about having the hip replacement because I am young and it is not suggested for young people because it is time-limited. But there was no choice." In addition, she no longer had the support that she had in the beginning. "After this surgery, I guess I was expecting people to come visit me and almost no one came to visit. I felt very abandoned. I really felt horrible."

Fortuitously, a friend gave Chana copies of Dale Carnegie's book *How to Stop Worrying and Start Living*.[1] "His book helped me very much and taught me to accept what I can't change. And I wasn't accepting. Now I accept whatever I can't change."

Chana's hip replacement and recovery were much faster than she expected. "Suddenly I was almost well physically. But then I began feeling that nothing was like it was before. I found myself at home and not going to work and without a lot of support." Living with the

---

1   Simon and Schuster, 1984.

fear of the Israel-Hezbollah/Lebanon War and the reality of soldiers dying brought on PTSD symptoms. For the first time, she went to a psychologist, "but it didn't really help me. I guess, because I was home for so long, I'm a very different person. I have detached myself from society to a certain degree and now I don't see myself fitting back into things like I was before. I don't feel comfortable. I always feel different. I guess something died within me that didn't die in the beginning, even though in the beginning the pain was much more severe."

After a very difficult year, Chana really wanted to help herself. She started working a bit. "I am teaching again – and a bit back to exercise. *Baruch Hashem*, I feel things are better now than they were last year. *Baruch Hashem*, we have a lot of things to be thankful for. But there is always this struggle. Things keep happening that take us backwards. We don't have the strength. We are tired." Her husband and daughter have recently discovered new health problems related to their injuries. "So we are not the young healthy people we were before. We have to be careful all the time. Meanwhile, we accept God's will and believe that He leads us to whatever will be and that it is all for our ultimate good."

Reflecting back ten years later, Chana felt "I was pulled back in time to the pain and struggle, and it took me a few days to get back to myself." Four years ago she began to learn art therapy, which ended up becoming a transformative process that gave her tools to deal with her difficulties. She is currently finishing her BA in teaching and will then become a licensed art therapist.

"There are always ups and downs." Nearly two years ago, Chana was fortunate to give birth to Menachem; she labored all day on Tehilla's birthday and gave birth the following day. A year later, around what would have been Tehilla's bat mitzvah, she had a very difficult time. Chana, Matanya, and Shoshana, as well as five-year-old Malka who was born after the attack, struggle with medical issues. Several times, Chana has discovered troublesome shrapnel throughout her body, "and each time it's a story to get it out, and deal with it emotionally." Lately she has been challenged again, requiring stressful decisions and travel to the United States for surgery to repair both her hip replacement and a painful condition in her healthy hip due to the strain placed on it. "It's really difficult to be at this point ten years after."

Nevertheless, "in general I feel stronger within, and I hope things turn out okay. Thinking back, I continue to feel how impossible it would have been to go on without *emuna*. That's of course what's keeping me going now too. And I guess our struggle is not over, we always have new mountains to climb."

Ora Cohen

The evening of the bombing, Ora and Shalom Cohen were celebrating their nine-year anniversary. With five small children – Meirav (7), Daniel (6), Orly (4), Shira (one and a half), and Elchanan (one month) – they did not get out of the house very often. The school year was about to begin so they decided to do something special with the children. The children very much wanted to go to the Kotel, and they too felt it was the best place they could be on their anniversary. "Once there, the kids ran around having the time of their lives. They each had a chance to pray by the wall and say some *tehillim*, and they still managed to make a playground out of the plaza, as they and other kids their age laughingly chased one another. Taking Elchanan, who had been born just a few weeks prior, and touching his small hands and body to the stones of the Kotel was a very special experience."

They boarded the crowded Egged bus no. 2 for the twenty-minute trip home to Ramat Eshkol and settled into seats near the middle of the bus. Elchanan was hungry, so Ora covered him up with a large baby blanket and began nursing, just as the bomb exploded.

Ora's eardrums were ruptured, and she was barely conscious. The roof of the bus fell on her, and she lay immobilized with broken bones in her nose and jaw and pain in her chest, ears, nose, and back. Shalom had been facing the bomber and was hit with metal, nails, and glass in the face and eye. Meirav, Daniel, and Orly had severe damage to their ears and shrapnel in their bodies, but miraculously escaped major injury. The youngest, Elchanan and Shira, were thrown from their parents' laps, and were missing for hours. They were rushed to Hadassah University Hospital–Ein Kerem, while their parents and the older children were taken to Shaare Zedek Medical Center, adding to the confusion and grief. Shira lost the vision in one eye but doctors succeeded in saving the second eye after numerous operations.

The children are still very badly traumatized. Ora still dreams about the attack and Arabs – "sometimes not on the bus and other places, but being chased on the street." For a long time, she tried unsuccessfully to ride on buses. All the members of the family continue to undergo psychological treatment and treatment for their physical conditions, especially for their damaged eardrums.

Ora, a housewife and full-time mother of five, was born in Iran and moved to Israel in 1994. Her family is widespread, so she had no one to turn to. Shalom learned in a *kollel* and was a part-time carpenter before the attack. A year after the attack, Shalom still wasn't able to work full afternoons and he had difficulty concentrating. He became very depressed because he could no longer do what he had done before. Ora's life was busy with frequent medical appointments for one or another of her children or for herself. Finding babysitters was difficult. She had "no time to do anything for me – to buy new clothes, go out, relax, or go on vacation alone." She worried so much more about her family than herself that she "almost forgot about myself." Psychologically, it was very difficult. She felt under a lot of pressure and lost some of her self-confidence. "I will never be the same as before. Life is very disappointing because of all the suffering. Everything is much harder."

The Cohens' story was widely publicized because it was the first time an entire family was injured and in the hospital. People came from all over the world to visit, which helped emotionally. "We had a good feeling that people were thinking about us." They were strengthened by the love and caring that people showed them. "When we had people around, it made it easier to get back to ourselves." Like Chana, Ora found that, over time, the support diminished. "There are new attacks, so people rightfully take care of new victims. There are not many visits anymore and less help, but when they do come, it gives me and my children a lot of joy and strength, knowing that we are not alone."

Like the Nathansens, religion played a very important role for the Cohens. They felt they were saved by "the prayers and *tehillim* said for our injured daughter. We pray more deeply now – more from the bottom of the heart."

Ora would like to help others. "Every time an attack happens, it takes us back to the time of our attack and the mood lasts for a while. We feel very bad for people who were attacked. I would like to visit them in the hospital and give them hope and my emotional support, but I don't do it because I am sure that by visiting them, my pains will come back and make me miserable. And then I persuade myself not to feel bad because I am sure that they have family and relatives to help them that I did not have."

Four years after the attack, Ora still faced many challenges. Some of the surgeries didn't help and even made things worse. She just wants to be herself and "sit home one day and do nothing. I would like to work, but no way. I would like to sleep enough hours. I want one day to see everything finished – a better, happier life, like before – seeing friends, going to weddings – going back to myself… It's a sad life, but I have to make it. I have to go through."

On the ninth anniversary of the attack, Ora and her children decided to visit the Kotel to thank Hashem for their survival. "We thought that a *pigua* could happen only once to our family," so they boarded the Egged bus no. 3 for the trip to the Kotel. While they were stuck in traffic for twenty minutes in an Arab neighborhood, their bus was pelted with big stones. The kids were screaming and sprayed by broken glass from the shattered windows. The police could not get to them, but waited at the gate of the Old City for them with ambulances and took them to Hadassah Hospital to be checked out. "The children are traumatized and won't go to the Kotel anymore; they are scared of buses and afraid to go for counseling."

Shira, who was one and a half at the time of the Children's Bus bombing, will celebrate her bat mitzvah soon. She needs more eye surgery and will be under treatment her whole life. Ora still suffers from pain from the hole in her ear, but has no time for herself. "My life changed; it never goes back to what I had before."

Chapter 8

In the Service of One's Country

growth, distress, and death

S ince Israel must be constantly on guard against attacks, the army is an important part of daily life. Most men and single women are inducted into the Israel Defense Forces (IDF) at age eighteen, women for two years and men for three. Men generally serve in the reserves up to age forty. Out of respect for their community's religious commitments, Orthodox women may be exempted from military service, although many choose to perform twelve months of national service in the civilian sector. Most ultra-Orthodox men are granted deferments while pursuing Torah studies.[1]

Arab Israelis are citizens of Israel with equal rights. In 1948, Israel's Declaration of Independence called upon the Arab inhabitants of Israel to "participate in the upbuilding of the State on the basis of full and equal citizenship and due representation in all its provisional and permanent institutions." The only legal distinction between Arab and Jewish citizens concerns civic duty. Since Israel's establishment, Arab citizens have been exempted from compulsory service in the IDF out of consideration for their familial, religious, and cultural affiliations with the Palestinians and the rest of the Arab world. Still, volunteer military

---

1   Jewish Virtual Library, "Israel Defense Forces (IDF) – An Introduction," http://www.jewishvirtuallibrary.org/jsource/Society_&_Culture/IDF.html   (accessed May 25, 2009). Note that there are currently plans to reduce the terms of service in 2015.

service in the IDF is encouraged and, at the request of their community leaders, is mandatory for Druze and Circassian men.[2]

This chapter begins with the story of a soldier in the service of his country: American-born Ken Sachs, who survived an attack by three terrorists on his military base. The chapter continues with the story of a Russian immigrant family who experienced a double tragedy – first they lost one young son to cancer and then a second son, a soldier, was killed in a suicide bombing attack while on patrol.

2   Jewish Virtual Library, "Arab Israelis," http://www.jewishvirtuallibrary.org /jsource/Society_&_Culture/arabs2.html.

Shooting attack at an army base, Gaza: June 8, 2003

Ken Sachs: Mental and Physical Toughness

"If I could take back anything, it would be to bring my four friends back to life."

Ken was on reserve duty – his first tour since completing the regular army – and coincidentally on the same base in Gaza where he had served for three months at the height of the Second Intifada. "I was in the First Response team and did guard duty from four to five in the morning. When I finished it was my job to wake up my unit at 5:20 for a scheduled patrol to make sure that no serious problems or infiltration had taken place overnight. I went back to my room and picked up a book just to kill time. Before my phone alarm went off, I heard the first shot. I knew it was close, but I assumed that it was one of our tanks inside of Gaza. It never occurred to me that it was someone shooting at my base."

Without thinking about it, "I loaded my gun, grabbed all of my equipment, woke up the other two people in my room, and ran to the APC (armored personnel carrier) where my unit is supposed to meet in case of an emergency. From the time that I heard the gunfire, my mind just kind of shut down and everything that I was ever taught in training just took over. When I got to the APC, my officer told us what to do and where to go."

Ken went straight to his post. "Looking around the corner, I saw the back of somebody wearing an IDF uniform. He turned around and shot. To my luck, the terrorist was not a good shot or I would not be here today. He shot about two rounds of bullets at me, between fifteen and twenty bullets, miraculously hitting me in the leg, my tibia, and my calf muscle, but not in my chest. It felt like somebody had thrown a rock at my leg. I was able to retaliate, shooting three or four bullets, knowing that I hit him at least once before he shot me a second time. My knee was almost completely destroyed, as well as two of my ligaments and 80 percent of my cartilage; my fibula and tibia were broken and my femur fractured in two. I'm not sure how I stood through the first two bullets; but then my body fell onto the APC, smashing my right shoulder. I had enough awareness, strength – I'm not really sure what – to get my body behind the APC. I grabbed my gun and waited for the terrorist. My mind was a blank. I just was in a state of waiting for him and nothing else – I don't think I blinked. Everything that I was ever taught became very efficient and normal and my instincts took over."

After seven or eight minutes, one of Ken's officers yelled and asked if he was in shock. "I told him I wasn't in shock, but I was hurt. It took the medic another seven or eight minutes to get to me and pull me back from the gunfire. He did everything that he could to stop the blood loss until the paramedics and doctors were able to do their job. It still hadn't occurred to me how serious this was."

Once the grenades were cleared from the base, Ken was taken by ambulance to the nearest hospital in Ashkelon. "X-rays were the hardest ordeal because I had to move my knee and the pain was the worst I have ever felt in my life." As he was being wheeled into surgery, Ken called his older brother Frankie and sister-in-law Mara in Jerusalem to tell them and his girlfriend what had happened. They were waiting for him after the surgery. "The first thing that I said to my brother was 'Congratulations on the New Jersey Nets winning game in the NBA finals.' He was shocked – it was the last thing he had expected me to say – but he felt good knowing that I was mentally with it. The first thing that I did when I saw my girlfriend was to apologize and I'm still really not sure for what." His parents flew in from the United States later that day.

Ken was transferred to Hadassah University Hospital in Jerusalem to continue treatment and begin physical therapy. Since then he has undergone five surgeries, including a state-of-the-art osteotomy and cartilage transplant, as well as intense rehabilitation and physical therapy. "I knew exactly how much I could deal with, physically and mentally, and I asked my doctors every last question that I could think of. They told me things that I never wanted to hear in my life, but they also said that I have surpassed where they believed I'd get to. While it's nice to be past the doctor's goal, I still haven't gotten to my goal."

Ken never thought that "I would be dealing with the effect of my injuries on so many levels for such a long period of time." About a month after the attack his nephew was born. "That's when my brother told me that he kept thinking of the possibility that he would have had to name his son after me. It was the first time that it really ever occurred to me how different the situation could have turned out… And on Memorial Day, when I visit the graves of the fallen soldiers at the cemetery, I get this weird feeling throughout my body because it occurs to me how close I was to being there."

Ken knows that he could not have done anything differently the morning of the attack to save the lives of the four other soldiers who were killed in the attack. "I know that my actions did not cause anything to happen to anyone else. I know that I did everything based on my training, the way I was supposed to do it. I couldn't have saved anyone else's life, although I wish I could have. If I could take back anything, it would be to bring the four of them back to life. I would live like this for the rest of my life, if it meant that the four of them were still living."

Ken had made *aliya* to Israel in December 1997 from Bayonne, New Jersey, at the age of twenty because "being in Israel always felt right." He first went to Israel on a family trip when he was ten. "I had a wonderful time. Three years later I went back to Israel for my bar mitzvah and again I had an absolutely wonderful time. I can't explain the feeling, but when I was in Israel everything just felt right, it felt normal, it felt like that's where I belonged. I knew from the time I was thirteen that I was going to move to Israel and I was going to go into the army."

For a few years, "the plan kind of changed in my head but never really changed. I played high school basketball and was supposed to go to college on a basketball scholarship. I figured I would get my education, and then move to Israel." But a knee injury from a car accident ended his plans. "So a month after I turned twenty, I packed my bags and moved to Israel." His brother Frankie was already there. "He went to Israel to do his freshman year abroad and after being in Israel for five or six months all of a sudden he also decided that's it."

Learning to speak Hebrew was very important for Ken because "I didn't want to become the American that moves to Israel and stays American. If I was going to live in Israel, I wanted to live as an Israeli with the Israelis." He took a job that kept him on the street and forced him to speak Hebrew with Israelis. "It really helped me to get into an Israeli mindset. Maybe I don't agree with everything because I still have a lot of American in me, but at least I know where they're coming from."

Ken went into an Israeli army infantry unit in the beginning of 2000. "There my Hebrew really moved up a level. I was forced to learn because when you deal with guns, you really don't want to take the chance of saying, 'I'm pretty sure I understand.' The first month my Hebrew improved a lot, but it was still shaky. My second month I didn't care about making mistakes because I knew I was going to make them. By the time I got out of the army I felt very comfortable with my Hebrew and had no problem going out into Israeli society and doing things."

Ken served in an IDF reconnaissance unit from 2000 to 2002, immediately after the start of the Second Intifada. He was stationed in Lebanon, the Gaza Strip, and the West Bank cities of Jenin and Tulkarem. "In the army, I really learned who I was. A lot of the things that I learned I took into my real world, into my real life. I spent eleven straight months in places where we were being shot at regularly. I learned to trust the people around me with every last bit of my life so that I could just do my job and not worry for a split second about what was going on behind me. I learned to trust my reactions and go out there and make the right decisions."

After the army, Ken worked in security for the Ministry of Education and started playing semi-professional basketball. "I knew it was going to take time to get my game back, but basketball was always my life and still is. I was focused and determined and stubborn enough to make sure that it was going to happen."

And then he was injured and his entire focus became "getting my life back." The mental toughness that Ken got from the army helped in his lengthy rehabilitation and acceptance of his new life. "I thought I knew who I was before I got to the army, but that's where I really learned who

I was. That's where I really learned what stress is, what is important in life. You have to learn how to deal with time and how much you can and cannot handle. You really don't have much of a choice. I learned what my body could take, how much I could deal with, and how much pain I could take. I am able to push myself to my limit now."

The army required Ken to see a psychologist. "I was released after five or six sessions. The therapist told me that, at that time, I didn't show any signs of a normal victim. She believes that the main reason is that I was so dedicated to my rehabilitation. That's often what happens with people who put everything behind them, to deal with what they have on their plate now. But when you finish everything on the plate, a lot of symptoms come up. She told me a few things that I should look out for and if they ever bother me to contact her or someone else. There's a day here or there that I might be in bad shape, but I've never felt the need to contact anyone."

Ken is unsure whether religion helped him during the recovery process. "I didn't grow up religious but I always have been very spiritual. I believe that everyone has a path in life and that God gives you direction and you wind up going in your direction. I always believed that everything happens for a reason and that if I do the right thing, the right thing will be done for me." He doesn't know the reason he was wounded and doesn't dwell on it. "But I hope that reason will be clarified in the near future."

Ken is grateful for the support he received from everyone around him. His brother and sister-in-law "were there for me every single day and they helped me do whatever I could not do for myself. That was the hardest part – knowing that I need someone else to do things for me. But over time I got used to it because I didn't have much of a choice and it brought me much closer to them. Maybe it's just seeing them from a different perspective." His father is more cautious about asking him to do things and "is scared that something might happen physically, even though I know exactly what my limits are. I understand because the morning he saw me in the hospital was the first time I ever really saw fear in his eyes." Right before the attack, Ken and his girlfriend started to have problems. "Our lives changed so suddenly after the attack.

Before I was helping her out with things and after she was helping me out. It put a lot of strain on our relationship. In the end, we decided to go our own ways."

Being part of Israeli society helped Ken deal with the bureaucracy and with the people around him. In addition to his family, his support network included friends from work and people he had played basketball with. "People went out of their way to help. I didn't have to ask them. They all volunteered. When I needed something I wasn't afraid to ask because I knew they would be there for me and take care of anything I needed done. My friends have gone to battle for me for things that I wasn't strong enough to do or when I couldn't get around."

While recovering, he met someone who had been similarly injured about three years earlier and is now one of his closest friends. "He helped me out more than anyone else with things that I was having trouble dealing with – whether it was bureaucracy or mentally or physically or anything else." Likewise, Ken helps other soldiers who were injured or had friends killed. "Since I had already dealt with my injuries, I was able to give them advice and be there for them and help them out." When he goes to physical therapy and sees people who complain, he realizes that "they have no idea how lucky they are. And then I see people who are much worse than I am and it reminds me how much worse it could be. It keeps everything in perspective for me."

Talking to groups has been therapeutic for Ken. "The first few times I spoke about it, it was very difficult. With time the words just became easier. I don't know how it helps; I can't explain it. I don't know the inside of a mind, although I'm fairly good with the inside of a knee." He has spoken to many groups from various synagogues and organizations like Hadassah and Hillel – first in Israel and then for a month each year in the United States – "to explain what happened to me, to make people aware of what really is going on here, not just what they see or read in newspapers or on television. People might not understand it for themselves but they can start understanding it through me. My message is to make them understand how my life has changed from top to bottom in one split second. As close to a hundred percent as I have become, drawbacks are always going to be there."

One thing has never changed for Ken, no matter when or to whom he tells his story. "The images in my head are there, they don't change. It's like I'm watching a DVD in my head over and over again with everything in slow motion. Everything is as clear as day – picture perfect. It's like I go back to the attack for that moment. It's something that I am never going to forget. I look at my leg and I think about it, not in a bad way, preventing me from living my life or causing me to be depressed. Instead I think about it as a constant reminder of how far I've gotten and how far I still need to go to get my life back. It's a reminder of how lucky I am to be alive and how sad I am that I lost four friends that day. It's a reminder of how great my friends are to help me do things and to make sure that I am where I am today. It's always in the back of my mind, but it doesn't control my life. It just forces me to continue working harder and stronger. It's part of my life now, motivating me to move forward."

Sixteen months after the attack, Ken spoke optimistically about his future. He looked forward to going back to his job, to reserve duty, and to his plans to study at the Wingate Sports Institute to become a basketball coach. "The person who shot me wasn't trying to ruin my life; he was trying to end my life. I can't let him get any satisfaction to any degree. The only way to make sure that doesn't happen is to take my life back into my own hands. And the only way I can do that right now is day by day. I can't worry about anything too far into the future, because I don't know what's going to happen."

Four and a half years after the attack, Ken still sees doctors every two months and has regular physical therapy twice a week and special exercise therapy once a month. Together with his doctors, he is planning his sixth and seventh surgeries. He has a wonderful girlfriend from England and two dogs he enjoys walking. "They are the newest part of my life, something that I've never had before. Their energy and excitement, and how happy they are to be with me, make me feel better about myself."

His physical condition has forced him to change his career plans. He sells wholesale shoes as an account executive for a company in New York. "I am in charge of one of their websites and in charge of international sales. I never thought I would be working at a desk job in my life and never thought I would be sitting in front of a computer, on the telephone all day long. But what I want to be doing, I can't do. You can't fight that sometimes, you have to just move along." He would love to go back to his old life, working security and playing basketball. "In my mind, I'm still twenty years old; I'm still that kid out of high school – just give me a basketball and a hundred dollars a day and I'll be happy the rest of my life. But that's not realistic."

Ken has learned what is important and meaningful in life. "A lot of things in life that I thought I understood and realized over the last few years, I really knew nothing about. And a lot of things are so much clearer to me today than they ever were before: What life is, how to enjoy it, what to do about it, what to take seriously, what not to take seriously, and how it doesn't pay to get upset about unimportant things. God forbid, if these things happen, you deal with them; you don't get too upset about them, you don't yell and scream at everyone. You learn that they are no longer important and life goes on no matter what."

Ken and Judith are married and the parents of two boys.

Son Ofir killed, suicide bombing, army patrol, Gaza:
June 21, 2001

Dina and Omer Kit: The Best Medicine Is to Keep Busy

Omer Kit: "The loss of one child is too much; two is incomprehensible."

Dina Kit: "The world fell apart, dreams were shattered."

Dina and Omer immigrated to Israel from Georgia, Russia, to "have our own family, a Jewish family, a good family, so that we'll live in this country and be citizens that give to the State and live in happiness." They were the very happy parents of three sons – Yisrael, Ofir, and Yair. Dina chokes up when she recalls: "All we wanted was to build a home and have children, to educate them, to give them love. And we succeeded, we had good boys. It was a great pleasure to be their mother. My Yisrael was a very clever boy, a quiet kid, a modest kid, full of wisdom; he was a good student, a sportsman, and a basketball player. Ofir was a different boy – a little more mischievous, very clever, but impulsive, very sharp tongued and very funny; he brought so much joy to our home – it was a pleasure to watch. Yair was a quiet kid. We were a family, expecting a pleasant future."

But in 1990, their oldest son, thirteen-year-old Yisrael, was diagnosed with cancer. After many treatments and operations, he died on May 21, 1993. "Of course it was very, very difficult for us because he was our first child, our first love. He was a very special boy. We continued our life – not life and not death, something in between – because, although we had lost our lovely, lovely boy, we still had the others. Ofir was twelve years old and Yair was eight. So we had to continue. We didn't have any choice."

Omer Kit

Omer tells Ofir's story, as Dina walks away overcome by the grief of her memories: "Ofir was a very good student and enjoyed literature and theater. He also played basketball and was very, very happy. He loved music and when he came home from school, the walls would come alive with song and with kisses for his mother and for me. He did everything for us so we could forget our tragedy." Then on June 21, 2001, Ofir and another nineteen-year-old sergeant, Aviv Iszak, were killed in a suicide bombing while they were patrolling the Shikma Beach area near Dugit in the Gaza Strip.

Ofir had chosen to join an IDF combat unit against his parents' wishes. "I was afraid all the time because of the Intifada and I already knew what it meant to lose a child. If my son were thinking only about me and his mother, he would have chosen not to be a fighter. But it was important for him to choose whatever was best for himself and his life. He had also lost a big brother, but he wanted to be a better human, a better citizen, a better soldier. He wanted to show other people that it's possible to be better even though he had lost a brother."

Just a few minutes before he was killed, Ofir had phoned Dina to wish her *Shabbat shalom*. He said "it's a beautiful place – beach and blue sea and sun" and she told him, "When you get off patrol you can go to the sea and swim there." They spoke some more and Dina heard him shout to Aviv, "Hey, wait for me. I'll come with you. Don't go alone." They had noticed a jeep with Israeli license plates, apparently stuck in the sand, and several Arabs beckoning for assistance. One of them was a suicide bomber who exploded as they got nearer, killing the two Israeli soldiers and himself.

Fifteen minutes later, Omer heard on the radio that two soldiers had been injured and taken to Soroka Hospital in Beer Sheva. "I didn't hear anything about my son, but I had an emotional feeling. I told my wife to call her sister in Beer Sheva and ask her to go to the hospital and find out who those soldiers were. Afterwards we understood it was too late – they were dead, not injured, the moment the terrorist exploded himself." When army officers came to tell him his son was dead, "it was very difficult just to hear, not feel, because in the first minute you stop feeling. You just hear, you really don't understand what happened."

Omer understandably worries about his youngest son Yair, who was drafted into the army. "On the one hand I'm afraid for my son, my last son. On the other hand, it's a terrible situation here in Israel and in the army and you can't keep him at home. You can't keep your son in jail. He has a life. And he wants to do everything, experience everything. It's not easy."

For Omer, a retired engineer, "it's terrible. It really is impossible to continue, because all the time I'm looking for my boys and they are not there. Every Shabbat is so difficult – I make *kiddush* (blessing on the wine) and I see just a wife and one son, and two are not there. Every holiday, it's like dying again because in Israel the holidays are family holidays. I think the loss of one child is too much; two is incomprehensible. When morning comes, I want to go to sleep. When night comes, I want to see morning; maybe to begin from the beginning. There is sunshine and everyone begins to wake up for a new day; but for me it is nothing new, nothing emotional. I feel dead inside."

Dina Kit

Dina was more emotional, twice attempting to take her own life. The first time she wanted to fall from the balcony – five floors. And the second time she drank fifty different medications near Ofir's grave, crying, "Ofir, this place is not for you! You are alive, you are a basketball player. What do you do there? Wake up and come out!" Luckily another parent who had also lost a soldier son was present; he heard her and called an ambulance.

Sometimes Dina wonders why she has to live in this world. "I'm tired. It's upsetting. It's a cruel world. I hear about many things that are not the way they're supposed to be, and it upsets me very much. We human beings don't appreciate what we have. Many bad things happen, and it makes me very angry. But on the other hand, I know that if whatever happened to me wouldn't have happened, I would have flown along with life, accepting everything as inevitable. Now I don't because nothing is obvious."

For Dina, "the world fell apart, dreams were shattered, and everything stopped. People say it gets easier with the passage of years. No, I feel now that it gets much more difficult. I'm afraid of everything; I'm afraid of the future. I worry a lot about my son who remains. I feel that it's not within our power to give him a better life. And I keep repeating to myself: 'Lord, help me, look after the son I've got left, let him have a good, happy life.' I think a lot about it. I'm very sad. I hurt plenty."

After Ofir was killed, Dina left her hospital job. "I found it difficult to get out of bed in the morning, to start living; it was difficult to hear people at work talking about kids, Shabbat, the family. It was difficult to do the job and to arrive on time, smile, talk with everyone. People are considerate for half a year, a year; afterwards it's enough. People think they understand, but they don't understand exactly. They try to understand, try to help in their way, but it's not always the right way for me. I left work because I couldn't take it any longer."

Avihu Cohen understands. Together with founders Chantal and Marc Belzberg he was instrumental in building and directing OneFamily,[1] an organization committed to helping Israel's victims of terrorism and their families, providing personal, financial, material, legal, and emotional assistance. The organization also provides social and therapeutic opportunities for the victims to aid in their recuperation and rehabilitation. OneFamily organizes workshops by professional psychologists and retreats for bereaved family members and those wounded in the attacks, as well as support groups all around the country.

Avihu's involvement with OneFamily started after his father, Tunisian-born Baruch Cohen, fifty-nine, was killed in a drive-by shooting on the Efrat-Jerusalem Road on March 18, 2001. Baruch was driving to work early in the morning when terrorists from a passing truck fired on him with an automatic weapon, hitting him with at least five bullets. He lost control of his car and collided with an oncoming truck. In an interview, Avihu poignantly told me that "everyone who lost someone has a big hole in his heart that needs to be filled. Most

---

1   OneFamily Overcoming Terror Together, http://www.onefamilytogether.org/.

are filled with agony and have no spark in their ideas."[2] Some, like Avihu, take action and choose a different path for their lives. Despite the heavy emotional burden and the time away from his young family, Avihu felt obligated through OneFamily "to take care of those people – they couldn't make it without us. In the beginning, it was therapy for me. I became the servant of the cause and felt the need to help other people and show them that there are other ways to cope."

For Dina, OneFamily has been a blessing. Together with Omer, she was invited to travel to the United States and Canada "to show the American Jews our problems, our situations, how we feel here, how we live here." Dina started to volunteer for OneFamily where she not only helps others, but also is helped in doing so. "I'm busy the whole time, but I don't forget, it's stuck in my mind." The people at OneFamily appreciate and accept her the way she is. "I help a lot, and the respect I get for what I do and how I do it gives me a good feeling. I learned that there are people who worry about and take care of people like us. I'm not the same person I was before, my moods are different, and I don't have the same aspirations. Sometimes I have very difficult days, but I make myself go there, because it helps a lot and it is pleasant to be there. Otherwise one can lose one's mind."

Dina struggles between positive and negative thoughts and feelings. She thinks about her two dead sons Yisrael and Ofir, wondering where they would be today. But she also worries about being a good mother to Yair. "There's another child, Yair, and he is miserable too – he lost two brothers. And in this case a kid loses his parents too. I'm not the same mother; I don't have the energy, the patience, the desire. I try not to show it, keep it inside, but it's impossible. When the longing and sadness take over my thoughts, my whole body falls apart and I feel heartsick. I feel that my life stopped at some stage, and I'm embarking now on a new life. It's hard, but I succeed."

The support of good people around her is extremely important for her survival. "When someone says a good word, helps, or supports, it strengthens. It's like medicine or a drop of water when someone

---

2   Avihu Cohen, in discussion with the author, July 1, 2004.

feels unwell; as a result, he gets better, and it's very important. True, I'm making an effort too, to go on, to function. I'm alive, and while I'm alive, I'm moving through processes – to live, to do pretty things, trying my best. I look for things that may make me feel better, but nothing whatsoever makes me happier. Although inside it's all ruins, when I'm among others I'm very strong." When she thinks about it, she realizes that "I derive a great part of my energy from within myself. With OneFamily I'm busy the whole time and I motivate myself. I'm receiving from my surroundings – from whatever it is that I'm doing."

Six and a half years after Ofir's death, Dina has become a cornerstone of OneFamily. She is the full-time office manager at OneFamily's main office in Jerusalem and also volunteers there in her remaining free time. She has gradually taken on more responsibilities and developed several projects. Dina's Boutique helps provide beautiful clothing at low or no cost to families in need. A men's choir, comprised of twelve fathers who lost their children in terrorist attacks or in the IDF, aims at coping with the pain and difficult loss. They perform upbeat Israeli songs about hope and happiness. Omer is a member of the choir and "doesn't sing because it makes me happy; but if I succeed in making someone else happy then I have done something. Our presence on the stage, our performances make our children remembered. We are seen and heard – but they are remembered."

Dina also organizes outings to the Dead Sea for rest and relaxation – to enjoy the tranquil, healing waters and to be treated like royalty at a local resort. "After going through what we have – losing our children or nearly losing our lives in terrorist attacks," says Dina, "we're desperate for a day like this every once in a while. It takes us out of our pain, away from everything we know, and shows us another world – a more peaceful world, where we are surrounded by people who care and love us."

That's not all. She also runs Feminine Empowerment Workshops for bereaved mothers. Dina understands that "the best medicine is to keep busy. I need energy, I need adrenaline." She personally runs many of the workshops and retreats for mothers. "They see that I lost two sons and I am productive and strong, and they get encouragement from this.

And they see that when the body begins to strengthen, the spirit begins to work with and take care of the body."

Yair finished the army and lives at home. He is studying business management in college. "He also went through a tough time and doesn't want any connection with these groups or the families who have lost family members. He wants to live a regular life." Omer is working part-time as a tour guide and his job gives them the opportunity to travel together, including recent trips to New York and Thailand. "We are allowing ourselves to live a little and to think a little positively. Although it's difficult to go out of the country, we did it!"

For Dina, memories of Yisrael and Ofir sadden her, but also inspire her to move forward. "I meet friends of theirs. I see things of theirs. Every day they appear in my eyes. Yisrael was so cute and Ofir was such a happy and good young man. It's very, very difficult to see them in my thoughts and in my eyes and to know that they are gone. But since I am left alive, I want to live with *kavod* (human dignity). I want them to know that I am a mom who wants to see the world. And when I meet my kids, I want to tell them how much I did and how many people I met and how many people remember them. I lost two amazing sons, and the country, and the whole world, lost two amazing people. We miss them and lost a lot because they could have changed so many things for the better. It's because of them that I do what I'm doing at OneFamily. They inspire me."

Chapter 9

Three Bereaved Mothers

helped through acts of altruism

These are the stories of three Jewish-Israeli mothers who made *aliya* from North America with their families; three mothers who lost their sons horrifically during the Second Intifada; three mothers, bereaved by terrorist violence, who recognized the importance of sharing their sorrow and overpowering feelings of loss and pain with other mothers whose grief they can understand in a special way. These three mothers help each other with support, comfort, and laughter, while providing others with support and hope through acts of altruism.

Sherri Mandell's young son Jacob (Ya'acov, Koby) was the innocent victim of a random act of terror, one of the first victims of the Second Intifada. The soldier sons of Susie Weiss and Cheryl Mandel, Staff Sergeant Ari Yehoshua Weiss and Lieutenant Daniel Mandel, were killed by terrorists while they were serving their country as members of the Israel Defense Forces (IDF). Sherri, Susie, and Cheryl volunteer to help other families, provide extra food for soldiers, and raise spirits in their community through the performing arts.

The lives of these three mothers are intertwined in a very special way. Six months after Ari was killed, the Efrat/Gush Etzion Raise Your Spirits Summer Stock Company,[1] which was originally conceived as a morale builder following several terrorist murders that rocked Gush Etzion and environs, brought their production to Ra'anana. It was a

---

1 Raise Your Spirits Theatre, http://www.raiseyourspirits.org/.

fundraiser for Ochel Ari, founded by Susie to "bring food to soldiers in the field with no kitchen facility and no warm food." During the intermission, Susie remembers that "Cheryl Mandel, this funny lady, sought me out and gave me a big hug. It was a very emotional evening and I was crying in front of everybody as we sang 'Ani Maamin' (I Believe). Oh God, she was so sweet and two weeks later her son was killed."

A few months later, Susie and Cheryl reconnected at a women's health retreat sponsored by the Koby Mandell Foundation, established by Sherri and her husband Seth. Cheryl invited Susie to "just come and we'll be roommates, and we did." They also saw each other at Nahal (an IDF army brigade) memorials, where they were well known, the only representatives from the English-speaking community. They keep in touch and are "kindred spirits." Cheryl called Susie just before Daniel's *yahrzeit*, because she "can't ask just anybody, 'But do you think that pink suit is too sexy for me to wear?'…So thank God we have each other to talk to and joke with." Cheryl adds: "We should do a stand-up comedy act called 'No one wants to be me!'"

For Cheryl, keeping her sense of humor is a positive. Before Daniel was killed, she and Sherri always joked about the confusion between the two of them. Cheryl would be introduced as "'This is Cheryl Mandel, the manager of the Gush Etzion Judaica Center for Alon Shvut,' and they would say, 'Ah, Sherri Mandell, I'm so sorry about your son.' And I would say, 'No, it's not my son. I'm Cheryl Mandel. She is Sherri Mandell, the author of *The Blessing of a Broken Heart*.'" After Daniel was killed, Cheryl and Sherri again were able to laugh together. "Now there is no need to clarify things." Now when people tell Cheryl, "Oh, I read your book," she replies, "No, I'm the dancer and she's the writer. She's the blonde." When asked if they are related, Cheryl laughingly responds: "We're sob sisters!"

Son Koby and his friend Yosef Ish-Ran stoned to death, Tekoa:
May 8, 2001

Sherri and Seth Mandell:
The Blessing of a Broken Heart

Sherri Mandell: "Moving *with*, not moving *on*."

Seth Mandell: "Every suffering has a purpose."

Thirteen-year-old Koby loved his family – parents Seth and Sherri Mandell, and siblings Daniel (11), Eliana (9), and Gavi (6). His family immigrated to Israel in 1996 from Maryland because Seth and Sherri loved Israel and wanted Judaism to be at the center of their family's lives. In 1998 they moved to Tekoa, a West Bank settlement on disputed land south of Jerusalem. Koby loved his countries – America and Israel – and his village of Tekoa. He also loved sports, learning, hiking, and, most of all, telling jokes and laughing. As his mother described him, "Koby had everything going for him. He didn't care what others thought. He was a normal kid."

On the morning of May 8, 2001, Koby and his friend Yosef (Yossi) Ish-Ran played hooky from school to hike in the dry riverbed of Nahal Hariton. Later that day Koby and Yossi were found in a cave about two hundred meters from Tekoa, bludgeoned to death with bowling-ball-sized stones, an act attributed to Palestinian terrorists.

Sherri and Seth not only had to cope with the loss of Koby, but also with the horrific way in which he had lost his life. "We had the advantage of living on a *yishuv* (settlement) with other people of similar belief systems – spiritual, not materialistic – and with very big hearts. It was a very strong community, reaching out to us, respecting our loss, and giving us energy to continue." Sherri recalls that "I appreciated just having people there. I had a need for them, to know it matters. I had no defenses. I was open emotionally and didn't care about people judging me." Sherri's friend, Shira Chernobyl, a grief counselor, came to see her every day. "It was tremendously helpful because she acknowledged my special position and that everything I was feeling was legitimate."

At first, Sherri couldn't do anything. It was painful for her kids to be around her and they were invited to a camp in the United States for the summer. She stayed home and people brought or sent in meals. She wasn't ready to be alive. "I needed to empty myself totally – the first step in building strength."

Sherri had become a *baalat teshuva* (a non-religious Jew who embraces Orthodox Judaism) when she and Seth married in 1985. "It was more practice-based than anything else. I didn't have the feelings for God or for prayer. But once Koby was killed, I couldn't bear to hear or speak ordinary language because it was part of ordinary life. There's a different language after you've been through a trauma – not just a verbal language. I needed the words of the prayer book and *tehillim*. Religion became a place to go for dealing with this – maybe more than the psychological – it was the spiritual."

She studied with many teachers, using stories from the Bible to understand grief as a sacred space and make meaning of her loss. "Death inscribes you; you can't get away from it. So the main thing is how to live with it as a place to grow from. There is pressure to move on, like closing the door and going on with life, but it is really *moving with* – moving forward with the experience. It's like if you are pregnant, you never forget you are pregnant. If you have pain, it's always a part of you; you always carry it around."

Seth was a rabbi and a university Hillel director in the United States before moving to Israel to direct an outreach program for yeshiva students from other countries. He noted that you "grow *because* of suffering, not in spite of suffering," citing Jewish theology that teaches that "every suffering has a purpose." Exercise and structure were very important to help him grow. For him, Judaism, especially studying Mishnah, in Koby's name was helpful, but "any existing system or one's own created structure could serve the same purpose."

Seth spoke at Koby's funeral from "sheer willpower – the will to live, the will to overcome – just doing it even though I didn't want to do it. I knew if I didn't do something, I would always regret not doing it. What I learned at the funeral and *shiva* became a theme of 'if you do it, you *may* regret it; but if you don't do it, you *will* regret it.'" Five weeks after Koby was killed, he was invited to Florida to speak about Koby and the situation in Israel. Sherri let him go, "in spite of needing him so badly because we had people from the community who slept at my house every night. I could not have been alone then; being alone just made the pain double."

Sherri had very different coping skills. "Willpower would kill me." As a creative-writing teacher, journalist, and author, she needed to do something creative to grow. Hearing the stories that Sherri kept telling about Koby throughout the *shiva*, her husband and friends encouraged her to write. After four months of doing nothing, Sherri began to tell the story – hers and Koby's – writing through her tears *The Blessing of a Broken Heart*,[1] "taking ownership of a story and telling it to others who will hear it and be transformed."

For Seth, bereavement increased his consciousness and he learned that "there's a certain clarity that comes when tragedy strikes. All the veils, all the nonsense of the everyday world are stripped away and you see life clearly. It's almost a form of prophecy. After the *shiva* and mourning you get caught up into everyday concerns and the veil returns; but every once in a while the veil lifts again and you see through the nonsense."

The Mandell family knew immediately that the tragedy of Koby's loss could easily destroy them. As Koby had said a month before his own death about another boy killed by terrorists, "it's sad for the boy, but it's sadder for those left behind." The Mandells knew that it was important and necessary to find meaning in their loss and to help others do the same. They knew that they had to fight against their despair and their pain and give their other three children "a full life, not one of just sadness. We wanted to "show them we are still their parents and models for them." They decided to create something special to honor Koby

---

1 Toby Press, 2003.

and keep his memory and spirit alive in the world. As Sherri explained, "although his body is dead, I'm not going to let him die."

Determined not to let their lives be ruled by hate, the Mandells established the Koby Mandell Foundation[2] to help bereaved families keep their hearts open and spirits alive. It was their way to take the cruelty of Koby's murder and transform it into acts of kindness and hope. They wanted to enable people like themselves, struck by terror, to return to life with strength, hope, and healing.

The Koby Mandell Foundation sponsors healing retreats for bereaved women, as well as a camp for children whose parents or siblings have been killed by terrorists. The programs create a network of support for grieving families to ease the isolation that bereaved children and adults are often struck with after the loss of a loved one, by providing emotional, physical, and spiritual healing.

Camp Koby, one of the cornerstone programs of the foundation, provides children of families struck by terror with a place where others understand. As Sherri explains: "Children are often the silent victims when the tragedy of terrorism strikes a family. They keep changing and developing and going in and out, yet they feel it just as much." Surrounded by their peers, trained counselors, and professional therapists, children share their stories and express their feelings naturally. They feel free to have an incredible time and most return to life with increased vigor and emotional stability. They know they are not alone.

Sherri also knows that mothers who lose a beloved child or husband experience overwhelming shock and trauma. "Each birthday, holiday, and family meal brings memories of the person who is missing. Dealing with the grief and the changed family is very painful, but dealing with it alone is even more devastating." The Mothers' Healing Retreat brings these women together and nurtures them physically, emotionally, and spiritually. They learn to understand and manage pain and are given strategies for self-awareness and self-transformation so they can return home with tools for healing themselves and their families.

---

2   The Koby Mandell Foundation, http://www.kobymandell.org/.

The Mandells were instrumental in having the United States government pass the Koby Mandell Act, which strengthens efforts to capture overseas terrorists. This bill, initiated by the Zionist Organization of America (ZOA) in 2001 with key Senate and House cosponsors, created a new office in the Department of Justice to capture all foreign nationals who have killed or harmed Americans overseas, including Palestinian Arabs.

I visited Sherri again six years after Koby's death. Sherri understood that she, her family, and others would continue to need help for a long time. "There is a tendency to think people move on, but they still need to be supported, to be taken care of because they deteriorate, especially when they weren't strong or have financial and medical problems." New programs are continually being developed to meet the ongoing needs of bereaved mothers, fathers, widows, kids, young adults, families, and friends, who years later still suffer from the trauma of loss.

In addition to directing the Koby Mandell Foundation, Seth and Sherri spread their important message widely. Sherri speaks publicly and is writing another book. Her first book, *The Blessing of a Broken Heart*, was made into a play, helping them reach a new audience. Periodically, she and Seth wrote a blog "Heart-Earned Wisdom" for the *Jerusalem Post Online*,[3] which now is on the website of the Koby Mandell Foundation and is sent out as an email of "This Week's Thought From The Koby Mandell Foundation." Seth continues to write articles for the *Jerusalem Post* and Sherri is studying to become a pastoral counselor.

While there are ravaged societies that turn their pain into hate, the Mandells responded to their pain by building a network of love, making meaning out of their suffering, creating a fuller and more engaged life, and helping others do the same.[4]

---

3   The Koby Mandell Foundation blog on *Jerusalem Post Online*, "Heart-Earned Wisdom," http://cgis.jpost.com/Blogs/wisdom/ (site now discontinued).

4   The author acknowledges the supplemental information gleaned from *Publisher's Weekly*, the Koby Mandell Foundation website (http://kobymandell.org), the Mandell's *Jerusalem Post Online* blog (http://cgis.jpost.com/Blogs/wisdom/; site now discontinued), and the article by Ruthie Blum, "One on One: You Want to Die, but You Don't" (*Jerusalem Post*, May 16, 2007), in addition to the three personal interviews conducted with the Mandells in 2004 and 2007.

Son Ari killed, military operation, Nablus: September 30, 2002

Susie Weiss: Food for Soldiers

"I am so grateful that I can remember him and smile, and not remember him and cry."

With all the heartache, Susie Weiss remembers her son with pride: "It matters to me that he died as a soldier fighting for his country rather than sitting on a bus and being blown up by a terrorist. There's a difference to me." Staff Sergeant Ari Yehoshua Weiss, twenty-one, was killed and his good friend Shai Haim was badly wounded when Palestinian gunmen opened fire on an army position in Hamas headquarters in the Nablus casbah. Both soldiers were members of the IDF's elite Palchan unit of the Nahal Brigade. Susie continues: "I don't consider myself or Ari, my son that was killed, a victim of terror. He was a soldier in uniform with a gun serving in an army. He was my little boy. He was scared and brave and sweet. And he was killed. I don't know what the definition of terror is. He shouldn't have been killed. He wasn't pointing his gun at anybody."

Ari was months short of being discharged from the IDF and had just spent the Sukkot holiday weekend with his family, including Susie's parents who are Holocaust survivors. "I took him and Shai back to the bus stop. He didn't have time to kiss me and gave me the look like 'Oh God, I've got to go.' And I gave him the look and said, 'Go.' I talked to him again on Sunday night and he called me Monday at 5:30, but I wasn't home. He was killed at 6:03 p.m."

Susie describes her son: "He was strong, but he wasn't one of these macho men. He was scared to death and he would always tell me where his money was hidden before he went on an operation so I could put money into the *tzedaka* (charity) box. Why does God take people like that? Why make way for one and not the other? I'm not bitter. I just pray that wherever he is, he is happy and that he is laughing at me saying, 'if you would know how happy I am, you would stop this.' I hope that's true. My husband says, 'If you start doubting that, you have to start doubting everything else you believe in. So why don't you just stop it.' Okay, and then I just stop it."

In 1992 the Weiss family made *aliya* from Dallas, Texas, where Stewart had been a pulpit rabbi. They moved because "I believe this is where God wants us to be." Stewart founded the Jewish Outreach Center, catering to the many English-speaking immigrants near his home in Ra'anana, a northern suburb of Tel Aviv. Ari was the third of six children – two older sisters, a brother Eli who was a year younger and a paratrooper, and two little guys. "The children are okay, I think. Of course you never know. And if someone says to me, 'Look, they only lost a brother, you lost a child,' they should talk to one of my girls."

When Ari first came to Israel, "he was twelve and didn't know what hit him. He was scrawny, he didn't know a word of Hebrew, and yet he became our Israeli." The army was the unifying factor and Ari's best friend Shai helped him become Israeli. "Ari was a little American, religious, insecure kid. Shai was the army-poster child – tall, dark, handsome, Sephardi, and a generations-old Israeli. The two of them looked ridiculous together. I used to tell Ari to stand behind Shai wherever he went. In the end, it was the opposite. Shai was shot and Ari went to help him, and then Ari was killed… As my husband says, 'That is a hero – someone who is scared and still does what he has to do.'"

At Ari's funeral, Stewart said: "Ari believed that serving in the army in a combat unit was not a burden of punishment, but a privilege. You were a shy boy, unsure of yourself, but in the end you were everything that your name was meant to be – brave and courageous as the lion (*ari*) and a leader like Yehoshua."

Susie and Stewart responded to the tragedy in different ways. "Before Ari was killed, I couldn't understand how tragedy tears families apart, and now I understand, because everybody grieves in their own way and it doesn't always jibe. Stewart is a man. He doesn't talk much about it publicly, but we are very open with each other. My husband is a crier – more than I am. At certain times he talks about Ari and cries and I talk about Ari and I smile. We have our differences, but as long as we are patient, tolerant with each other, and know what we need, thank God, it is okay."

After Ari was killed, Stewart put a lot of effort into creating a community learning center in Ra'anana that could house a number of different programs and institutions simultaneously. Called Ohel Ari,[1] which means "the tent of Ari," it welcomes and offers spiritual and physical sustenance to both citizens of central Israel and IDF soldiers looking for a friendly smile, a hearty meal, and a bit of strengthening.

Susie can't associate a building or bricks with Ari. Instead she has started a project called Ochel Ari, which means "the food of Ari." "Ochel Ari, I can do. When it comes to food and feeding and moms, I can do that." In fact, thirteen days before Ari was killed, Susie had organized a huge delivery of food donated by local shops and people to Ari's unit. "I was on the phone with him and it was right after Rosh Hashanah. 'Mom, we're starving here. We were out in the field. There's nothing to eat. I can't stand pickles and olives and corn anymore.' And there I am sitting looking at his favorite shawarma place. I said to Ari, 'All right, give me a few minutes,' and I said to them, 'I need about thirty-five shawarmas now. These guys are starving.' He said, 'Just tell me what time you need it.' And I walked down to a wholesale grocery and got eighty drinks. And a little further there was a bakery, I got the cakes. Friends called and by the time I walked home, I had a carload of stuff. By the time we got it to him, it was quite a feast. When he called at midnight, the guys were screaming and laughing and grabbing the phone."

The story was written up in the *Jerusalem Post* and it became a very big deal. "Ari was concerned about what picture I put in and did he have the three stripes on his uniform because if he didn't have any stripes, they would just think that he was just some soldier but he was an officer. I said, "Don't worry, Ari, you look adorable." Then two weeks later he was killed. "And they used the same picture and it was awful. But that article seemed to have just taken off and people recognized that this was just a kid whose mom wanted to give him something warm to eat."

---

1   Beit Knesset Ohel Ari, http://www.bkohelari.org/.

Susie is still associated with this mission. "Between pity and my persuasive powers, Ochel Ari has gotten food and wholesale prices and donations from all over Israel and America. It gives me a little bit of satisfaction to do this in Ari's name. And I know that he is proud of me up there." It is hard for people to say no to Susie. "People are very gentle with me, sometimes too gentle. They are too scared that I will break." For Susie, Ochel Ari is fun. "I don't know if Ochel Ari is what I was meant to be. It seems to have snowballed and everyone says you've got to take it and run with it. I'm very nervous. I'm scared. I don't know what God has in mind for me. I'm just doing what I can. And that's okay." A medical technologist by education, Susie is now a tour guide in Beit Hatfutsot (the Diaspora Museum) in addition to running Ochel Ari.

If anyone had told Susie that she could do such things after the death of a child, she wouldn't have believed them. "I would say I will curl up in a ball until I die. I will not breathe. I will not eat. During the *shiva*, other women came and told me that this happened to them and I looked at their earrings and their makeup and I said: 'You put on makeup after something like this? Everything matches? How do you do this? Why do you do this?' I lost a lot of weight. I couldn't do it. I just didn't want to do anything. I function, I always function, but I just couldn't picture life. Even the obituary signs with his name – get it off, what is that doing there? I couldn't believe that I was part of it."

Susie is a strong person. "I guess you don't know that until you are tested. I would have thought I would have stopped living." Her other children give her strength. "Thank God, I still have many reasons to get up in the morning and I am very grateful for that. I still have more than what most people start out with. So I am grateful that I have the strength somehow to keep going and to tell a joke and to do projects and be there for my husband and my kids. I'm generally a happy person, but my level has come down. I am very sad. I lost my boy and we were very, very close."

Although she keeps busy and is upbeat, Ari is never far from her thoughts. "When Ari was in the army, my day was either I had spoken to Ari already or I hadn't yet. I sent him packages. I sent him jokes. I put liquor in one of the packages at Purim and I didn't know you couldn't have liquor on the base. Apparently he was a big smoker. I filled a box of cigarettes with bubble-gum cigarettes. He needed cigarettes and he thought I was so cool that I had sent them and he opened the box and found bubble gum in there and he went nuts. I thought he was going to kill me. So we were very close. I am so grateful that I can remember him and smile, and not remember him and cry. And I think that is a gift from God, because I wouldn't have thought I would be able to do that."

Being religious helps Susie. "I have a lot to hold onto, but lately I'm obsessed with wanting to know. 'Okay, where is Ari now? Where is his soul? Does he hear me? Does he not? Is he in another person?' I don't know. And the biggest of rabbis can't tell me. So I will delude myself into thinking what I want to think for the rest of my life. And if it's true, great, and if it's not, it still served its purpose." She wants to think that "Ari is smoking his head off. I want to think that everything I do in his memory brings him an extra steak. I want him to be happy. And this is what I say to God, 'Whatever it is that makes us all happy, I don't know what it is, but he deserves it.' He was a wonderful, good, sweet boy."

Often she feels that Ari is giving her a hand, even though he is gone. "I talk to Ari and he talks to me. I like to believe that he is watching me and he's proud and saying, 'All right, Mom, don't fall apart, it's very embarrassing.' So I'm not… Things can start me off. I can hear a song and think about something and start to cry. If I see a package of Parliaments on the sidewalk, I think it is a hello from Ari. I really need to write down all the ways he signaled me, like his name appearing on my phone. It's bizarre. People are going to think I'm nuts. But that's okay. It gets me through the day… I look up and say, 'Now Ari, they are writing songs about you and projects about you and basketball teams have T-shirts with your name on them.' It's pretty unbelievable what he has caused and I just keep telling God, 'Okay, there's a boy who changed the world for the better in his life and after his life. Now You need to change the world in his merit. Thank You.'" On Ari's grave, Susie and Stewart inscribed the Hebrew saying "When a righteous person dies, he truly begins to live." "And that is Ari. He changed the world."

Like other bereaved families, Susie felt that people did not know how to relate to her after Ari's death: "I'd walk down the street and it was just a lot easier for people to cross the street than to have to actually face me and think of something to say. Sometimes I would really make it harder and I would cross the street too and then they had no choice… How many times did I hear, 'Just let me take you out for a cup of coffee'? I used to say, 'If coffee could bring Ari back, he would have been back a long time ago…' Even now, everybody is being so nice. I just want them to treat me like a normal person. But then again, if they did, I'd say, 'What is this, everybody has forgotten?'"

The Israel-Hezbollah/Lebanon War and seeing so many more bereaved mothers triggered her emotions. "I lost Ari and has it gotten any easier or better? I don't think so. I was hoping that it would. I realize it's never going to be finished. It's like a constant mourning. It is a second curse of God. First he takes away my son and then he makes me wake up every morning to the same reality. I realize that nothing will ever be the same. And it is a terrible reality to know that we will never be as happy as we once could have been. And that's awful… Every mother's nightmare happened to us. Even though I talk about it, I still can't believe it. And I hope that I go to my grave not believing it, because the reality is just horrible… I'm not afraid of dying anymore. Although my life is important, if I die, I will see Ari… Hopefully one day this will all make sense, but I don't think that this will make sense. And people say about Ochel Ari, 'At least something good came out of it.' And my brain says, 'Nothing good can come out of this.' So many acts of kindness and wonderful things have been done in his memory because he was such a wonderful person. I hope that every act done will elevate where he is. I just hope he is having a ball somewhere, because he deserved it."

Son Daniel killed, military operation, Nablus: April 15, 2003

Cheryl Harmony Mandel: Dancing through Life

"I have been handed the machine gun to carry."

B efore dawn on the day before Passover, Lieutenant Daniel (Mendel) Mandel, twenty-four, the commander of "the Mendel Platoon," an elite IDF reconnaissance unit, was in the field leading his soldiers. They were on a mission to capture three terrorists believed responsible for two earlier bombings that killed more than thirty and injured over one hundred and forty Israelis. Daniel was killed in battle on the streets of the West Bank town of Nablus. Two other Israeli soldiers were injured. Daniel was a charismatic leader, dedicated to his soldiers, his staff, and his army service, all of which he truly loved. At his funeral his mother Cheryl spoke about his peace of mind and positive attitude. "When bad things happen, you can make sure something positive comes out of the tragedy. When bad things happen, people can go up or down." His family was determined to go up and make a difference for others: "to be strong, to build ourselves, and to help others."

Cheryl and David Mandel and their five children – Nicole, Yonah, Daniel, Gabriel, and Shlomo – came on *aliya* from Toronto, Canada, in 1987. The change of location was part of another change. "Our family chose to be an Orthodox religious family, which involved a change in lifestyle patterns. We had the best time in Israel and loved it when we spent a year here. On a gut level we felt totally at home, and like it was the right place to live. I loved being in a country that was all about me – who I was – as opposed to the other." The Mandels settled in Alon Shvut in Gush Etzion, a small West Bank community not far from Jerusalem.

The Mandels were preparing for Passover, a joyous family holiday, when the army came to notify them of Daniel's death and "everything went into a surreal mode." Cheryl was helped by the presence and support of other people, both in the first horrific hours and the weeks and months that followed. "Most helpful to me were people who had gone through a tragedy, who showed up at my door; also thinking about people who had gone through a tragedy and grew from it. Unfortunately here in Israel, we are no stranger to tragedy. Then there were my two close friends – Sharon Katz and my next door neighbor who I can call in the middle of the night and just say, 'I need you to do this' and they say, 'I'll be right there.' They were just there and did everything for me, mothering me and bringing nourishing food, just quiet nurturing… And my husband was phenomenal – still is phenomenal. David's been like a rock. He is a man who has deep spiritual beliefs and he accepted it with a total, deep *emuna*, deep love and trust that this is what God did – not that it was okay, but that God knows what He is doing and this is the way things are meant to be."

Cheryl admires David's acceptance, but she is a fighter. "If something can be changed, I will fight to get it changed. I can be very, very much of a bulldozer and very aggressive to get what I think is right. If something cannot be changed, only then do I accept it." After giving a beautiful eulogy at Daniel's funeral, "people couldn't understand how I had such strength and was so positive at my son's funeral. They would ask, 'How can you be so strong?' I would look at them and say, 'If I thought crying day and night would bring Daniel back, I would cry.' So I just accepted it because there was nothing within my power that I could do to bring Daniel back and there was just no sense in breaking down. It's like somebody who has lost an arm; you adjust, not to the fact that you don't have an arm but you adapt, you figure out how to do things with only one arm. But it doesn't mean that every minute of every day, you don't wish you had that arm back and you don't remember how great it was with it."

Cheryl demanded "a lot of myself and now I keep on going." She and David very quickly decided to keep going out to *semachot* (joyous occasions). "We somehow felt that it mattered a lot to people that we keep going, that our community needed us to be strong." She kept a strong public face, but "during the night is when I had to deal with it." She had problems sleeping and got sick. "Obviously I was internalizing it to the point that I got a stone in my kidney. Now I try to write a lot and not block what I am feeling."

Cheryl went back to work managing the Gush Etzion Judaica Center about a month after Daniel was killed. She instructed her staff that "if somebody is coming in to buy a gift, that's what they want. They don't want your emotional baggage with it. You have to keep it out because people won't like to come and shop with us."

With Daniel's death, she became more sensitive to other people, and that has been good for her. "It definitely opened my own ability to feel pain and my own compassion. It gave a new depth to my understanding of other people. I think I developed more patience and more understanding. I've probably become a lot less judgmental. I see that things happen in life and they change you and I understand the fact that most people don't have the strength and the support system and a partner that I have that enable me to go through this the way that I have."

Grief books did not help. "I hated them all. I found that I couldn't relate to them." Instead, she related to books about overcoming adversity. "I found them more inspiring. I think there are a lot of crappy situations in life and I identified more with 'I can handle a crappy situation' than with grief. I somehow didn't allow myself to break down. I forced myself to keep going. I'm not sure if it's good or bad. I'm not sure how much one can control the way one responds to a tragedy."

She tried therapy a few times but "I realized it wasn't for me. I had successfully solved all the development issues, growing issues, interpersonal issues that I had twenty or thirty years ago and I didn't want to deal with stuff like that again. Now I was seeking therapy because I had a specific problem. My son was killed. If my son hadn't been killed, I wouldn't have shown up at the psychologist's door. And I wanted a specific solution." She also went to an army therapy group. "I didn't like that either. I prefer to be in a group that is positive, happy, and not focused on grief. I'm always looking to find the positive interpretation of any situation, looking at the cup half full, and growing from adversity."

About her family, she says, "although everybody suffers privately and basically goes through it alone and in their own way, we all sort of cling to each other to give strength and to get strength. There's a greater closeness. I try to help them by showing them an okay example and by trying to be available for them. My daughter Nicole is open, but the boys are more silent and so it's a lot harder."

Nicole is "this amazing, amazing, amazing daughter. She is so incredible. She is such a good daughter. She cooked for me. She brought her kids around a lot. At the beginning, she told me, "*Ima* (Mother), it's really hard for us when you are so down." But I just couldn't help it… Four weeks after Daniel was killed there was a *brit* (Jewish ritual circumcision) for my new grandson. I used to be known as a person who dressed very, very colorfully – colorful scarves, colorful jewelry, and colorful clothes. As soon as Daniel died, I took off all color. And Nicole said, 'Don't become one of those eccentric old bent-over ladies. You don't want people saying, "She used to be the most colorful woman; you should have seen her until her son was killed."' She said, 'Don't do it. You are coming to the *brit* and you are dressing up and you are putting on makeup and you are putting on jewelry.' And I did. And thank God, with time things come back. My positive energy did come back" – as did wearing her signature colorful scarves.

Two days after the baby was born, Nicole developed a high fever and, although she fully recovered, Cheryl thought she might lose her daughter. "I could not believe it. I thought that not only do shitty things happen in life, but when one shitty thing happens, it doesn't mean you have had your quota. I always used to think that because I was sick as a baby and my family poor, I was guaranteed to have *nachas* (pleasurable pride); and basically that's what happened until Daniel was killed. Since then we've had all these horrible things happen to us. My understanding of how the world works is relatively primitive. I don't see myself as a spiritual person, but I accept that there is an order and a balance. Now I have more of an acceptance that I'm not running the world and that I can't prevent these things from happening. Yet, I'm still pretty positive."

She helps her sons by "engineering opportunities that I think might be good for them. Shlomo went with OneFamily on a big trip to the United States. And it was very, very positive for him to be with other kids who had also experienced a tragedy as a result of the war and to be with wonderful, giving, caring adults." Gabriel also went for a week to London and then he met a friend from his army unit for a week in Ireland and that was "just wonderful for him, just so positive."

She speaks to each one of her children almost every day, feeling a stronger need to keep the connection. "It takes a lot more energy to take care of a dead child than a live child. A live child you can forget during the week. They are busy doing whatever. But you are reminded of a dead child all the time – whether it's being invited to a ceremony from the army, to speak to a group, to attend Daniel's friends' weddings, or to build a park dedicated to Daniel's memory. Your dead child never leaves you alone. I wasn't just leading my life, it felt like I was leading my life and Daniel's too. So you are constantly putting energy there. You have to be really smart to figure out how to not shortchange your other kids; your dead child is not more important than the wonderful children that you still have left."

Her experience has strengthened her resolve to live in Israel. "Now my son is buried here, no way I'll leave here. With Daniel's blood we have become real Israelis and the connection I feel now to Israel is really much, much, much deeper. I am connected by blood now with 22,500 other mothers who have lost a child."

She is steadfast in the belief that "the enemy had a victory over me when they killed my son and they will have another victory over me if I go down with him. I have chosen not to give it to them." On the first anniversary of Daniel's death, Cheryl told the group gathered at his gravesite how he had to carry a heavy machine gun for ninety kilometers (56 mi.) although he had not been prepared physically or intellectually to do it. But he did it because his commanding officer told him to do it. "As a bereaved mother, I feel like I am in the middle of a trek that is called life, and now I have been handed the machine gun to carry. I wasn't trained to carry this heavy load and I certainly have not been prepared to do it, not physically and not emotionally. How does one prepare to be a bereaved mother? But I am carrying it because that is what my commanding officer, Hashem, has commanded me to do. And I am doing it with as much dignity and as much positiveness as I can for two reasons: out of love and respect for my beloved son Daniel and out of love and respect for all *am Yisrael* (Jewish people)!"

Cheryl makes other people happy. She volunteers as a lactation counselor, giving breast-feeding advice and support to nursing mothers to help them form positive relationships with their new babies. "It just feels like such a gift." And she performs with the Raise Your Spirits Summer Stock Company, started by her good friend Sharon Katz when people were being killed on the road to Efrat. "We wouldn't drive on the roads because there was a *pigua* almost every day. We wouldn't leave our houses and sat in front of the news, eating junk food and crying as we watched all the funerals. Sharon, a very charismatic woman, said, 'Let's put on a play. We'll have fun doing it, and it will make people happy.' Now people travel from all over the country to see our shows."

It took a few years for Cheryl to realize that she no longer had the energy or the interest to be doing what she was doing. "I was very aware that often people make major life changes after they have been through a loss or a tragedy and I decided that I was going to hold onto the reins of my 'ordinary' life and just keep going. I kept waiting for it to be over, to get back to who I was. Finally I felt sufficiently strong, sufficiently clear enough to realize that this is it; this is now your story." She left her job "to be with my family, doing things that are good for me, taking care of my health, and spreading the message that I feel I have to spread."

The first thing she did to help herself and others was to travel to Poland with the Israeli army's officers' training course. "They take bereaved parents with them on every trip to add a very important perspective. It was unbelievable. It was a major, major experience." When she came back, she decided to study for her real estate license and worked for two months for the top real estate agency in Jerusalem. "I hated every minute. It was just very hard for me to come to the understanding that what I thought was right, really wasn't right." Since she was not ready at age fifty-seven to be a stay-at-home grandmother, she took a job as an administrative assistant at NDS – a high-technology company – using her skills as a facilitator.

Cheryl Harmony – yes, that is her actual middle name – has always loved performing and dancing. "A dancer is who I am and who I will always be. I'm older and wiser, but I still love to dance. And the more people watch me, the happier I am. I think I was always a mover. I've learned that whatever you were before your tragedy, you are after your tragedy." She performs in an annual dance show with her troupe of dancers.

As she approached her sixtieth birthday, Cheryl wanted to mark it in a significant way. A close friend suggested putting on a dance show for charity and Cheryl said, "Let's go for it!" She decided to tell the story of her life through dance – from life as a teenage go-go dancer in Toronto to a religious life in Alon Shvut, with many interesting stops along the way. She also decided to film the performance as an example to others of the beauty and freedom of an autobiographical film, to offer food for thought about the mysterious paths that life takes us on, and as a gift to her family for generations to come. "I want them to be able to say, 'This was Cheryl Harmony and she was a cool grandmother!'"

Cheryl continued her new career in high tech for six months after her sixty-fourth birthday. Since then, she has had a long speaking tour in Australia with travels also to New Zealand, Thailand, New York, Canada, and Poland. "Most of this is a result of the positive way I have dealt with the death of our son Daniel and the determination to maximize my situation. During this time, our children have grown, married, had children; we are awaiting our eighth grandchild and enjoy a lot of family time together. As much as possible, David and I appreciate what we have and cherish each moment of health and love." As she is quoted often as saying, "I have more left than most people start out with."

Chapter 10

Every Suffering Has a Purpose

making a difference through extraordinary action

There is no greater grief than losing a child; but when a child dies suddenly as the result of a terrorist attack, there is no time to prepare for the worst or somehow make their farewells. These parents may have a very difficult time in finding closure; yet some turn their grief into doing good for others, turning the most negative episode in their lives into something infinitely positive.

The three families of victims in this chapter find meaning and are committed to making a difference through extraordinary action. Although they have experienced inhumanity, they do not hate or seek revenge. They respond to pain and suffering by building, growing, making meaning out of suffering, and choosing life. They want to help people like themselves, struck by terror, be able to return to life with strength, hope, and healing. Through their stories and deeds, these parents honor the memories of their beloved children and truly make a difference in the lives of others.

Arnold and Frimet Roth remembered their daughter Malki, killed in the Sbarro Pizzeria bombing, by creating Keren Malki, the Malki Foundation, to help children with special needs. Amin Hassan honored his daughter Maysoun – the first Druze woman to be killed in a terrorist attack – by dedicating his life to advancing peace between Israel and the Palestinians. And Elaine Hoter, whose son Gavriel was killed when terrorists infiltrated his yeshiva, helps other families cope with bereavement.

Daughter Malki killed, Sbarro Pizzeria bombing, downtown Jerusalem: August 9, 2001

Arnold Roth: Survive, Go Forward, Make a Good Life

"The therapeutic value of speaking and writing about terrorism... and of promoting Keren Malki..."

Life-long friends and neighbors, Malka Chana (Malki) Roth, fifteen, and Michal Raziel, sixteen, spent the morning together decorating the bedroom of a neighborhood friend about to return from vacation. Like Peggy Kern and her daughter Gail, they too decided to stop for lunch at the Sbarro Pizzeria, on the corner of King George Street and Jaffa Road in the center of Jerusalem. They were standing next to each other at the counter when the twenty-three-year-old terrorist, Izz al-Din Shuheil al-Masri from the West Bank village of Aqaba, entered the unguarded restaurant just before 2:00 p.m. He was dressed as a tourist and carried a guitar case containing a five- to ten-kilogram (10–20 lb.) bomb, which was packed with nails, screws, and bolts. The explosion gutted the restaurant, killing Malki, Michal, and thirteen other innocent people, including seven children, and injuring about 130 others inside the restaurant and on the busy nearby streets. Malki and Michal were buried in simple graves next to each other in Jerusalem's Har Menuchot cemetery.

Arnold and Frimet Roth made *aliya* from Melbourne Australia with their family in 1988, shortly before Malki's third birthday. The middle child between three older brothers and three younger sisters, Malki was an amazing young woman. She was devoted to helping people and played a major role in the care of her profoundly disabled sister, Haya-Elisheva, serving as her mother's constant and ever-reliable right hand. Caring, sweet-natured, talented, vivacious, and musical, Malki brought happiness into many lives. She was especially good with special-needs children and their parents, seeking out opportunities to give the kind of practical help that a young teenager can.

During her last week of life, Malki was a youth leader at a camp for special-needs children and adolescents run by Etgarim, the Israeli Outdoor and Recreation Association for the Disabled. She was a much-loved *madricha* (counselor) of nine-year-old girls through Ezra, an Israeli religious youth movement, and had completed tenth grade at the prominent Horev Girls School in Jerusalem. A gifted musician who played the classical flute, she composed the words and music for what is now known as "Malki's Song." The song is upbeat, optimistic, and happy – just as Malki always was – reminding us that "we each have hope and a future, and a place in the World to Come."

Arnold explains that his parents were Polish Jews who survived the Holocaust and settled in Melbourne, Australia, in the late 1940s. With few material possessions, they raised him and his brother in a homogeneous community in which there were many Holocaust survivors. "Because of what the Nazis did to them, they were obliged to rebuild their lives without the help of extended families. Yet the life of our community, and especially the lives we children lived, was optimistic and positive. The motto of the family, although it was never expressed in this way, was 'Survive. Go forward. Make a good life.'"

In his university years Arnold became active in Jewish communal and Zionist organizations, eventually becoming the head of the Australian Jewish Students Union and a community activist. "Then I headed off in my own direction, going to Yeshiva University in New York after I finished law school. It was a formative stage in my Jewish life." That's where he met Frimet, a native New Yorker, who married him with the understanding that they would live for a very limited time in Australia before making *aliya* – which they finally did twelve years later.

After making *aliya*, Arnold requalified as a lawyer and found a niche managing technology companies, particularly start-ups. Frimet, who completed her law studies in Melbourne, is also a very talented artist. However, she maintained a deliberately low profile career-wise. "We made a conscious decision in life that we wanted to raise a family and have the children be at the center of our lives. Frimet is still there now."

Everything came under intense stress with the death of Malki. "Our normal lives were turned upside down by our child's murder. When Malki died… was killed… was murdered, all of us – the kids and Frimet and I – felt we had to do something that would associate Malki's life with acts of *chesed* and sensitize other people to the value that all of us can bring to the lives of special-needs children." Haya-Elisheva, the youngest of the Roth children, suffers from profound disabilities. Her parents had fought the government health-fund system and what they perceived as a misguided emphasis on institutionalization. "That is an unacceptable approach for the many families like us who are simply unprepared to have government bureaucrats tell us how to look after our child."

Based on their own experiences and challenges, the Roths created Keren Malki (the Malki Foundation)[1] to provide "solutions for the special needs of families in Israel – Christian, Muslim, Druze, and Jewish alike – who wanted to give the best possible home care to their child with severe disabilities." Arnold explains: "We want these families to feel empowered, to resist the pressure to hand off their child to institutional care just because of the lack of a reasonable alternative. We want the families to feel that they can do what's right for the child, in their eyes." Keren Malki delivers essential medical and rehabilitative equipment in partnership with Yad Sarah, a well-established voluntary organization in Israel, and provides subsidies to enable paramedical therapies, allowing families to choose physical, occupational, horse-riding, water, and speech therapies for their home-cared special-needs child. More than thirty thousand such therapy sessions were enabled owing to the work of Keren Malki in its first decade of activity.

Arnold explains that for Frimet and himself, "creating a foundation in our daughter's memory has been helpful in giving us a constructive focus to ameliorate the grief and pain and anger that came with our daughter's murder. We feel a need to use acts of goodness to offset the almost incomprehensible hatred that was visited on our lives by these monsters. And we want the goodness to be out there in the world.

---

1   Keren Malki, http://www.kerenmalki.org/.

We are glad for the opportunity to be agents for something positive, constructive, and personal. It certainly has been helpful for me in the ongoing task of trying to make sense of life after Malki's murder. I'm pleased that we are doing it. It's not an end in itself. It's a process that I hope will go on as long as we are alive."

Arnold thinks it does him more good than it does Frimet, basically in two ways. "One is, on a day-to-day basis, my wife is coping with two almost incomprehensible loads. One is that the most beloved person in her life was taken away from her in an act of hatred. How can she ever reconcile herself to that? I don't say it's been easy for me, but I have learned that the emotional load is different for my wife, heavier and harder to bear. The second is that every day she deals with a child, our youngest, who has no communication with the world, who is constantly at medical risk. It's a difficult life with no expectation of a happy, Hollywood-style ending."

Frimet writes and publishes a good deal "and much of it is angry. She writes frequently about terrorism to alert people everywhere to its ugliness, pain, and pervasiveness and to the failure of Israeli society and other societies to come to terms with the challenge of terrorism." They both "feel like the terror victims are often the only people who fully understand the danger and the impact, and can sense how badly the fight against terrorism is going, even today." They believe that "the willful forgetfulness, the need to sweep up the broken glass, to re-open the stores by morning, and to make sure the buses are running so we don't hand the terrorists a victory, is a strategic mistake and a moral mistake. Very few people get up and shout about this. That's why we feel we have to do that. We need to remind people of the power of remembering and figuring out what needs to be done in the face of ongoing terrorist barbarism."

Arnold has spoken at numerous international gatherings and conferences, often representing Israel. "For me, this has considerable therapeutic value – including the opportunity to meet people from widely different backgrounds who have been thrust into the same bitter kind of story when someone they love is hurt or worse by the practitioners of terror. Being able to look people in the face and say, 'You know you've just got to understand. Something very serious is going on here. And it is getting worse. It's not getting better.' That kind of thing is important for me to do. I believe it."

The Roths speak out as parents of a child who was murdered. "Not because our child was more important, not because our pain is greater, but because we have experienced this, we have learned things that people should never have to know. So please listen to us. You don't want to listen only to the politicians. You don't want to place too much faith in the analysts and commentators. Hear us too. We have something to say, something we learned in the hardest way." They share their views through the Malki Foundation website, which contains a selection of magazine and news articles, speeches, interviews, and essays by the Roths. In addition, they write a blog called "This Ongoing War"[2] that expresses their deep concern at what they believe is the dangerously inaccurate, partial, and agenda-driven journalism that explains to the world the events that are happening in Israel. The title really reflects what they feel. "We believe we are in an ongoing war. The murder of our daughter wasn't the beginning of it and it certainly wasn't the end of it. And it is most certainly not limited to this neighborhood."

Each member of the Roth family has experienced the loss in a different way – a full spectrum of suffering, of paying a price. Each of them has a story; some feel compelled towards action. One of their daughters attended the same school where Malki had gone, but for years after the Sbarro massacre no attempt was made to bring Malki's death into the life of the school – not in the days immediately after her murder or on its anniversary, not even on Yom Hazikaron (Israel's national memorial day for the fallen soldiers and the victims of terror). Their daughter was troubled and began acting up, yet the school treated it as nothing more than a discipline issue. Fortunately the Roths were able to identify the problem, get first-class help for their daughter, and move her to a new school with a far better outcome.

---

2   Frimet and Arnold Roth, *This Ongoing War* (blog), http://thisongoingwar .blogspot.co.il/.

But they aimed for more. Realizing that the teachers and the principals were not being adequately prepared, the Roths approached officials of the Ministry of Education, requesting to present their understanding and to suggest that intervention was needed for the benefit of the other children and for Israeli society. "Their response was terrific. They quickly convened a meeting of school counselors from all over Israel to address the issue of war and death and loss and grief – not death as a result of illness, but in an environment of ongoing risk. Frimet spoke at that conference and the educators and counselors were, I think, floored by the power of her message. Very likely, they had not heard a parent articulate the problem until then. They had failed to grasp the size and acuteness of the problem. It was a turning point. We realized that if you explain this difficult experience in a way that is understandable and insightful, there is a good chance people are going to listen to you and respond."

The Roths are committed to living in Israel, and hope their children will choose to stay and make their lives there. In the intervening years, they have been blessed with weddings and grandchildren, but in significant ways, life has remained challenging in the wake of Malki's death.

As also experienced by other bereaved families of victims of terror attacks, it was disturbing to Frimet and Arnold to see, for example, how many of their friends disappeared from their lives, "even in certain cases to the point of crossing the street when they would see us coming. I understand this to be a matter of their not knowing what to do. They feel bad, perhaps awkward. So often they will do nothing. For myself, I don't begin to know how one ought to act in the presence of other people's grief. I only know that finding so many of our friends no longer involved in our lives when we needed them the most has been very hard to come to terms with." Now the Roths have a number of new friendships; people in the same situation, families who have lost children. "The single most valuable dimension has been hearing other people saying that everyone has had this experience – family members who don't understand, friends who don't understand, things that are not easily spoken about or shared. It's a universal aspect of a situation that I have heard over and again when meeting people whose lives were impacted by the terrorists. Yet it's rarely discussed and never adequately addressed. You could say it's a 'winning' dimension of the strategy followed by the terrorists."

Another aspect, as the Roths see it, was the 2011 decision to release from Israeli prisons three of the people who carried out the Sbarro massacre. The political campaign leading to the final decision evolved over a period of some years, and with growing intensity. When in October 2011, the mass release took place of 1,027 terrorists, most of them guilty of murdering Israelis and Jews, the Roths found themselves again in a minority – not just as victims of terrorism but also as part of the minority camp of Israelis deeply disturbed at the injustice of releasing unrepentant killers, many of them deeply ideological and on record as being ready to kill again.

"For years, we had written and spoken publicly against the suggestion that the woman who brought the bomb to Sbarro should be released as part of a deal with the terrorists. It was a private campaign: us against the *New York Times*, us against the camp that said if only we let the terrorists out of prison, we can expect good times and peace. We were voices in the wilderness, and while there were responsive notes of sympathy and understanding to our message from certain quarters, particularly outside Israel, we were ignored. And worse – while we believed we were speaking in the name of the fundamental notion of *justice*, we found ourselves, along with others like us, being publicly called *vindictive* and *vengeful*. In the week leading up to the actual release, a terrible time for us, Frimet and I were interviewed in some of the most public parts of the media many dozens of times. Much less by the Israeli media, by the way. But in the end, our voices were ignored and we were left, once again, to ponder the loneliness of losing a child to an act of barbaric hatred and to find how little this is understood."

None of this has caused the Roths to think about taking an active role in politics, a domain to which they feel no affinity. But as parents of a child whose beautiful life was cruelly stolen from them, they have carved out a nonpolitical role in society that, in small ways, offsets some of the challenges that have intruded into their lives.

Daughter and sister Maysoun killed, daughter and sister Jihan injured, Egged bus no. 361 bombing, Meron Junction: August 4, 2002

Amin, Farida, and Ghoussoun Hassan (Father, Mother, and Sister): Druze Family Values

Amin Hassan: "You have to be strong. Everything is bound up in love and peace."

Farida Hassan: "Everything changed, like a fire in our home. Like a wound, it is still bleeding."

Ghoussoun Hassan: "She will be with us forever."

Maysoun Amin Hassan, nineteen, was a beautiful young woman – with blue eyes, red hair, and glasses. She was always happy, smiling, and laughing. She was self-confident, talented, and a gifted student – graduating from high school with honors and looking forward to beginning her studies in psychology at Haifa University "because she wanted to help others." She was special – the driving force in her home and in her own family.

The Hassans are a well-known family from Sajur, one of twenty-two Druze villages in northern Israel. The Arabic-speaking Druze people are a separate cultural, social, and religious community, and serve in the Israel Defense Forces. Amin Hassan and his wife Farida were the parents of three daughters – Ghoussoun, Jihan, and the youngest Maysoun – and four sons. Amin was a former senior police officer in the IDF and the Border Police – the military branch of the Israeli Police – and served as the director of the Israel Olive Board since 1997.

On the morning of August 4, 2002, twenty-two-year-old Jihan had an exam at the Safed Regional College. Maysoun went with her so that they could shop afterwards for clothes for Jihan's forthcoming wedding.

Before leaving home, Maysoun kissed her sleeping father on the cheek, and gave her mother a special look as she was going out the door. Later, some said that she had a premonition that something bad was about to happen. Ghoussoun's husband Ronny dropped them at the bus stop located just outside their village on the route that connected Sajur with Haifa and Safed.

Meanwhile, Jihad Hamadeh, a Jordanian by birth and a resident of the West Bank village of Burkin near Jenin, was with Ibrahim Bakhri and Yasin Bakhri, Israeli Arabs from the neighboring village of Ba'aneh. They housed Jihad for two days, helping him select a target, buying the batteries to detonate a bomb, and dropping him at the Sajur Junction bus stop where he boarded Egged bus no. 361. Just before 9:00 a.m., Jihad exploded the bomb at the crowded Meron Junction near Safed. The blast blew off the roof of the bus, which then burst into flames, killing nine people – three soldiers, four Israeli civilians, and two Filipino women – and wounding fifty others. Maysoun and Jihan had been forced to sit apart because the bus was crowded. Maysoun was sitting directly behind the bomber and was killed instantly; Jihan, who was sitting further back in the bus, was seriously injured and traumatized by the death of her sister.

Jihan's family tells her story: "She flew around the bus. She was injured in her eyes, ears, and everything in the body. The soldier near the terrorist was cut totally, others lost their heads and parts of their body. There was a lot of blood and many parts of people were everywhere, including in Jihan's hair. She underwent surgery on the right side of her body. She remembers that every day she is not the same Jihan. Jihan was strong, not like she is now. She has trauma. She lives the event again and again. She lost her memory and she loses control whenever she sees the color blue – the color of the bomber's clothing. She was in a wedding, for a relative, and in our traditions they celebrate by a gun. She totally collapsed. She feels afraid every moment. She feels that someone is following her."

Jihan received psychological treatment in the hospital and as an outpatient. For the family, "there was nothing that we could do other than speak to Jihan and give her goodwill." As soon as she was well enough, her father and mother arranged for her marriage to go forward.

"We made a celebration for Jihan – we made a good wedding. That was very important for Jihan because if we let her stay here without anything, she would speak about the situation and she wouldn't feel well. So we gave her a wedding very quickly to feel better and avoid a terrible situation in the future… It took several years to make a baby and now she is very busy and happy with her son. It's good for her and brings great joy to our family." However, she still suffers from nightmares as a result of the *pigua* – "There is no medicine for that." The Druze community and families are very close and this has helped Jihan recover. Her family continues to help her. "She comes here and takes whatever she needs from our home. Everybody gives her all the opportunities we have. We don't close any door on Jihan."

Amin Hassan had a strong personality and a reputation for toughness. For the first time, Amin's children saw him cry. His wife Farida "brought him something and put it in his eyes to encourage him to cry." Ghoussoun remembers that "it was difficult for my father to cry and express his feelings. It was very difficult for us to see my father cry." For Amin, "it was a terrible situation for a father to see one daughter killed and the other injured. It was very hard to see Jihan in the hospital and to tell her that Maysoun had been killed in the same explosion." Three days after the attack, "I went to the hospital and told Jihan that Maysoun had been killed. I said, 'That's what God wanted to do. So we have to pray to God and thank Him for everything that He's done and accept it whether it is good or bad. And we have to pray to God that you are still alive because you and Maysoun were close to the murderer and she was killed and you were not.'"

Amin knew that he had to be strong for his family. "It's very important to be strong because I am the head of the family and I have four sons and three daughters. I might have let this destroy me but we have to be very strong to continue forward. I give the whole family strength and encouragement to be strong in this situation to face the problems, because if we were weak it wouldn't be good for anybody in our family. We have to be very strong to handle this situation because it is very hard and very difficult." He adds: "That's a good solution for everybody who has a problem in his family."

His Druze faith and belief in fate helped him. "Everybody who is born has to reach the end of his life – younger and older people. We Druze serve in the army like the Jewish community. Soldiers are killed – very young men – and there are very terrible accidents in the roadways every day. But you have to be strong." He believes that it is necessary to accept and learn how to live with both the good and the bad. "Maysoun had to die when and where she died, because it was decreed. Many things help us and prevent us from going mad in such situations. Fate helps us. We also derive comfort from the Druze belief in reincarnation and from our love for the Israeli flag that we serve. I truly believe that Maysoun was fated to die. True, I dreamed about the day on which she would start her university studies and about the day on which she would receive her degree and about the day of her wedding. However, fate wanted something very different."[1]

Amin's brother Gideon explains the Druze belief that saying good-bye to a person's body does not mean that you are saying good-bye to that person's soul. On the contrary, he feels that Maysoun's soul will always be with them.[2] Ghoussoun believes that Maysoun's soul visited her when she gave birth. "I saw a figure around my child and I woke up my husband to see. Jihan, in the morning, told me that she dreamed that Maysoun visited my child. You can see the telepathy… She is always with us."

For Maysoun and Jihan's mother Farida, "everything changed, like a fire in our home. Sometimes I feel my head fly around. This situation affects me extremely. I lose my memories. I forget and feel disconnected. It's very strange." Although she is being helped by a psychologist, she still lives the trauma strongly, experiencing fear and sometimes hyperventilating and shaking. "I feel very bad. Like a wound, it is still bleeding. Since the attack, I am not the same as I once was. I used to be strong, without these problems. I used to travel with Amin to Europe, but now I can't leave. I feel distant from my husband. I am still near

---

1   Daniel Ben Simon, "Fate Decided to Take Her," http://www.haaretz.com/fate -decided-to-take-her-1.37424. Reprinted with permission.

2   Ibid.

Jihan; she lives the situation. We lost Maysoun, a decision of God, but to see Jihan suffering is very complicated. I'm constantly afraid that something will happen to Jihan. I think about her, about whether her husband is angry at her, or if she will have an attack."

Farida proudly, but humbly, describes how all of the children have "special qualities and capacities." Ghoussoun is studying drama therapy at Tel Hai College in Kiryat Shmona "as a result of what happened to us." One son is studying to be a lawyer at the Academic Center of Law and Business in Ramat Gan and the younger boys attend Kadoorie – a prestigious boarding school that reflects the diversity of Israel's population. Only one child still lives at home. Although it is a tribute to their children's self-reliance and their parents' confidence in their abilities to send them away to school, it is unusual in the Arab society to get such freedom. It makes it harder on Farida not to see them and she worries that something bad might happen to them. "It is very difficult to be alone at home, everything deteriorates. It is difficult to see the beds empty. I don't go outside the home. A mother is very special, no doubt about that." What helps her most "is to see my children at home."

After the attack, Amin felt he had two options: either he could allow his bereavement to control him or he could utilize his loss to do something positive. So he decided to dedicate his life to advancing peace between Israel and the Palestinians. "It's unusual for two daughters in one family to be targeted. I spoke about this situation very much on Israeli radio and television and wrote for other media as well. I spoke about peace and about reform and tolerance between people."

To promote peace between people he met with the bomber's family. "It was very important to speak about the situation in order to create a good atmosphere for people here in our village and other Druze villages in the Galilee and for our neighbors here. I met with the Bakhri family because we have been neighbors with Ba'aneh village for many, many years, and this issue can cloud relationships between the people in my village and our neighbors in Ba'aneh." It was critical to Amin that all his actions – speaking about what had happened and preventing the situation from collapsing – be done according to God's will. "I spoke with them and said that what happened here happened from God and we don't blame anybody from our area. These are innocent people who go by bus to learn in the college – not in the army or anything else." Farida adds that the bomber was "also a victim of the situation and we don't know what passed in his life."

As the director of the Israel Olive Board, Amin was determined to honor his daughter's memory by strengthening the ties with his Palestinian partners. Since Maysoun's death, "I support the peace process between Israel and Arab people. In my work I put a lot of effort into creating a good atmosphere between people, like my help to the Palestinian Authority in the olive fields." He explains that "we have about two hundred thousand dunam (49,000 ac.) of olive trees in Israel, and the Palestinians have about one million dunam (247,000 ac.) of olive trees – more than five times that of Israel. Palestinians come here to pick and harvest the olives. And we invite the Palestinian people to join us in the courses we teach in Israel – to learn with us and to form connections with us in order to promote peace in the world."

In April 2006 Amin and his counterpart on the Palestinian Olive Board, Khaled Junaidi from the West Bank city of Nablus, visited an oil and wine exhibit in Verona, Italy. "He was standing near me with the flag of the Palestinians behind him and the flag of Israel was behind me. I spoke, saying that we had a good relationship between us – the Arabs and the Jews in Israel and between Israel and the Palestinian Authority. In spite of the fact that Mr. Hamadeh killed my daughter, I continue to help the Palestinians, opening the doors of Israel and giving them all of our information concerning the development of olive trees. And as you can see we are working together as one unit – Israel and the Palestinian Authority. It is very difficult to be here, but we choose the route that gives everybody the opportunity to change their ideas about what the future of people here in the Middle East will be. We read about the situation with the Palestinians and the Israelis and we think that there is constant war in the Middle East. But it is not true; we have good relationships between Arabs and Jews here. We are constantly working on creating an atmosphere for peace. We hope we can reach peace as soon as possible because peace means love, peace means a good life, peace means good work, peace means a good education – everything is bound up in love and peace." They received a standing ovation.

Before his death on October 9, 2008, a year after being interviewed for this book, Amin dreamed of building the National Center for the Olive Culture in Israel at Chanania Farms, the headquarters of the Olive Board near Meron in the Galilee. "I want to build an educational center for peace and tolerance, under the symbol of the olive branch, as a center for cooperation between all religions – Muslims, Druze, Christian, and Jew. The center will include a museum about olive trees, as well as lecture and meeting halls, a laboratory for analyzing olive oil, a center for agricultural research and development and for collecting information about everything written about olive trees, an amphitheater, and an archeological garden showing how olive oil was produced from early history until now." The garden would be dedicated in memory of his daughter Maysoun and the eight innocent victims who were murdered with her as a reminder that "all people suffer from terrorist attacks."

Son Gavriel killed, shooting attack, Otniel Yeshiva:
December 27, 2002

Elaine Hoter: *My Brother Was...*

"The tremendous impact it had on us... and the tremendous
responsibility we've felt since..."

Elaine Hoter, a fifty-six-year-old mother of six, moved to Israel from
the United Kingdom when she was eighteen. She believed that she
would be spared from the increasing terrorism all around because "God
only gives people a burden to bear if they can bear it. He knew that I
couldn't do that. I am not a strong person. I knew it wasn't going to
happen to me because I couldn't cope with it. And then suddenly it
happened... And I discovered that I was stronger than I had thought...
It was my third son who was only seventeen. He didn't take risks. He
wasn't even in a dangerous place. He had volunteered to replace a
friend on kitchen duty... The event is really powerful not only because
it changed *our* lives; it impacted so many people's lives because of the
person Gavriel was."

Gavriel was one of four yeshiva students murdered at the Otniel
Yeshiva near Hebron by two terrorists from the nearby West Bank
village of Dura. Wearing Israeli army uniforms and carrying M-16 rifles,
ammunition, and hand grenades, the terrorists cut through the fence
surrounding the Jewish school. About one hundred students were in the
ground-floor dining hall, enjoying the Friday night Shabbat meal. The
terrorists sprayed the building with bullets before entering through the
kitchen service entrance. All four young men in the kitchen were killed:
Gavriel Hoter (17) of Alonei Habashan, Staff Sergeant Noam Apter (23)
of Shilo, Private Yehuda Bamberger (20) of Karnei Shomron, and Zvi
Zieman (18) of Reut. Before they were shot dead, the boys managed to
bolt the door to the adjoining dining room, preventing an even greater

loss of life. The terrorists were later killed by IDF forces. Ten others, including six soldiers, were wounded in the attack.

Gavriel was born on Holocaust Day – April 17, 1985 – in Kfar Adumim, a village outside Jerusalem in the Judean Desert. A gifted student, he skipped eighth grade and went on to study at the yeshiva high school for science and technology in nearby Maale Adumim. He decided to remain and board in the dorms when his family moved to Alonei Habashan in the Golan Heights the following year. While still in high school, he studied science and ecology at the Open University and planned to finish his Bachelor of Science degree before joining the army. That summer, he joined the *hesder* program – a five-year program combining religious studies with army service – choosing to attend the Otniel Yeshiva in the Hebron Hills, where his older brother Sephy was studying. He devoted himself completely to Jewish studies, but always made time to help and support his many friends. He was the third child of Chaim and Elaine and is survived by five siblings – Ben-Yishai, Sephy, Michal, Orit, and Avichai.

His mother explains why during Gavriel's short life he influenced so many people: "He was just such a good person. Even when he was young he led us. He was the rabbi of the family. It was something that you didn't talk about. If someone had told me there was such a thing, I probably wouldn't have believed them. When you see someone like that, then you believe that people don't come to this world equal. They come bringing everything they've got from worlds they've been to before. He was funny and he was brilliant. The important thing was he lived his life through the Torah. He lived here in this world to help others and to be a better person. From a very young age, he had a natural instinct to help anyone who had a problem. Students always came to the house to study with him – this was the person they wanted to be – it's amazing."

Gavriel was "a child who was never a child." His kindergarten teacher told Elaine that she had twenty-nine children in the class "but one man – one little man. From first grade he would go to all the adult lessons every night. He always had questions and was part of the lessons, but in a quiet way. He never raised his hand. He would come up afterwards and add something, if they asked him. He would never push himself. To keep from being bored at school, he explained that 'I listen to the lesson and I see if there is any new material and I see if the teacher is presenting it a different way. And if that is not interesting, I look at the pupils and I see how they are behaving and how the teacher relates to them. But if that's not interesting, then I think how I could teach the lesson a different way to make it more interesting. So how can a lesson be boring?'"

After the funeral and the *shiva*, Elaine felt that the family had a "tremendous responsibility because the person who is gone is the person who is supposed to make the world a better place and he's not here anymore. And we are not like him. We've tried in our own way to continue what Gavriel had done so it wouldn't stop with him. And it's hard to do because you can't stop your life and just think about what you are going to do and what would Gavriel want to do."

Elaine learned that "we can't be happy and sad together. It takes a long time to be happy. According to *halacha* (Jewish religious law), in the grieving process you go through several stages and things become easier." The first year "I felt the need to talk about Gavriel all the time. I never spoke about him when he was alive. It was like how do you speak about someone like that? So I would speak of the other children, little funny things they were doing. Afterwards, I had to speak about him all the time… The first year or two – my whole identity changed. I was Gavriel's mother even before I was my other children's mother. Slowly things get back into perspective and I really don't have to tell everyone I see and it's not written on my forehead – 'Hey, this is me.'" She tells her story with much love and laughter, easily expressing her emotions.

Elaine feels that she has changed "a lot" from this experience and is "sure that as time goes on there will be even more changes. On the one hand, I don't have energy to do all the things that I used to do. I used to invite loads of people each Shabbat to the house and now that is difficult to do. On the other hand, I've got much more strength and power in my life than I had and I can do more to help other people." She is still not thinking about long-term priorities or goals. "I take each day as it comes, working on my projects."

The first year or so, Elaine "was so busy trying to do things – memorial things." She did a lot of work on Gavriel's memorial internet site,[1] including a video of Gavriel's life. "I found that video has a tremendous impact on people compared to when they hear you speak. When you see the video from all the different angles, you get the picture of who he was." Israel television also chose to make a documentary movie for Memorial Day about the four boys together "to show how each family goes through bereavement in a different way but with lots of similarities – with no hatred or revenge – and doing good things in that person's name. It was very positive."

From the beginning, the Hoters did not take Gavriel's death as their own personal tragedy. "It was a national tragedy and everyone who knew Gavriel also looked at it that way. Obviously everyone has a role in this world. I do not know our particular role here, but I still think that we have to go and do things." They created a book in memory of Gavriel based on Pirkei Avot (Ethics of Our Fathers), chapter 6, about the forty-eight traits needed in order to study Torah. "That was Gavriel, all forty-eight together. So we asked forty-eight rabbis and other people who knew Gavriel to write about what each trait tells us about living our lives to make the world a better place. Each trait is illustrated by a story from Gavriel's life, showing how he lived his life according to these traits, including his own self-accounting diary of what he wanted to do to improve himself."

The Hoters also established Midreshet Gavriel, a learning center, to encourage young people to follow in his footsteps by improving their personal character traits and behaviors. It sponsors learning workshops for high school students. "They take time out to be in nature and think about their lives and where they are going and about themselves and whatever it is they want to improve about themselves." Gavriel's father, Chaim, is a tour guide and now works with Midreshet Gavriel. "Every tour he does, he tries to bring something of Gavriel into the tour because Gavriel was a part of nature. People who go on the tour appreciate thinking about things beyond the tour, about themselves."

---

1   Gavriel Hoter, http://www.gavriel.org.

Elaine believes strongly that "I am guided in what to do." She dreamed she "wrote a children's book – to help other children who have lost a brother. And the dream was exactly what had happened to Avichai, my four year old, whose exuberance kept the family going after the tragedy. He is very verbal about everything. I woke up and wrote the story from the dream." *My Brother Was…*[2] expressively and movingly describes the way young children cope with loss and mourning and helps families cope with bereavement. The book is illustrated with clay models, Gavriel's favorite medium, as a way to put a little bit of humor into the story and because real pictures can be frightening for children.

The book tells the story through Avichai's eyes – "everything he went through and the stages that children go through. Things they normally can't talk about with their parents because parents don't understand what they are going through. So many children need this book – children who have lost siblings through suicide, illness, or car accidents and not one book is on the children's market to help brothers." And the books about the loss of parents make it even more traumatic for a child to think they can lose a parent too.

Avichai has become more fearful of his parents leaving him. "He has a recurring dream that the police shoot Chaim, his father. He told me, 'I keep thinking about this dream and I think it's terrible to lose a brother, but it's even worse to lose a parent because a parent is everything.' And he said, 'That's my secret. That's why I run away from kindergarten every day to see if you are alive, if you are okay.' I hugged him and said, 'You know that we really love you and anyway it's usually old people who die.' And he said, 'Yeah, but I know things can be different.'"

As the first terror-victim family in the Golan, there was almost no organized support infrastructure to help the Hoters, except for two families living nearby. Like so many other survivors and bereaved families, they were amazed that "a lot of people don't know how to react to you, how to help. People avoid you. I wasn't prepared for that. I did not have the energy to go up to them and say, 'It's okay, you can talk to me. Come over and have coffee, I need you to be there.' I couldn't

---

2   Elaine Hoter, *My Brother Was…* (Israel: Midreshet Gavriel, 2005).

say that. And so I didn't have that support system, because I couldn't make the first step. And I think you have to make it in that situation."

Fortunately, Almagor-TVA, the Terror Victim's Association, "came to our house personally in the *shiva*. Almagor is run by terror victims for terror victims, which is very important because you can try and sympathize but if you haven't been there you are still one step away… I find the most support comes from people who have been through it seven or eight years ago – someone who has been there and you can see they are continuing their lives." The same was true for her children. "When they go away to camps, I can see the difference. One of my daughters goes to OneFamily, where she has great friends. And my other daughter went to the Koby Mandell camp and it's great for her to have people to talk to who have been through it a long time before us."

Almagor sent Elaine to the United States for a weeklong speaking engagement and she realized that she has the power to give strength to other people. As an instructor at Talpiot College of Education in Tel Aviv, she was no stranger to lecturing, but "in America, people came up to me afterwards and said things like 'You changed my outlook on life.' When you've been through something like this, you come out with an understanding of what you didn't have before and with the ability to help other people. When it is put the right way, you can influence people a lot – not just people who have gone through a terror attack, but people who have been sick or are having problems in their lives." She doesn't know how she got this power, but supposes that it came "probably from just knowing that I was the mother of Gavriel."

Elaine also lectures on bereavement to help people understand how to act. She has been invited to speak to youth programs and schools, and many people and groups come to her home. "I use the book to speak about empathy and coping after a tragedy and I go through the book with people and tell them what happened behind the scenes and how it was written. It is quite moving because it's like a window into a world that they obviously never want to enter. They have a new level of understanding, particularly people who are so frightened of death or frightened to go to a *shiva*. I give them a lot of information to make it easier when they have to face the situation. Near the very end, I spend a few minutes telling them about Gavriel so they can take a little bit of him with them. That's sort of my thing – I get something out of it too."

Elaine now volunteers with a new organization for terror victims, L'hamshich Lichyot B'yachad (Together We Will Continue Our Lives), in which "people can be in a non-threatening environment and be themselves, not putting on a mask and pretending that everything is okay." She also volunteers for the Ministry of Defense, recently helping a mother who lost her son in the Israel-Hezbollah/Lebanon War. Although she likes to help people, "I find that we are all limited to the number of relationships we can put a lot of effort into and the amount of time that we can spend. You can't spread yourself so thin because you have to be able to be there when one of them needs you."

Elaine admits that she has "an overdose of creativity" and is constantly developing new ideas and new projects. She was an advisor for the Ministry of Education for using the Internet and technology to combat suicide attempts and has introduced digital storytelling as a way for people to tell their own stories for healing. She has moved forward to action by promoting multiculturalism and battling hatred through videoconferences connecting her religious college, a secular college, and an Islamic Arab college so they can understand each other and work collaboratively. Over the last nine years, this project has grown into a national project where thousands of students and pupils have experienced online collaborative learning with people from different religious and cultural backgrounds. Elaine received the 2013 Award for Achievements in Teacher Education for a pedagogical initiative that makes a unique contribution to teacher education. She has lectured on her research on these projects around the world.

The rest of the family has reacted "according to where they are in their lives." Each has found special and meaningful ways to do good things to honor Gavriel's memory and, in the process, found meaning and purpose for their lives in the aftermath of such a horrific event and their grief over the loss of Gavriel.

Chaim and Elaine look at things differently. Elaine thinks the difference has to do with gender and personality. "If you are open and you talk, it helps. If you close yourself up, it eats your heart out."

Looking back on the years since Gavriel's murder, Elaine says, "it's been very hard. Basically Chaim became depressed because of the tragedy. And it is very difficult to live with someone who is depressed. It pulls you down. He went to a psychologist. He didn't get along. He isn't a talking person. He would probably do well with someone who gives a hands-on massage or would throw him around. Everyone needs their own therapy... And sometimes time can heal. Today, thank God, Chaim is back to his old self, but it took a long time."

Their youngest son Avichai "is doing okay now. He still gets upset if we go out or leave him, but he's improving." The four older children are all doing very well. "Each one has taken something from Gavriel with them on the way. It changes their life a lot."

Their oldest son, Ben-Yishai, lives in Kfar Adumim and is a *mohel* (trained in the practice of ritual circumcision), a *chazzan* (Jewish cantor), and a tour guide. He has six children. His first daughter, born two weeks after the murder, is named Noga, the first light. The Hebrew letters spelling her name stand for *ner Gavriel v'Hashem* – in the light of Gavriel and God.

Nine months after Gavriel was murdered, their second son Sephy had his first daughter Pe'er. "And we say, *'pe'er tachat efer'*[3] – out of ashes shall come beauty and lightness again." Sephy is a spiritual advisor and junior high school teacher and studied to be a film director. He now has five children.

Michal, when in the army, took new immigrants through their basic training and taught in the Jewish studies course. She studied in Rimon, the school of music and jazz, and is a very talented composer and a singer.

Orit, the Hoter's youngest daughter, has the personality of a psychologist and is "very much into helping people. She used to spend hours on the phone with other bereaved kids. She's amazing. She just looks at people and tries to help them." Orit also is very spiritual. "She

---

3   A quotation from Isaiah 61:3, calling for joy and comfort for those who have mourned over Zion's destruction.

raises everyone's spiritual level wherever she goes." She is now married and has a daughter.

Composing and singing songs have always strengthened the whole family and given strength to other people. All of the Hoter children are trained singers and they sing in close harmony. "Even at the funeral they sang songs for Gavriel and through the *shiva* they sang." Michal, who was fourteen at the time, "feels that the music comes to her from somewhere and she wrote two amazing songs." One song, translated into English, is "Give me the strength to go on, to bind my burning wounds, to know that I won't see him again, to continue in spite of the pain." The other song is from the *haftara* (weekly reading from the Prophets) for the week when Gavriel was killed. Michal took the words from Ezekiel 16:6 and wrote a song "In Thy Blood, Live," which draws on her father's Yemenite heritage. The family created a disc of all the songs in Hebrew and in English. "People who hear the songs and have gone through a crisis of any type just feel the songs. They have a lot of power to them and give them strength."

The Hoters continue to sing together and have made a new disc, which is much more upbeat than the first one. The songs and tunes are mostly written by the Hoters. It includes a song written by Orit – a metaphor for how she and her family are trying to move forward in the aftermath of pain and suffering. She chose the words from Psalms 30:12 – "You have taken my sorrow and turned it into dance."

Chapter 11

Ongoing Losses, Trauma, and Suffering

not just statistics

Terrorism is unexpected and indiscriminate and can strike any one at any time and any place. "At the end of the day, we are all victims of terror. It doesn't make any difference that my mom and sister were killed eight years ago or someone was killed maybe two weeks ago. For the people who are left behind, they are also statistics – it's exactly the same thing. They are still people; they are also victims of terror."

This book ends with the story of a mother and daughter who were victims of an attack that took place on the eve of the Purim festival in 1996 between the First and Second Intifadas. Paul Bernstein and Marlyn Butchins share the Bernstein family story to ensure that their mother, Sylvia Bernstein, and sister, Gail Belkin, and all of the other victims of terror – whether old, recent, or future terrorism – are not *just* statistics and are remembered and treated equally. "People talk about the Second Intifada and about how many people have been killed *since* the Second Intifada – recent terrorism. When they talk about that, they aren't talking about people like Sylvia and Gail and all the people who were killed *before* the Second Intifada – old terrorism – and do not appear to really be a part of it."

Mother Sylvia Bernstein and sister Gail Bernstein Belkin killed,
suicide bombing outside Dizengoff Center, Tel-Aviv:
March 4, 1996

Paul Bernstein: Old Terrorism
Marlyn Bernstein Butchins: A Celebration of Life[1]

"At the end of the day...we are all victims of terror."

In the nine days leading up to the festive Jewish holiday of Purim in March 1996 sixty people died in five acts of terrorism throughout the country. Fearing more terrorist attacks, many of the usual Purim parties were canceled and children stayed home. As a result, many young Israelis remember 1996 as the year without Purim.[2]

At 3:56 p.m. on the eve of Purim, a suicide bomber detonated a twenty-kilogram (44 lb.) bomb laced with nails and screws at the intersection of Dizengoff and King George Streets, outside the Dizengoff Center shopping mall in downtown Tel Aviv. Five children in costumes were among the thirteen victims, who included a young soldier, two friends out for coffee, a journalist on his way to work, an elderly woman due to meet her son at an Israel Philharmonic concert, a woman on her way home from shopping, and a mother and daughter.

Seventy-three-year-old Sylvia Bernstein and her forty-eight-year-old daughter Gail Belkin were out with Gail's daughter for her wedding-dress fitting – she was to be married a week later. Sylvia, a widow, had three other children: her son Paul and her daughter Marlyn Butchins in Israel, and her son Darryl in Australia. Gail was survived by her

---

1   Marlyn's husband, Larry Butchins, contributed to this story.
2   Michele Chabin, "Jews Will Recall '96 as Year We Lost Purim," JWeekly.com, March 8, 1996, http://www.jweekly.com/article/full/2687/jews-will-recall-96-as -year-we-lost-purim/.

husband Larry Belkin – an American to whom she had been married for a year; her two daughters; and two stepchildren.

The Bernstein family was originally from Bulawayo, Rhodesia. Paul, his wife Sharon, and their sons Jason and Richard were the first to make *aliya* in 1986 because "what I breathe and see, what and who I am every day is a Jew, and I'm living in my home. Israel is the place to bring up Jewish children." Marlyn, her husband Larry Butchins, and their three children Camilla, Craig, and Aliza followed eighteen months later, as did Gail and her youngest daughter. Sylvia came later and was "really well integrated into, not Israeli society per se, but certainly into a kind of new immigrant society. She taught Israeli high school students to speak English. She was a very sparkly person, and had every reason to still be walking around with her 'granny book' with pictures of all the great things in her life."

Paul and Marlyn do not speak Hebrew well enough to participate in the counseling sessions offered by Bituach Leumi. "It's not the fault in any way of Israel and society; I'm one of these Anglo-Saxons who have never really perfected the language. So my sister and I are kind of isolated from the victims-of-terror groups and we've been very much left to our own devices." Paul would have liked to meet with a group of English-speaking families of terror victims, "to sit together and really talk it out. I think that would really be helpful to talk to someone who actually had one of their own killed like that, and be part of the experience."

Paul and Marlyn have reacted differently. Paul is a very private person and "I kind of live with it." Even with his immediate family, "I have had brief discussions about it, but we haven't gone into how we are really feeling. I just don't see too much of a purpose in trying to rehash it because it's over and I don't really see anything positive that will come out of it. When the peace comes, if it ever comes, I'll feel a little bit easier. I may be able to see some kind of purpose in the bombing. But it's just gone on and, for now, it's just a difficult thing to live with."

Paul seeks closure through accountability. "I don't think I will ever really get closure as such unless there is some way that some accountability is apportioned. I still have a certain amount of anger. I think culpability must be shown at some stage by the Palestinian Authority. And I think a lot of things can make me rest a little easier. Those things haven't happened. Whether they will happen or not, I don't know."

Paul continues: "Meanwhile, I believe I'm taking it in my stride. Now there's really not a hell of a lot I can do about it. I don't change my life in any way whatsoever. Because what happened to Sylvia and Gail is something that just happened to my family – that's all. If I have to go to Dizengoff or anywhere, being blown up by a suicide bomber has as much chance of happening to me as to the people who are visiting Paris or visiting Spain being hit by terrorists. Terrorists hit people whenever and wherever they decide. I still don't feel this danger in Israel, although it may be here. There have been suicide bombings and various other incidents since then. Every time these things happen it is sort of like reliving our past. But the big thing overall is that it is just not nice being a statistic."

Marlyn and her sister Gail were best friends and exceptionally close. For Marlyn, "it was nine years until I started doing something about it. For me it doesn't have to be closure. I heal – I don't like the word closure, because there is no closure really. It's something that you think about all the time. I was extremely close to my sister. I had virtually never lived without her our whole lives. And for me it was earth shattering… I eventually came to the acknowledgment and understanding that life does go on. Despite the pain and the hardship of the loss, I realized we must continue to move forward, otherwise we hand a victory to those who would seek to destroy us."

Marlyn describes her journey of healing. "Since the day of the tragedy, we have attended the commemoration service held on the corner of Dizengoff and King George streets in the heart of Tel Aviv. Every year there have been speeches by the mayor of Tel Aviv, by a representative of a family, a poetry reading or song by a sister or brother, a dedication by another family member, *yizkor* (memorial prayer), and many, many tears. The ceremony has always been, thankfully, short and dignified. *Yahrzeit* (memorial) candles are lit, the names on the stark stone memorial erected under the ancient tree that stands on the sidewalk are touched with loving fingers…and we have gone home to mourn once again." As for Paul, "I go and buy two red roses."

It bothered Marlyn that she didn't know who was killed alongside her mom and sister. "And it worried me that I used to go the ceremony every year and I just didn't know who else was involved there." When she became passionate about quilting, she found it exceptionally therapeutic and enjoyed working closely with other quilters. This led her to embark on a personal mission to create something significant – the Dizengoff Memorial Quilt[3] – to bring the stories of the victims of Dizengoff, Purim 1996, to life. She did so with the help of volunteers from the Accent Quilters Guild of Herzliya.

Conceptually, she decided to create thirteen individual quilts – one for each victim. Each quilt would tell the personal story of the victim's lives, achievements, hopes, and ambitions. "Each of these people had their own stories; they each left their own personal legacy, known mainly to their families and friends. I felt that the thirteen victims – out of the thousands who have perished at the hand of terrorism in Israel and abroad – could become powerful symbols and guiding lights as to how we can honor and cherish the memories of our loved ones." And finally, as a poignant symbol of the holiday, she included a piece created by Paul's wife Sharon – a Purim mask with tears of blood staining its cheek.

Marlyn knew that she "would need to gather personal information from each of the families in order to build up a narrative of each victim's life, to get to understand them as individuals, and to transform this information into a piece of fabric art." The family members came alive during these meetings as they started to remember things about their loved ones and brought out photographs and things they had made and were interested in. As Marlyn was doing the interviews and making the quilt, "everything started coming right for me. And I honestly and truly felt a healing. It was such an incredible feeling."

The quilt was a celebration of life and not a memorial. "The memorial

---

3   "The Dizengoff Memorial Quilt," http://www.geocities.com/dizquilt/.

ceremony at the Dizengoff Center in 2005, the first time that the quilt was presented in public, took on an entirely different nature: whereas before it had been a somber, painful ritual, the atmosphere changed to one of excitement and animated discussion. The quilts guided each of the families through the lives of their loved ones, as significant symbols and elements in the designs personifying each person were instantly recognized. There were exclamations and anecdotes: 'Remember when she did this....' 'Look at how he wrote that....' 'It's her poem....' 'That's the picture of his dog....' 'Here are the beads she loved....' This project has taught me how families coped with this tragedy and it has taught me that loving-kindness and good deeds are more powerful than hatred."

For Marlyn this was a personal achievement, as well as a journey of healing. "I felt an amazing uplifting of my spirit. I was actually taking control of the tragedy and saying: 'No, you will *not* control my life any longer; I choose to celebrate the lives of my loved ones and the lives of all those who were lost; I will *stop* the sadness and replace it with joy – joy in that I was privileged to know those who were close to me, that I learned so much from them, that I loved them and they loved me.' I have been enriched and empowered, and I felt an indescribable lightness, a relief, as if an enormous weight had been lifted from my soul and I was free to remember my mother and sister in the best of ways. I was inspired by the strength of the people I met, by their indomitable spirit and most of all, by the lack of bitterness, the absence of hatred, and the determination to move forward."

Unlike Paul, Marlyn shares her feelings very easily with people. For her, "the best thing is that I am able to speak about it." Together with her husband Larry, she has taken the quilt abroad to Jewish communities in the United States, United Kingdom, South Africa, and Australia and talks to them about victims of terror and what terrorism has done to families. At the same time, they demonstrate the power of the human spirit and the determination to keep alive the memories of terror victims in meaningful and creative ways.

The quilt serves to ground Marlyn – and her audience – "in the reality of where I was living – never once have I felt the need to run, to turn my back on my new homeland, or to escape from my personal history. *This* was my escape; this is what loosened the clutches of the tragedy on my heart. In fact, if anything, through engaging with the families, I felt strengthened in my commitment to my homeland and to the struggle for survival. I was now part of the struggle – and part of the amazing success story that is Israel – in ways that I could never have imagined." Whenever she speaks, it always ends on a positive note for Israel.

The quilt not only helped Marlyn, but also caused "hundreds of thousands of people to know about Dizengoff. I am absolutely certain that anybody who sees that quilt and hears me talk about it will never ever think of Dizengoff as a statistic. They will know the name of an incident that happened at the Dizengoff Center on *erev* Purim 1996; the quilt will tell the world about the victims and let everyone know that our lives were enhanced by their presence – however brief – among us. People may not remember all the names and all their details, but I know they will never forget that incident and I know they will always speak about it. And I also know that by doing what I have done, I've touched other people who have also had traumatic things happen to them and they have gone on to do something."

Marlyn's project has helped her entire family. Her oldest daughter Camilla documented Marlyn's story and the creation of the quilt in the film *Patches*. "My film is about memory, as opposed to being a memorial. In a lot of ways it is more about the people living than about those who died." Marlyn adds that it also is "just an angle of a kid who loved her granny." Marlyn's project also helped her husband Larry, who feels that "despite the fact that I've written the speeches and written the brochure and I've heard Marlyn talk maybe sixty times, every single time it gets to me, in a very positive way. I think it has helped the entire family. The whole family has moved forward. It's like a wound. It doesn't hurt any more, but the scar is always there. That scar will always be there as a reminder. It will always be felt, but without the anguish and the immediate pain, because it obviously dissipates over time."

The family continues to gather and remember. Larry sums it up: "It is now up to us to ensure that the third generation, our grandchildren, can have a real relationship with Sylvia and Gail – and we can do this by continually celebrating their lives: telling them stories, showing them photographs, telling them who they were, what they did, how they spoke, what they enjoyed doing, where they came from, and who they loved. We can help them get to know Sylvia and Gail as real people, people who would have loved them and been excited and intrigued by them, and would have played a very meaningful role in their young lives – and who, in this way, can still play a meaningful, positive role."

Sadly, on February 7, 2008, in a ghastly twist of fate, Paul and his wife Sharon lost their elder son Jason to the ravages of an appalling disease – streptococcus A toxic shock syndrome. Jason died after being in hospital for just five days; the same hospital where his baby daughter had been born three weeks earlier. "Once again, our family was immersed in sudden tragedy and had to try and pick up the pieces and carry on living. The pain for Sharon and I, and our second son Richard, has been crushing. Our granddaughter Mika Angie has become the light of our lives. Our daughter-in-law Leanne established a library in the children's wing of Meir Hospital in Jason's memory."

Conclusion

Making Sense of Their Lives and Moving Forward

Learning to Live with Life Crises

The stories in the previous chapters provide answers to some of the important questions raised earlier: How do Israeli survivors and families of survivors and victims live with the constant threat of terrorism and the social and economic disruption of their lives? How do they develop coping skills and adapt to their situation? What do these changes look like and how are they manifested? What accounts for the fact that so many of them did as well as they did? Was their recovery due to certain pre-trauma personality traits and inner resources and/or to their post-trauma environment – their families, their communities, and the organizations with which they had contact?

All of the people in this book have struggled with highly challenging life circumstances – the traumatic experiences of terror acts – either personally or through the lived experiences of a loved one. For some, these events are of seismic proportions – "my private holocaust" – a term not used lightly by those who are often related to survivors and victims of the Shoah (the Holocaust). Some may continue to suffer from physical and psychological distress due to their terrorism-related injuries and/or to the natural aging process for the rest of their lives. How they respond to the trauma and stressors ranges from those who experience little change (*stress resistance*), to those who survive with impairment (as in *posttraumatic stress*), to those who bounce back after experiencing hardship and adversity and move on with life as usual (as in *recovery* or *resilience*), to those who move forward, surpassing what was present before the event occurred (as in *posttraumatic growth*, *growth following adversity*, or *thriving*).

While most readers will never directly experience a terrorist attack, life crises are inevitable for almost everyone. In our struggles, we can learn from others how they have been able to continue life with new vitality, purpose, insights, and productivity. While there are some unique circumstances in the way these Israelis have responded to their challenges, there are valuable lessons to be learned from each of them – victims, survivors, and thrivers; those who have personally experienced terrorist attacks and those who are family members; those who were civilians and those who were soldiers; those who are Jews and those who are Muslims, Christians, or Druze – for how to deal with our own challenges.

The way that each person experiences such an event results from his or her own personal characteristics, past experiences, and present situation. Changes may be experienced in the physical, emotional, and/ or spiritual dimensions or in personal beliefs and social and societal values. No single factor or magical combination ensures a positive outcome, however certain qualities have been shown to enhance stress resilience and growth. Some may be internal factors, such as optimism, hope, self-confidence, hardiness, sense of coherence, flexibility, creativity, humor, acceptance, religious beliefs and spirituality, altruism, exercise, and the steeling effect of having weathered the storm of prior traumas.[1] Other enabling factors may be external, especially the support of friends, family, other traumatized people, and professionals, as well as the broader society and culture.

Lessons Learned: Collective Wisdom

The people in this book who have survived and thrived share some common qualities – ones that we may cultivate to master any crisis. The following vivid description of these qualities evolved from the in-depth narrative analysis of the interviews, questionnaires, and survey responses on which these stories are based.[2]

They struggle, confront, and ultimately integrate painful thoughts and emotions. As they struggle with highly challenging life circumstances, they confront their trauma-related thoughts, feelings,

---

1 Richard G. Tedeschi and Lawrence G. Calhoun, *Trauma and Transformation: Growing in the Aftermath of Suffering* (Thousand Oaks, CA: Sage Publications, 1995); Lawrence G. Calhoun and Richard G. Tedeschi, "Posttraumatic Growth: Future Directions," in Tedeschi, Park, and Calhoun, *Posttraumatic Growth: Positive Changes*, 215–238; Ronnie Janoff-Bulman, "Posttraumatic Growth: Three Explanatory Models," *Psychological Inquiry* 15, no. 1 (2004): 30; Steven M. Southwick, Meena Vythilingam, and Dennis S. Charney, "The Psychobiology of Depression and Resilience to Stress: Implications for Prevention and Treatment," *Annual Review of Clinical Psychology* 1 (2005): 255–291; and Calhoun and Tedeschi, "Foundations of Posttraumatic Growth," in Calhoun and Tedeschi, *Handbook of Posttraumatic Growth*, 3–23.

2 See Appendix A for an overview of the data analysis and findings.

and images, seeing all aspects of the trauma – negative and positive. While they do not forget their traumatic experiences nor minimize their suffering, they are able to integrate and own the painful emotions of their situation, make them part of their story, and live with them in a productive way. They have learned how to "live next to" and "move forward with" their feelings of grief, pain, and helplessness.

They adjust their future expectations to fit their new reality and focus on the important things in life. Although they may experience severe distress, including physical limitations, stress symptoms, and anxiety, at the same time they move forward in their lives, going beyond moving on with life as usual. They develop visions for the future, identify new possibilities, and actively seek solutions for dealing with challenges, rather than waiting passively for something to happen. In struggling to make sense of the event, they realize a greater appreciation of their existence in the world, along with a sense of reordered priorities. They manifest growth as warmer, more intimate relationships with others or with God; recognition of new possibilities for life; a greater sense of personal strength; spiritual and existential change; and a greater appreciation of what is really important and meaningful versus what is trivial.

They call on their inner strength, core beliefs, and values. They recognize the power or strength from within, as well as in the context of their external world. They take the time to reflect and go deeply into their selves and discover who they are and what is important and share these thoughts and feelings with others. They develop their own coping strategies to reconstruct their shattered assumptions and establish a comfortable, integrated world that incorporates the traumatic experience. While who they are does not change, they deepen and clarify their core values and beliefs. They are helped to move forward by their future visions and goals. By discovering their strengths, their self-perception improves, as well as their self-respect.

They stay in control and do not fall apart. Many demonstrate self-reliance. Staying in control during and immediately after an attack often contributed to saving their lives and the lives of others, even though they may have experienced serious injuries.

They are helped to move forward with strength gained from their past experiences and prior adversity. Although life crises, loss, and trauma are undesirable, successful past adaptation may have a steeling effect or provide psychological preparedness, which increases the likelihood of effectively meeting future challenges. While some attribute their changes to having experienced a trauma, others think these changes might be due, at least in part, to the natural process of maturation.

They are helped by spirituality or grappling with fundamental existential questions. Some may experience deeper faith; for others, religious or spiritual beliefs and practices have become more meaningful. Often individuals who face trauma are more likely to grapple with fundamental existential questions about death and the purpose of life; as a result they may experience life at a deeper level of awareness. They may ask themselves, *Why me? Why did I survive while others died?* or *Am I immune now that I have been in one attack?* Some conclude that *It was destiny* or that *God had a plan and was testing me*, while others find no answers.

They stay healthy and focus on their body image. Living well – a good diet and regular physical activity – provides crucial buffers against stress. Some focus on their body image as an attempt to control what they can and normalize their lives, helping them organize their thoughts about their experiences and cope with stress. As a result, they develop a stable sense of self-worth and enhanced self-esteem, which are related to well-being and greater stress resistance.

They are creative, find the silver lining and give back, moving forward with action. Many survivors find meaning by their deeds, experiences, and the attitudes they take towards unavoidable suffering, acknowledging the human potential to grow. They may find meaning by creating a work or by doing a deed. Some construct meaning through self-transcendence or altruism. They see negative events as an opportunity to help others, contributing to society and turning tragedy into action or activism. In the wake of grief, many bereaved family members also create meaning through altruism; others create memorials to meaningfully recognize and honor their loved ones. Out of their disappointment in others who do not know how to react to their bereavement, they create opportunities to educate and raise awareness. Through these acts of healing others, they heal their own hearts and souls, and leave a legacy for future generations.

They stay connected and seek outside resources to help them survive rough times. Recovery can be enhanced by the availability of psychosocial, social, and material resources to the individual both during and after the event – sometimes not accessed until many years later. Often, most helpful are other people *who have been there* and *just understand it*, legitimating painful experiences and feelings.

They tell their stories and make sense of their lives. Storytelling helps everyone gain perspective on their life and redefine their identity, while their narratives help them rebuild coherence. Over time, their narratives become more consistent and coherent, reflecting a great degree of processing of their thoughts and feelings. Recovery is supported by disclosing their personal narratives to interested and supportive listeners – including family, friends, other traumatized people, professionals, and general audiences. Expressing feelings and concerns and receiving supportive suggestions facilitate coping.

They are hopeful, optimistic, and celebrate life. The tone of their narratives goes beyond acceptance and appreciation of life; hope and optimism replace despair. People who have a sunny outlook do better at managing crises. They frequently use expressions like *positive*, *I can do it*, *I will do it*, and *a glass half-full* and feel their survival is *fortunate*, *good luck*, or *a miracle*; they understand the healing power of laughter and a smile. They celebrate life and the important events in their lives, especially the anniversary of the attacks. Remarkably, many report feeling little or no resentment or hatred toward their attackers.

They discover who they are. In the process of healing, they come to understand and change their self-identity; they identify themselves as survivors and are not defined by victimization or by survivor's guilt. In the face of overwhelming disaster, these otherwise ordinary people call forth courage they never knew they possessed; find meaning from their deeds, experiences, and attitudes; and turn tragedy into triumph, allowing growth and wellness to thrive. They become survivors! And they discover for themselves that the meaning does not lie in the disaster, but in the way they respond to the disaster!

As we reflect on these qualities, we can think about how they may enhance or detract from our own ability to experience positive psychological changes or even to grow and thrive as we struggle with life's challenges. Each of us may draw our own conclusions and think about how we might be inspired to find new meaning in the way we respond. Perhaps we too may find the strength to be able to use the trauma itself to advance our own healing process and find new enrichment by focusing on the important things in life, by staying healthy and fit, by the attitudes and actions we take, by obtaining and fostering resources that help buffer the effects of stress, by seeking out others who have been there and understand, and by sharing our own trauma stories and experiences with sensitive and empathic listeners in a safe, respectful, and supportive environment.

Roberta Bernstein, an Israeli social worker, expressed it to me so beautifully: "There is so much destruction and devastation and yet if one begins to look, there are people out there who somehow find the strength to move onwards despite the ongoing deep pain in their hearts. These people do rebuild their lives in new ways that they had never known before."

Appendix A: Research Methodology and Findings

Some of the stories that make up this book are part of a research study that was both interpretive and empirical, with qualitative data in the form of narratives or stories and quantitative data collection in the form of survey results. The methodology and findings are summarized below and fully documented in my doctoral dissertation[1] and related journal article.[2]

Participants

The participants were recruited by word of mouth and via paper postings, newspaper ads, and trauma newsletters and websites. A few who were contacted decided not to participate because it might bring back unwanted memories that they did not wish to confront.

The study sample included twenty-four Israelis, ages twenty-two to sixty-three, who personally survived suicide bombings and other attacks on civilians between 2001 and 2003. Twenty-three of the participants were Jewish and one was a non-Jew who had lived in Israel for fifteen years and "feels more than Jewish." The interviews were conducted in 2004, eleven to forty-four months after the attacks. The seven shooting incidents took place in or on the road to West Bank communities; the suicide bombings were in urban areas. Nineteen participants were personally injured in the attack; three lost a family member; and three were with relatives who were injured.

---

1 Zieva L. Konvisser, "Finding Meaning and Growth in the Aftermath of Suffering: Israeli Civilian Survivors of Suicide Bombings and Other Attacks" (PhD dissertation, Fielding Graduate University, 2006, ProQuest/UMI Dissertations/Theses, publication number 3234197).

2 Zieva Dauber Konvisser, "Themes of Resilience and Growth in Survivors of Politically Motivated Violence," *Traumatology* 19, no. 4 (2013): 292-302, doi:10.1177/1534765613477500.

These individuals were interviewed again in 2007 to engage them in an ongoing and widening conversation, to probe for changes in levels of functioning – positive and negative – and for factors facilitating sustained or continued positive growth, and to learn the impact of the 2006 Israel-Hezbollah/Lebanon War.

Data Collection

Qualitative data were elicited via an in-depth interview protocol to obtain "the rich descriptive detail and deep understanding of the individuals who have faced major life crises."[3] Interviews were conducted in English and/or Hebrew.

Quantitative data was collected in the form of survey results: (a) Pre-Interview Questionnaires to understand participant demographics; (b) the twenty-one-item Posttraumatic Growth Inventory (PTGI)[4] to assess changes in functioning over time in five domains of growth: relating to others, new possibilities, personal strength, spiritual change, and appreciation of life; and (c) the twenty-one-item Posttraumatic Stress Disorder Symptom Scale self-report survey (PSS)[5] to assess changes in posttraumatic stress disorder symptoms: reexperiencing, avoidance, and hyperarousal. All questionnaires were provided in English and Hebrew.

Data Analysis

Interview data was analyzed using a narrative analysis approach to identify common factors, themes, and concepts and to discover how survivors found meaning in and grew as a result of the traumatic events they experienced. Quantitative data was analyzed using the SPSS software package to perform: (a) correlations and relationships among variables; (b) sequencing and grouping of PTGI scores; (c) hierarchical cluster analysis; and (d) principal components analysis.

---

3   Calhoun and Tedeschi, "Foundations of Posttraumatic Growth," 16.
4   Tedeschi and Calhoun, *Trauma and Transformation*, 139–141.
5   Edna B. Foa et al., "Reliability and validity of a brief instrument for assessing post-traumatic stress disorder," *Journal of Traumatic Stress* 6, no. 4 (1993): 459–474.

Results

The data analysis and findings are illuminated by the literature on posttraumatic growth, which provided the theoretical lens through which to examine the data. While quantitatively almost all participants reported positive growth, clearly there were varying degrees or gradations to which they reported having experienced growth. Almost all reported some concomitant distress as well.

Similarly, in the qualitative data, many of the concepts from the literature were manifested in some or many of the narratives. The manner in which each individual experienced the event, the meaning which each ascribed to the event, and the actions each has taken resulted from his or her personal characteristics, past experiences, present context, and physiological state.

Thus, although all of the participants in this study have struggled with the highly challenging and traumatic experience of a terror act against civilians – and manifest many of the characteristics of growth – only a subset of these people can be described as having experienced *posttraumatic growth*. The responses of the remaining study participants were characterized into three other groups: (a) those reporting little or no growth, continuing to perform at the same high levels as before the attack; (b) those who are still struggling with and *living the attack*; and (c) those who returned to the pre-adversity level of functioning and are moving on with life as usual (*resilience*). Two groups were treated as exceptions – survivors who suffered from brain injuries and those who lost other family members in the same attack. While they report varying degrees of growth, their pattern or process of growth may be different, requiring a more comprehensive understanding of the literatures and therapeutic practices in the fields of traumatic brain injury, grief, and bereavement.

Twelve themes emerged from the individual narrative voices of those who are characterized by posttraumatic growth or resilience. These themes and a composite vivid description of each are presented in the conclusion to this book.

Furthermore, the findings provide deeper insights into various aspects of posttraumatic growth: the distinctions between posttraumatic growth and resilience, in particular the primacy of the domains of new possibilities and personal strength; the focus on action growth or moving forward and finding meaning through self-transcendence or altruism, going beyond moving on with life as usual; the critical role that the integration of cognition and affect – thoughts and feelings – plays in the development of posttraumatic growth as demonstrated by intellectual and emotional awareness; and the therapeutic and healing value of telling one's story to an interested and empathic listener.

Longitudinal Study

For the follow-up study, in addition to qualitative interviews, the previously administered self-report questionnaire, the Posttraumatic Growth Inventory (PTGI), and the Posttraumatic Stress Disorder Symptom Scale self-report survey (PSS) were readministered.

The approach to analysis included the following: (a) qualitative narrative case analysis; (b) quantitative data analysis of PTGI and PSS survey scores and demographics, using SPSS and a repeated measures design; and (c) regression analysis of 2004 and 2007 PTGI and PSS scores.

The quantitative and qualitative analyses both continued to reflect the same patterns as in 2004, with some moderation at the extremes over time.

Appendix B: Chronology of Major Events

May 14, 1948: Proclamation of the State of Israel

November 29, 1947–July 20, 1949: 1948 Arab-Israeli War

known by Jewish Israelis as the War of Independence and by Arabs as the Nakba (The Catastrophe)

After the Arab rejection of the 1947 United Nations Partition Plan for Palestine (UN General Assembly Resolution 181) – which would have created an Arab state and a Jewish state in what had been British Mandatory Palestine – irregular forces increased attacks to prevent the establishment of Israel. When Israel declared independence the armies of five Arab nations (Egypt, Iraq, Jordan, Lebanon, and Syria) joined the attack. Israel survived but the Arab state within Palestine was never created, with Jordan annexing the West Bank and Egypt occupying the Gaza Strip. Hundreds of thousands of Arabs became refugees. An armistice agreement ended this phase of what would become the ongoing Arab-Israeli conflict.[1]

1967 Six-Day War/an-Naksa (The Setback)

Almost two decades of continuous unrest, including thousands of terrorist attacks against Israel and brutal reprisals, occurred before Egypt closed the Straits of Tiran to Israeli shipping, ordered United Nations peacekeepers out of the Sinai Peninsula, and massed troops against Israel. An Israeli preemptive strike against Egypt and Syria (which had placed their militaries under joint command) led to the Israeli capture of the Sinai and Gaza Strip from Egypt and the Golan Heights from Syria. Jordan attacked Israel and consequently lost the West Bank, including the Arab section of Jerusalem containing the holiest Jewish sites – the

---

1   "1948 Arab-Israeli War," http://en.wikipedia.org/wiki/1948_Arab%E2%80%93 Israeli_War.

Western (Wailing) Wall and Temple Mount.[2] The Arab defeat was seen as a humiliation and termed the an-Naksa. In its wake, hundreds of thousands of Arabs found themselves under Israeli military rule and tens of thousands became refugees.[3]

1967–1970 War of Attrition
Low-level warfare continued between Egypt and Israel with frequent border skirmishes, bombings, and incursions; it ended with the death of Egyptian president Nasser.

October 1973 Yom Kippur War/Ramadan War
A surprise attack against Israel on the holiest day of the Jewish year saw early Egyptian and Syrian gains which were repelled by Israel after suffering heavy casualties.

1979 Israel-Egypt Peace Treaty
Following secret Egyptian-Israeli negotiations, Egyptian President Anwar Sadat called for peace and traveled to Israel. After two years of talks with American involvement a peace treaty was signed. Egypt regained the Sinai Peninsula but it took years for Arab nations to restore diplomatic relations with Egypt.

June 6–August 23, 1982: First Lebanon War
A Palestinian "state within a state" in Lebanon helped precipitate a Lebanese Civil War in the mid-1970s and cross-border terrorist attacks brought on an Israeli occupation of southern Lebanon that lasted from 1978 to 2000.[4]

---

2 Netanel Lorch, "The Arab-Israeli Wars," http://www.mfa.gov.il/MFA /AboutIsrael/History/Pages/The%20Arab-Israeli%20Wars.aspx.

3 Ahmad Baker and Nadera Shalhoub-Kevorkian, "Effects of Political and Military Traumas on Children: The Palestinian Case," *Clinical Psychology Review* 19 no. 8 (1999): 937.

4 "1982 Lebanon War," http://en.wikipedia.org/wiki/1982_Lebanon_War (accessed May 13, 2010).

December 8, 1987: Start of the First Intifada (Palestinian Uprising)

The First Intifada (1987–1993) was a mass Palestinian uprising against Israeli rule in the Palestinian territories; Palestinian actions escalated from civil disobedience and stonings to murder. An estimated thirteen hundred Palestinians were killed (both in fighting with Israelis and in interfactional fighting) and 160 Israelis were killed.[5]

September 13, 1993: Signing of the Oslo Declaration of Principles (DOP) between Israel and the Palestine Liberation Organization (PLO)

The First Intifada was dying down by the time Israel and the PLO signed the DOP on the White House lawn. While not a peace treaty, both Israel and the PLO officially recognized each other and committed themselves to a peaceful resolution of their disagreements via direct negotiations. Not all segments of Israeli and Palestinian society, or the Arab world, were accepting of the accord.[6] Despite the Palestinian commitment to renounce terrorism, terrorist attacks continued, killing another 269 civilians and soldiers until September 2000.[7] This book addresses one attack that occurred during this time:

- March 4, 1996: Suicide bombing outside Dizengoff Center, Tel Aviv (Sylvia Bernstein and Gail Belkin, mother and sister of Paul Bernstein and Marlyn Bernstein Butchins)

September 27, 2000: Start of the Second Intifada/al-Aqsa Intifada

The Second Intifada was instigated and directed by the Palestinian

---

5   "First Intifada," http://en.wikipedia.org/wiki/First_Intifada (accessed April 27, 2009).

6   Ephraim Yaar, "The Historical Roots of the Middle-East Conflict," Arik Institute, http://www.arikpeace.org/post.php?id=48.

7   Israel Ministry of Foreign Affairs, "Fatal Terrorist Attacks in Israel since the Declaration of Principles," http://mfa.gov.il/mfa/foreignpolicy/terrorism /palestinian/pages/fatal%20terrorist%20attacks%20in%20israel%20since%20 the%20DOP%20-S.aspx.

Authority (PA) after the failure of the Middle East Peace Summit at Camp David, convened by United States President Clinton. Israel experienced politically motivated violence on an almost unprecedented scale. Its citizens lived in fear of being blown up by suicide bombers or shot to death by Palestinian gunmen. Rejectionists like the PLO's al-Aqsa Martyrs Brigade, the Islamist Hamas, and the secular Popular Front for the Liberation of Palestine (PFLP) opposed negotiations and urged a return to "armed struggle" to eliminate Israel. Others simply wanted to improve the PA's bargaining position by wearing down Israeli resistance and attracting greater Arab and international support for Palestinian demands.[8] Between September 2000 and October 2013, 1,236 people were killed by Palestinian violence and terrorism[9] and many thousands more were maimed or psychologically scarred for life. In addition 5,181 Palestinians were killed and 33,117 were injured in the West Bank and Gaza between September 30, 2000, and August 31, 2008.[10]

Attacks that occurred during this period include:

- February 27, 2001: Shooting attack on the road from Atarot Industrial Park (Shoshana Gottlieb)
- March 18, 2001: Drive-by shooting on the Efrat-Jerusalem Road (Baruch Cohen, father of Avihu Cohen)
- April 12, 2001: Shooting attack, Efrat-Jerusalem roadblock (Jacki Glassman)

---

8   Shaul Shay and Yoram Schweitzer, "The Al-Aqsa Intifada: Palestinian-Israeli Confrontation," Institute for Counter-Terrorism, April 4, 2001, http://www.ict .org.il/Articles/tabid/66/Articlsid/60/currentpage/36/Default.aspx.

9   Israel Ministry of Foreign Affairs, "Victims of Palestinian Violence and Terrorism since September 2000," http://www.mfa.gov.il/mfa/foreignpolicy/terrorism /palestinian/pages/victims%20of%20palestinian%20violence%20and%20 terrorism%20sinc.aspx. This figure includes eighteen Israelis killed abroad in terror attacks directed specifically against Israeli targets, as well as three American diplomatic personnel killed in Gaza. It does not include the nine IDF soldiers killed during the ground operation against Hamas terror in Gaza (Dec. 27, 2008–Jan. 18, 2009).

10 Palestine Red Crescent Society, "Total Numbers of Deaths & Injuries - West Bank & Gaza," http://www.palestinercs.org/en/reports.php?page=16.

- May 8, 2001: Stoning, Tekoa (Koby Mandell, son of Sherri and Seth Mandell, and Yosef Ish Ran, friend of Koby Mandell)
- May 13, 2001: Shooting attack on the road from Petach Tikvah to Karnei Shomron (RH)
- June 21, 2001: Suicide bombing, army patrol, Gaza (Ofir Kit, son of Dina and Omer Kit)
- August 9, 2001: Sbarro Pizzeria bombing, downtown Jerusalem (Peggy and Gail Kern; Malki Roth, daughter of Arnold Roth)
- August 27, 2001: Shooting attack, Elah Valley, on the road from Efrat to Jerusalem (BD)
- October 3, 2001: Shooting attack at a concert in Hebron (Feige Fishman Glasomitsky)
- January 27, 2002: Suicide bombing, Jaffa Road, Jerusalem (Sonia Dibeh)
- March 27, 2002: Park Hotel (Passover Massacre) bombing, Netanya (Amiram Hamami, husband of Corinne Hamami)
- March 31, 2002: Matza Restaurant bombing, near Grand Canyon Mall, Haifa (Bat-sheva Schaul)
- May 19, 2002: Suicide bombing, Netanya market (Andalau Elad Wassa)
- June 5, 2002: Egged bus no. 830 bombing, Megiddo Junction near Afula (Avraham Robinson)
- June 11, 2002: Jamil Shawarma Restaurant bombing, downtown Herzliya (Isaac and Jonathan Ashkenazy)
- June 18, 2002: Egged bus no. 32 bombing, Patt Junction, outside Gilo, Jerusalem (Ronit Elchayani; Ronit Tubul)
- July 31, 2002: Suicide bombing, Hebrew University cafeteria, Mount Scopus campus, Jerusalem (Dror Sullaper; Ariela; Roza)
- August 4, 2002: Egged bus no. 361 bombing, Meron Junction (Maysoun and Jihan Hassan, daughters of Amin and Farida and sisters of Ghoussoun Hassan)
- August 10, 2002: Moshav Mechora shooting, Jordan Valley (Yafit Harenstein, wife of Arnaud Harenstein and daughter of Iris Yihichya)
- September 30, 2002: Military operation, Nablus (Ari Weiss, son of Susie Weiss)

- October 10, 2002: Dan bus no. 87 bombing, across from Bar-Ilan University, Ramat Gan (Aharon)
- December 27, 2002: Shooting attack, Otniel Yeshiva (Gavriel Hoter, son of Elaine Hoter)
- March 5, 2003: Egged bus no. 37 bombing, Moriah Boulevard, Haifa (Sharon Stav, Ismini Soyvadzogloy, and Molly Shwisha)
- April 15, 2003: Military operation, Nablus (Daniel Mandel, son of Cheryl Mandel)
- April, 30, 2003: Mike's Place bombing, Tel Aviv promenade (Joshua and Arlene Faudem)
- May 19, 2003: Suicide bombing, Amakim Shopping Mall, Afula (SY)
- June 8, 2003: Shooting attack, army base, Gaza (Ken Sachs)
- June 11, 2003: Egged bus no. 14 bombing, downtown Jerusalem (Sarri Singer)
- August 19, 2003: Egged bus no. 2 (the Children's Bus) bombing, Jerusalem (Ora Cohen; Tehilla Nathansen, daughter of Chana Nathansen)
- September 9, 2003: Café Hillel bombing, German Colony, Jerusalem (Shai Ben Tzur)
- October 4, 2003: Maxim Restaurant bombing, Haifa seashore (Nir Regev, friend of Ola Korol; Gil Carmely)

July 12–August 14, 2006: Israel-Hezbollah/Lebanon War

The Israel-Hezbollah/Lebanon War began on July 12 with the killing of eight Israeli soldiers and the kidnapping and subsequent killing of two Israeli soldiers on the border with Lebanon, and concluded on August 14 with a United Nations brokered cease-fire. Hezbollah fired hundreds of rockets a day – over four thousand in total – against Israeli civilian targets including homes, hospitals, and infrastructure. Approximately one-third of Israel's population – about two million people – were within striking range. Thousands of civilians required medical attention for injuries and shock, an estimated four to five hundred thousand civilians fled south out of rocket range, and about one million people were confined to bomb shelters. Forty-four Israeli civilians and 121 IDF soldiers were killed.[11] Lebanon suffered a significantly higher death toll and infrastructure damage due to Israeli attacks against Hezbollah fighters and rockets located in civilian areas.

Attacks during this period include:

- July 17, 2006: Rocket attack, Leon Blum Street, Haifa (Sharon Stav)
- August 6, 2006: Rocket attack, Wadi Nisnas, Haifa (Nabila, Mounir, and Fahima Khouri)

The Israel-Hezbollah/Lebanon War took a heavy toll on the Arab community in Israel which comprises 1.658 million people, about 20.7 percent of the Israeli population.[12] Eighteen Israeli Arabs from ten cities and villages were killed by rockets during the shelling of northern Israel – a full 46 percent of Israel's total civilian casualties.[13] While victimized by the indiscriminate Hezbollah rockets, many also had friends and family in Lebanon under Israeli attack.[14] Today about four hundred thousand Palestinian refugees and their descendants live in Lebanon.

December 27, 2008: Operation Cast Lead
November 14–21, 2012: Operation Pillar of Defense

In response to escalating attacks by Hamas and other terrorist organizations, making normal life impossible for over one million Israelis, surgical strikes were conducted against the Hamas terrorist infrastructure in Gaza. Preceding these operations, over sixty-one hundred rockets hit Israel since the Hamas takeover of Gaza in 2006.[15]

Violence, including stonings, shootings, bombings, and rocket attacks, continue to terrorize, injure, and kill innocent civilians and soldiers.

---

11 Israel Ministry of Foreign Affairs. "Behind the Headlines: The Second Lebanon War - Three Years Later," http://mfa.gov.il/mfa/foreignpolicy/terrorism/hizbullah/pages/the-second-lebanon-war-three-years-later-12-jul-2009.aspx.

12 Israel's Central Bureau of Statistics, April 14, 2013, http://www1.cbs.gov.il/reader/?MIval=cw_usr_view_SHTML&ID=705.

13 Mossawa Center, "The Arab Citizens of Israel and the 2006 War in Lebanon: Reflections and Realities," (Haifa: Mossawa Center – The Advocacy Center for Arab Citizens in Israel, 2006), 7.

14 Ibid., 6, 12.

15 Israel Ministry of Foreign affairs, "Operation Pillar of Defense – Selected Statements," http://mfa.gov.il/mfa/pressroom/2012/pages/operation_pillar_of_defense-statements.aspx.

Appendix C: Organizations Supporting Terror Survivors and Families

The following is a selected list of organizations in Israel and abroad – professional, governmental, and voluntary – as well as medical centers – that provided loving care, services, and support to the terrorism survivors and families in this book and/or supported the author in her research efforts. Additional information is available at the organizations' websites.[1]

Professional Organizations

Amcha: The National Israeli Center for Psychosocial Support of Survivors of the Holocaust and the Second Generation (Jerusalem and thirteen centers throughout Israel; http://www.amcha.org/indexEn .htm):

Focuses on nonmaterial, psychosocial, and largely preventive support for Holocaust survivors; provides a framework for mutual aid, memory processing, and grief resolution, as well as a place where survivors and their families feel at home and are understood; and offers support groups, phone help, professional aid, and home visits to those who cannot come to the center.

Center for the Treatment of Traumatic Stress and Anxiety Disorders, Department of Psychiatry, Hadassah University Hospital– Ein Kerem (Jerusalem, Israel; http://www.hadassah-med.com/medical -care/departments/psychiatry/units/research-units/center-for-traumatic -stress-and-anxiety-disorders.aspx):

A specialty treatment center for anxiety disorders, offering diagnosis and focused treatment plans for trauma victims using cognitive-behavior therapy, as well as pharmacological options.

---

1   These websites were active as of June 9, 2013, and are subject to change.

CHERISH: Child Rehabilitation Initiative for Safety and Hope (Ramallah, Palestinian National Authority):

Conceived to ease the present realities of Israeli and Palestinian children by helping them regain their confidence, their ability to function in daily life, and their hope for the future; focuses on psychological and social rehabilitation; and addresses the professional community as well as children and their families.

Child and Adolescent Psychiatry Unit, Hadassah Medical Organization (Jerusalem, Israel; http://www.hadassah-med.com/medical-care /departments/psychiatry/units/child-and-adolescent-psychiatry.aspx):

Offers immediate psychological and psychiatric treatment and follow-ups during the recovery process to children under eighteen years old who experienced trauma, as well as community outreach to educate and train doctors, teachers, and social workers to identify children and adolescents with PTSD; conducts research on the impact of terrorism on children and adolescents to ensure the most effective treatment.

Enosh: The Israeli Nonprofit Mental Health Association (Ramat Hasharon and fifty-five centers around Israel; http://www.enosh.org.il /Index.asp?CategoryID=360):

Promotes mental health issues for individuals dealing with a psychiatric disability and their families; provides rehabilitation services and support during the recovery process; helps improve functioning skills in order to live as independently as possible in the community; and fights stigma.

ERAN: Emotional First Aid Telephone and Internet Hotline (ten centers throughout Israel and an internet service; http://www.eran.org.il/):

Operates an anonymous and confidential twenty-four-hours-a-day service, providing unconditional, nonjudgmental, and unrestricted emotional support for all, regardless of gender, age, nationality, religion, or race; staffed by over a thousand volunteers, speaking Hebrew, English, Russian, Amharic, and Arabic.

Israel Center for Treatment of Psychotrauma (ICTP), Herzog Hospital Latner Institute (Jerusalem, Israel; http://www.traumaweb .org/):

Provides training for mental health professionals to meet the diverse needs of trauma survivors; develops programs using advanced methods for treating posttraumatic symptoms and reinforcing natural coping mechanisms; provides integrated treatment and recovery programs through the Metiv Trauma and Crisis Treatment Center to help survivors develop vital coping mechanisms to deal with the emotional and psychological fallout of trauma; and develops and implements resilience-building programs in schools and for first responders in the Israeli police, firefighters, and Magen David Adom.

Israel Community Stress Prevention Center (ICSPC) (Kiryat Shmona, Israel; http://www.icspc.org/):

Founded in Kiryat Shmona to support the population of Israel's northern border by addressing the consequences of prolonged exposure to terror; expanded to provide psychotrauma treatment and clinical services, disaster management and training, cross-cultural work, and multidisciplinary resilience research.

Israel Trauma Care (Safed, Israel; http://www.israeltraumacare.org/):

Develops and provides physiologically based trauma-relief techniques for both emergency relief and improved quality of life for the Israeli general public, including abuse, war, and terror victims; trains individuals and groups to use their trauma-relief tools for themselves and others to restore inner calm, stability, and a sense of safety.

Magen David Adom (lit., red Star of David; http://www.mdais.com/):

Israel's national first-aid and disaster-relief organization.

Mahut Center for Preparedness and Coping with Emergency and Crisis (Shomron, Israel):

Works with families and communities uprooted from Gush Katif, and those threatened and injured by terror attacks in Judea and Samaria.

Maytal: Israel Institute for Treatment and Study of Stress (Haifa, Israel):

Outpatient mental health clinic serving individuals suffering from psychological stress ranging from performance anxieties to occupational stress and deep emotional trauma (such as those caused by war, terror, violence, or sexual abuse).

Nord COPE Center (Tivon, Israel):

Works with mental health workers in traumatized communities and trains professionals in the use of therapeutic associative cards to promote communication and creativity.

Palestine Red Crescent Society (http://www.palestinercs.org/):

National humanitarian organization, catering to the health and welfare of the Palestinian people and others in need in the West Bank and Gaza Strip and the Diaspora; provides humanitarian, health, cultural, and social services when and where needed.

Post-Traumatic Stress Disorder Clinic, Schneider Children's Medical Center of Israel (Petach Tikvah, Israel; http://www.schneider.org.il /Eng/):

Offers focused treatment for children and teenagers suffering from anxiety following a traumatic event.

Governmental and Related Organizations

Amuta: The Non-Profit Organization for Emotional Support of Girlfriends (Fiancées) of Fallen Soldiers of the Israel Defense Forces (Kiron, Israel; http://www.girlfriendsidf.org.il/eng/eng.htm):

Offers support groups to help girlfriends or boyfriends of IDF soldiers who were killed during their service to cope with the terrible tragedy that has befallen them and helps them rehabilitate themselves.

Beit Halochem Centers of the Zahal Disabled Veterans Organization (Tel Aviv, Haifa, Jerusalem, Nahariya, and Beer Sheva, Israel; http:// www.zdvo.org):

Fosters the full reintegration of disabled veterans into society by establishing sports and rehabilitation centers and by offering a comprehensive range of services to its members to improve their quality of life and to safeguard their legal rights and promote their interests through legislation or economic and social measures.

Bituach Leumi: The National Insurance Institute of Israel (http://www.btl.gov.il/English%20Homepage/About/Pages/default.aspx):

Responsible for social security in Israel; guarantees a financial basis for existence for families and individuals in need, including victims of hostilities and their families who are entitled by law to monetary remuneration and various benefits that are designed to assist and support them in their recovery.

FIDF: Friends of the Israel Defense Forces (http://www.fidf.org/):

Initiates and helps support social, educational, cultural, and recreational programs and facilities for the young men and women soldiers of Israel who defend the Jewish homeland; provides support for the families of fallen soldiers.

Ministry of Defense, Rehabilitation Division (http://www.mod.gov .il/); **Ministry of Health, Mental Health Services** (http://www.health .gov.il/); and **Ministry of Social Affairs** (http://www.molsa.gov.il /MisradHarevacha):

Provide rehabilitation, mental health, and social services for trauma victims through their own branches and agencies throughout the country, as well as through local authorities, public institutions, and volunteers.

Shekel Community Services for People with Disabilities (Jerusalem, Israel; http://www.shekel.org.il/):

Provides community services for Jerusalem children and adults with special needs to enable people with disabilities to enjoy a better quality of life and integrate naturally into the community.

Terror Victims Association (Tel Aviv, Israel; http://www.irgun.org.il/):

Since 1947, provides information and activities for bereaved families, orphans, and handicapped people who received recognition from the country as terror victims.

UNRWA: The United Nations Relief and Works Agency for Palestine Refugees in the Near East (http://www.unrwa.org/):

Provides basic services (education, health, relief, and social services), protection, and advocacy for some five million registered Palestine refugees in Jordan, Lebanon, Syria, and the occupied Palestinian territory, pending a solution to their plight.

Voluntary Organizations

All4Israel (Staten Island, New York, USA; https://www.all4israel .org/):

Provides emergency funds for the immediate and long-term needs of Israeli terror victims that the government agencies do not provide; assists victims through the bureaucratic process of qualifying for and maximizing government assistance; helps victims get top medical care and legal assistance at the best prices; and helps unemployed victims of terror and their families find good jobs.

Almagor Terror Victims Association (Jerusalem, Israel; http://www .al-magor.com/):

Founded in 1986 and largely supported by victims of terrorist attacks and their families so that people whose lives have been damaged by terror can heal through the mutual support of others who know their pain; organizes and represents terror victims, ensures welfare services for terror victims and their families, disseminates information about terrorism and its victims, conducts research about terrorist organizations and the anti-Zionist movement, and memorializes terror victims.

Atzum: Justice Works (Jerusalem, Israel; http://atzum.org/):

Helps families who have suffered significant trauma and serious economic difficulties following death or injury in terrorist attacks to regain stability, particularly those whose major wage earner has been incapacitated; provides educational resources and quality dental care that are the stepping-stones to their and their children's recovery and secure future.

CAF: The Challenged Athletes Foundation (San Diego, CA, USA; http://www.challengedathletes.org/):

Provides opportunities and support to people with physical disabilities so they can pursue active lifestyles through physical fitness and competitive athletics, believing that involvement in sports at any level increases self-esteem, encourages independence, and enhances quality of life.

Caritas Jerusalem (Jerusalem, Israel; http://www.caritasjr.org/):

Represents the socio-pastoral services of the Catholic Church in the Holy Land; and serves the social-familial, economic, health, and emergency needs of individuals from all religious backgrounds in the occupied Palestinian territories.

Chabad Terror Victims Project: Together, We're Rebuilding Shattered Lives (Kfar Chabad and 280 Chabad Houses throughout Israel; http://www.ctvp.org/):

Aids and assists in all ways possible – financial, practical, spiritual, and emotional – victims of terror and war in Israel and their families to help them reclaim and rebuild their lives successfully.

Elem: Youth in Distress in Israel (Bnei Brak, Israel; http://www.elem .org/index.php):

Helps at-risk youth become productive citizens with a variety of innovative and relevant programs targeted toward different population groups.

Ezer Mizion: The Israel Health Support Organization
(http://www.ezermizion.org/):

Offers an extensive range of medical and social support services to help Israel's sick, disabled, elderly, and underprivileged populations; provides specialized programs for children with special needs, cancer patients, the elderly, and terror victims.

Guardians of Israel: The International Fellowship of Christians and Jews (Chicago, Illinois, USA; http://www.ifcj.org/site/PageNavigator /eng/programs/guardians_of_israel):

Provides food, clothing, shelter, housing and other urgent needs for all Israelis, including children and the elderly, who are suffering due to poverty, terrorism, and war.

Hineni Jerusalem (Here I Am; Jerusalem, Israel; http://hinenijerusalem .org/en/):

Provides recovery programs and therapies for survivors of terror at the Hineni Center in Jerusalem and takes groups of survivors on trips abroad to help them deal with their fears and strengthen their sense of safety, through support and compassion.

Israel Trauma Coalition (Jerusalem, Israel; www.israeltraumacoalition .org/):

Leverages diverse resources to initiate, prioritize, and optimize trauma services, while working towards strengthening community resilience and ensuring national emergency preparedness; harnesses the collective knowledge, expertise, and experience of Israel's leading NGO's and government organizations to deliver a continuum of trauma services in a timely fashion.

Jewish Agency for Israel – Fund for the Victims of Terror (Jerusalem, Israel; http://www.jafi.org.il/JewishAgency/English/Making+History /Terror-Fund/):

Provides Israel's victims of terror with direct financial assistance, complementing the monetary relief they receive from government agencies and offices. The support provided by the fund is designed to improve the quality of life for the victims and their families in order to ease their recovery and rehabilitation.

Keren Malki – Malki Foundation (Jerusalem, Israel; http://www .kerenmalki.org/):

Founded as a living memorial to fifteen-year-old terrorism-victim Malka Chana Roth; empowers families of special-needs children in Israel to choose home care; provides long-term lending of essential home-care equipment, grants funds to subsidize the cost of paramedical therapeutic care, and provides home-based therapies.

Kids for Kids (Jerusalem, Israel; http://www.kidsforkids.net/):

Encourages active participation and help of overseas children in doing tangible acts of kindness for Israeli children affected by terrorism; fosters tangible supportive activities and humane services for children who have been left orphaned, maimed, and traumatized.

Koby Mandell Foundation (Efrat, Israel; http://kobymandell.org/):

Founded in memory of thirteen-year-old terrorism-victim Koby Mandell; initiates programs that bridge the isolation that bereaved children and adults experience after the loss of a loved one; and provides emotional, physical, and spiritual healing to engender a support network for grieving families.

Camp Koby (Israel; http://www.kobymandell.org/story/13463787 /camp-koby):

As a Koby Mandell Foundation program, Camp Koby provides youths and teens of families struck by terror with a place where others understand; surrounded by their peers, specially trained counselors, and professional therapists, children naturally share their stories and express their feelings; includes follow-up reunions during the year and an ongoing Big Sister/Big Brother program.

L'hamshich Lichyot B'yachad: Together We Will Continue Our Lives (Jerusalem, Israel; http://www.terrorvictims.org.il/?lang=en):

Founded by families of terror victims to help other families who have lost a close relative in a terror attack.

Midreshet Gavriel: Center for the Development of *Midot* (Personal Character Traits and Behavior) (Alonei Habashan, Israel; http://web.macam.ac.il/~elaine/gavri/midrasha.htm):

Founded in memory of seventeen-year-old terrorism-victim Gavriel Hoter; encourages young people to follow in his footsteps by adopting one of the outstanding personal qualities that characterized him and to strive to become an even better person; offers workshops about terrorism, coping with terror, and the strength to go on after terrorism has struck; and offers musical performances and guided tours throughout Israel by the Hoter family.

Natal: The Israel Trauma Center for Victims of Terror and War (Tel Aviv, Israel; http://www.natal.org.il/english/):

Provides emotional and psychological treatment and assistance to any Israeli suffering from posttraumatic stress disorder as a result of the Arab-Israeli conflict; offers a hot line staffed by mental health professionals; trains professionals and at-risk populations throughout Israel in prevention and coping mechanisms for PTSD; and advances awareness and knowledge about national psychotrauma and terror- and war-related PTSD in Israeli society.

Navah: Uniting Broken Hearts (Jerusalem, Israel; http://www.navah.org.il/index.html):

Offers emotional support to terror victims and bereaved families through therapeutic and rehabilitative weekend retreats, support groups, counseling help line, home visitations, and Jewish holiday events.

Ner l'Tehilla (A Candle for Tehilla; Zichron Yaacov, Israel):

Founded in memory of three-year-old terrorism-victim Tehilla Nathansen; supports women after childbirth.

Ochel Ari (Ra'anana, Israel):

Founded in memory of Staff Sergeant Ari Yehoshua Weiss, twenty-one, to provide food packages for IDF combat soldiers serving in the field, away from their base.

OneFamily: Overcoming Terror Together (Jerusalem, Israel; http://www.onefamilytogether.org/):

Empowers victims of terror in Israel and their families to rebuild their lives, rehabilitate, and reintegrate through emotional, legal, and financial assistance programs; facilitates a resilient Israeli society through healing retreats, workshops, support groups, and youth and young adult programs.

One Heart – One Hope (New York, NY, USA; http://oneheartonehope .com/about.html):

Founded in memory of Israeli victim-of-terrorism Rami Kimchy; aims to heal victims/survivors of terrorism and other traumatic crimes and their families through social support, shared experiences, and finding a sense of community.

Operation Embrace (Potomac, MD, USA; www.operationembrace .org/):

Offers direct financial assistance for medical, therapeutic, and rehabilitative needs to injured survivors of terror attacks in Israel to help them rebuild their lives; provides emotional support through posttraumatic stress disorder programs at various hospitals and counseling centers throughout Israel.

Parents Circle – Families Forum (Ramat-Efal, Israel, and Beit Jala, Palestinian National Authority; http://www.theparentscircle.com/):

Spearheads face-to-face reconciliation programs and dialogue meetings between Israelis and Palestinians who have lost close family members as a result of the prolonged conflict.

PRIME: Peace Research Institute in the Middle East (Beit Jala, Palestinian National Authority; http://www.vispo.com/PRIME/):

Established by Palestinian and Israeli researchers in 1998 with the help of the Peace Research Institute in Frankfurt, Germany; pursues mutual coexistence and peace building through joint research and outreach activities.

Project Tikvah – Maccabi World Union (Ramat Gan, Israel; http://maccabi.org/):

Offers special sports programs with qualified instructors to restore hope and joy to the lives of terror victims who choose whichever personal sports-therapy program suits them – fitness room, horse riding, swimming, sailing, hand cycling, outdoor challenges, waterskiing, kayaking, and others; helps victims of terrorism overcome their fears and regain self-confidence and belief in themselves and their abilities.

Raise Your Spirits Summer Stock Company (Efrat/Gush Etzion, Israel; http://www.raiseyourspirits.org/):

Formed by a group of women in Gush Etzion to raise their spirits, amid an atmosphere of grief and terror, by putting on musical shows based on the classic stories from the Bible to give them a positive outlet for their feelings and emotions.

Seeds of Peace (New York, NY, USA; Tel Aviv, Israel; and Ramallah, Palestinian National Authority; http://www.seedsofpeace.org/):

Inspires and equips new generations of leaders from regions of conflict with the relationships, understanding, and skills needed to advance lasting peace.

Selah: Israel Crisis Management Center (Tel Aviv, Israel; http://www.selah.org.il/):

Provides compassionate support, as well as financial and practical aid, to help new immigrants and their families who have experienced trauma cope with unexpected tragedy, both in an emergency and in the longer term.

Strength to Strength (New York, NY, USA; http://stosglobal.org/):

Founded by terrorism-survivor Sarri Singer; supports victims of terrorism around the world with long-term psychological needs, enabling victims of terrorism to share experiences and empowering them to live life to their best potential and move forward with their lives despite the trauma they have been through; "survivors healing survivors."

VAT: Victims of Arab Terror International (Jerusalem, Israel; http://www.victimsofarabterror.com/):

Raises consciousness by publicizing the crucial issue of Jewish victims in the Arab-Israeli conflict who are often ignored and forgotten; provides aid and comfort at funerals, during *shiva* (the seven-day Jewish mourning period), and at hospital bedsides, as well as moral and financial support for victims and bereaved families.

Yad Sarah (Jerusalem and 103 branches throughout Israel; http://www.yadsarah.org/index.asp?id=61):

Provides a spectrum of free or nominal-cost services designed to make life easier for sick, disabled, and elderly people and their families and to enable the ill and the elderly to remain in their homes and out of institutions as long as possible; lends medical and rehabilitative equipment on a short-term basis free of charge and provides a wide range of other services to anyone who needs it; and provides equipment and services for new mothers, infants, recently discharged hospital patients, and others in need.

ZAKA (Hebrew acronym for Disaster Victim Identification; Jerusalem and throughout Israel; http://www.zakarescue.org):

Nongovernmental, humanitarian voluntary organization in Israel, providing rescue, life-saving, and recovery services and working alongside law enforcement and emergency personnel in responding to incidents of terrorism, accidents, or disasters.

Medical Centers

Alyn Hospital, Jerusalem (http://www.alyn.org/)

Bnai Zion Hospital, Haifa (http://www.bnaizion.org/bz_medicalcenter .php)

Emek Medical Center, Afula (http://hospitals.clalit.co.il/hospitals /emek/en-us/Pages/EmekMedicalCenter.aspx)

Hadassah University Hospital-Ein Kerem, **Hadassah University Hospital-Mount Scopus**, and **Hadassah Offices in Israel**, Jerusalem (http://www.hadassah-med.com/)

Hillel Yaffe Hospital, Hadera (http://hy.health.gov.il/eng/)

Loewenstein Hospital Rehabilitation Center, Ra'anana (http://www .clalit-global.co.il/en/loewenstein_rehabilitation_center.html)

Rabin Medical Center (Beilinson and Hasharon Hospitals), Petach Tikvah (http://hospitals.clalit.co.il/Hospitals/Rabin/en-us/About/Pages /AboutRabinMedicalCenter.aspx)

Rambam Hospital, Haifa (http://www.rambam.org.il/Home+Page/)

Sarah Herzog Hospital, Jerusalem (http://www.herzoghospital.org/)

Schneider Children's Medical Center of Israel, Petach Tikvah (http:// www.schneider.org.il/Eng/)

Shaare Zedek Medical Center, Jerusalem (http://www.szmc.org.il/en /Home/tabid/395/Default.aspx)

Sheba Medical Center at Tel Hashomer, Tel Aviv (http://eng.sheba .co.il/About_Us/)

Soroka Medical Center, Beer Sheva (http://www.soroka.org/)

Tel-Aviv Sourasky Medical Center (Ichilov Hospital), Tel Aviv (http://www.tasmc.org.il/sites/en/Pages/default.aspx)

Glossary

Note that other terms can be found in the description of major events in Appendix B, as well as in the list of major organizations supporting terror survivors and families in Appendix C. In addition, key Israeli cities and locations of the attacks are shown on the map. All terms are Hebrew words, unless otherwise noted.

Abba. Father.

al-Aqsa Intifada. The Palestinian uprising that began in September 2000, named for the al-Aqsa Mosque in Jerusalem.

aleph-bet. Hebrew alphabet.

aliya. The immigration of Jews to Israel.

Allahu Akhbar. Arabic for "Allah (God) is great"; a general Muslim statement of faith but also what a "jihadist" seeking martyrdom shouts when attacking a target.

am Yisrael. The Jewish people.

Amida (lit., standing prayer). Central prayer of the Jewish liturgy recited in each of the three daily prayer services.

an-Naksa. Arabic for *setback*.

azaka. Siren or other alarm that warns of impending danger.

baal teshuva, baalat teshuva (fem.). A nonreligious Jew who embraces Orthodox Judaism.

balagan. Confusion; chaos.

bar mitzvah, bat mitzvah (fem.). The initiation ceremony recognizing a Jewish child at the age of twelve or thirteen; the age of religious duty and responsibility.

baruch Hashem. Blessed be the name of the Lord; thank God.

bashert. Destiny, often used in the context of one's divinely foreordained spouse or soul mate.

b'seder. In order; fine.

bikkur cholim. Visiting the sick; providing comfort and support to people who are ill, homebound, isolated, and/or otherwise in distress.

bitachon. Trust in God; also security, as in the Israel Security Agency "Shabak" (Sherut Habitachon Haklali).

brit mila. Jewish ritual circumcision performed on eight-day-old male infants.

chazzan. A Jewish cantor or musician trained in the vocal arts to help lead the congregation in songful prayer.

chesed. Act of kindness.

emuna. Belief or faith.

Eretz Yisrael. The biblical Land of Israel.

Haftara. The weekly reading from the Prophets.

halacha. The collective body of Jewish religious law, including biblical law and later Talmudic and rabbinic law, as well as customs and traditions.

Hamatzav. The situation or the overall state of affairs; in this context refers to the Israeli-Palestinian conflict.

hantzacha. Commemoration process; perpetuation or immortalization.

Hashem (lit., the Name). A reference to God.

hashlama. Acceptance.

IDF. Israel Defense Forces; also known by the Hebrew acronym Tzahal.

Ima. Mother.

Intifada (lit., shaking off). Arabic for *uprising*.

jihad. Arabic for religious or personal struggle; in our context a "holy war."

Kabbalah. Discipline and school of thought concerned with the mystical aspect of rabbinic Judaism.

kavod. Human dignity; individual honor.

kibbutz. A communal farm or settlement in Israel.

kiddush. Blessing made on wine to sanctify the Sabbath or holiday meal.

Knesset (Israeli Parliament). Legislative branch of the Israeli government.

Kotel, the Western Wall. The western wall of the Second Temple complex destroyed by the Romans in 70 CE and located in the Old City of Jerusalem; the most sacred spot in Jewish religious and national consciousness and tradition.

madrich, madricha (fem.). Counselor or leader, often of youth.

matzah. Unleavened bread made of flour and water, eaten on Passover.

mazal. Luck.

minyan. Quorum required for Jewish communal worship that consists of ten male adults in Orthodox Judaism and usually ten adults of either sex in Conservative and Reform Judaism.

Mishnah. The first major compilation of Jewish oral law, redacted ca. 200 CE.

mitzvah. A commandment of the Jewish law; a meritorious or charitable act or deed.

mohel. Jewish person trained in the practice of ritual circumcision.

moshav. Cooperative settlement of small individual farms in Israel.

nachas. Pleasurable pride, especially in the achievements of one's children.

Nakba. Arabic for *catastrophe*; commonly used to refer to the establishment of the State of Israel.

neshama. Soul.

nitzolei Shoah. Survivors of the Holocaust.

Pesach, Passover. Jewish holiday commemorating the ancient Israelites' exodus from Egypt.

pigua, piguim (pl.). An attack; commonly refers to a terrorist attack or a suicide bombing.

Rosh Hashanah. Jewish New Year.

sabra. A native-born Israeli.

schlemazel. Yiddish for luckless person.

schlep. Yiddish for tedious or difficult journey.

Seder. Ceremonial dinner observed during Passover.

Sephardi. Descendant of Jews from Spain and Portugal, including the majority of Jews from North Africa and Middle Eastern/Arab countries.

seudat hodaya. Festive meal of thanksgiving.

Shabbat, Shabbos. The Jewish Sabbath, lasting from Friday sundown until the appearance of three stars in the sky on Saturday night.

shaheed, shaheeda (fem.). Arabic for a Muslim martyr who died for the sake of Allah.

shalom. Peace; used as a Jewish greeting and farewell.

Shema, Shema Yisrael (Hear O Israel). First two words of a section of the Torah (Pentateuch) that is the centerpiece of the morning and evening Jewish prayer services.

sheitel. Yiddish for wig, especially for married women.

shiva. Traditional Jewish seven-day period of mourning the dead.

shawarma. Arabic for slow-grilled, shaved meat served in pita bread or a wrap.

shuk. Market.

simcha, semachot (pl.). Festive or joyous occasion.

Sukkot (lit., booths, huts). Jewish holiday that gives thanks for the fall harvest and commemorates the forty years of Jewish wandering in the desert after Sinai.

tachlis. Purpose, essence, substance, worth, basics, "brass tacks."

tefillin. Phylacteries, containing scrolls of parchment inscribed with verses from the Torah worn by Jews during weekday morning prayers.

Tehillim. The book of Psalms.

tikkun. Repairing or healing, as in *tikkun olam* – repairing the world; *tikkun halev* – repairing the heart; *tikkun haneshama* – repairing the soul; and *tikkun hador* – repairing the generation.

Torah. The Pentateuch; also refers to the entire corpus of Jewish learning.

tzedaka. Religious obligation to perform charity and acts of justice.

tzemicha v'pericha. Growing and blossoming.

ulpan. Intensive Hebrew-language study program.

yahrzeit. Annual commemoration on the anniversary of the death of a Jew by a mourner (the child, sibling, spouse or parent of the deceased).

yeshiva. An Orthodox school for studying Jewish texts.

yishuv. Settlement.

Yizkor. Judaism's memorial prayer recited by mourners in a *minyan*.

Yom Haatzmaut. National Independence Day of Israel, commemorating its declaration of independence in 1948.

Yom Hazikaron. National Memorial Day of Israel, commemorating the soldiers who lost their lives to establish or defend the State of Israel and all those soldiers who died subsequently defending the state of Israel; since the Second Intifada, it has been extended to remember victims of terrorism.

Yom Kippur. Day of Atonement; the holiest day of the year for religious Jews.

z"l. Abbreviation for *zichrono livracha* or *zichrona livracha*, honorifics for the dead, meaning may his/her memory be for a blessing.

Selected Bibliography

The idea that great good can come from great suffering is ancient, appearing in literature, philosophical inquiry, and religious thinking. In the mid-twentieth century, clinicians and scientists in the fields of psychology, counseling, psychiatry, social work, and others began to address the ways in which critical life crises offered possibilities for positive personal change. Major pioneers included Viktor Frankl on *logotherapy*, a humanistic and existential approach to psychotherapy, and the search for meaning in life; Aaron Antonovsky on *salutogenesis* and the origins of health; Irvin D. Yalom on *existential psychotherapy*; Abraham Maslow and Martin E. P. Seligman on *positive psychology* or the scientific study of optimal human functioning and its emphasis on what is right with people rather than what is wrong with them; and Mihaly Csikszentmihalyi on *flow* – the psychology of optimal experiences.

The focus on growth per se began in earnest in the 1990s with the publication of research by Jeanne Schaefer and Rudolf Moos on crisis and personal growth, Virginia O'Leary, Jeanette Ickovics, and Charles Carver on resilience and thriving in response to challenge, and Crystal Park, Richard Tedeschi, and Lawrence Calhoun on stress-related or *posttraumatic growth*. Currently, a great deal of interest and scholarly conversation is taking place on these important topics.

The following is a selected bibliography in the areas of trauma, stress, resilience, and growth of some of the works used in the making of the book; others may be found in the footnotes in this book or in the ever-growing body of literature available through the research libraries.

Aldwin, Carolyn M. *Stress, Coping, and Development: An Integrative Perspective*. New York: Guilford Press, 2000.

Antonovsky, Aaron. *Unraveling the Mystery of Health: How People Manage Stress and Stay Well*. San Francisco: Jossey-Bass, 1987.

Brom, Danny, Ruth Pat-Horenczyk, and Julian D. Ford. *Treating Traumatized Children: Risk, Resilience, and Recovery.* London: Routledge / Taylor and Francis, 2009.

Calhoun, Lawrence G., and Richard G. Tedeschi. *Facilitating Posttraumatic Growth: A Clinician's Guide.* Mahwah, NJ: Lawrence Erlbaum Associates, 1999.

——. *Handbook of Posttraumatic Growth: Research and Practice.* Mahwah, NJ: Lawrence Erlbaum Associates, 2006.

Folkman, Susan, ed. *The Oxford Handbook of Stress, Health, and Coping.* New York: Oxford University Press, 2013.

Frankl, Viktor E. *Man's Search for Meaning.* Translated by Ilse Lasch. Boston: Beacon Press, 2006.

——. *Man's Search for Meaning: The Classic Tribute to Hope from the Holocaust.* London: Rider Books, 2004, 2011.

Herman, Judith Lewis. *Trauma and Recovery: The Aftermath of Violence – from Domestic Abuse to Political Terror.* Rev. ed. New York: Basic Books, 1997.

Janoff-Bulman, Ronnie. *Shattered Assumptions: Towards a New Psychology of Trauma.* New York: Free Press, 1992.

Joseph, Stephen, and P. Alex Linley. *Trauma, Recovery, and Growth: Positive Psychological Perspectives on Posttraumatic Stress.* Hoboken, NJ: John Wiley, 2008.

Neimeyer, Robert A., ed. *Meaning Reconstruction and the Experience of Loss.* Washington, DC: American Psychological Association, 2001.

Schiraldi, Glenn R. *The Post-Traumatic Stress Disorder Sourcebook: A Guide to Healing, Recovery, and Growth.* 2nd ed. New York: McGraw Hill, 2009.

Southwick, Steven M., Brett T. Litz, Dennis Charney, and Matthew J. Friedman. *Resilience and Mental Health: Challenges Across the Lifespan.* Cambridge: Cambridge University Press, 2011.

Southwick, Steven M., and Dennis S. Charney. *The Science of Mastering Life's Greatest Challenges.* New York: Cambridge University Press, 2012.

Tedeschi, Richard G., and Lawrence G. Calhoun. *Trauma and Transformation: Growing in the Aftermath of Suffering*. Thousand Oaks, CA: Sage Publications, 1995.

Tedeschi, Richard G., Crystal L. Park, and Lawrence G. Calhoun. *Posttraumatic Growth: Positive Changes in the Aftermath of Crisis*. Mahwah, NJ: Lawrence Erlbaum Associates, 1998.

Van der Kolk, Bessel A., Alexander C. McFarlane, and Lars Weisæth. *Traumatic Stress: The Effects of Overwhelming Experience on Mind, Body, and Society*. New York: Guilford Press, 1996.

Although an extensive literature exists on the identification and treatment of the psychological consequences of trauma, my interest is focused on the specific challenges caused by terrorist activities. Several recent edited volumes influenced my thinking and provide useful information aimed at helping readers understand the psychology of terrorism and the therapeutic needs of survivors and victims of terrorist attacks and their families. The many contemporary experts within these volumes present a broad and deep array of exceptionally useful information from academic, medical, military, and clinical settings and from a wide range of historical events and geographical locations.

Bongar, Bruce Michael, Lisa M. Brown, Larry E. Beutler, James N. Breckenridge, and Philip G. Zimbardo, eds. *Psychology of Terrorism*. New York: Oxford University Press, 2007.

Danieli, Yael, Danny Brom, and Joe Sills, eds. *The Trauma of Terrorism: Sharing Knowledge and Shared Care; An International Handbook*. Binghamton, NY: Haworth Maltreatment and Trauma Press, 2005.

Knafo, Danielle. *Living with Terror, Working with Trauma: A Clinician's Handbook*. Northvale, NJ: Jason Aronson, 2004.

Kuriansky, Judy, ed. *Terror in the Holy Land: Inside the Anguish of the Israeli-Palestinian Conflict*. Westport, CT: Praeger, 2006.

Moghaddam, Fathali M., and Anthony J. Marsella, eds. *Understanding Terrorism: Psychosocial Roots, Consequences, and Interventions*. Washington, DC: American Psychological Association, 2004.

Stout, Chris E. *Psychology of Terrorism: Coping with the Continued Threat*. Condensed ed. Westport, CT: Praeger, 2004.

Living Beyond Terrorism goes well beyond the stories reported by newspapers, television, movies, and other modern media and the many books published about the Israeli-Palestinian conflict during the past decade. A selected few of these titles describing how Israelis – Jewish and Arab – live with the threat of terrorism and the psychological impact of politically motivated violence may be of interest to the readers of this book:

Cole, Leonard A. *Terror: How Israel Has Coped and What America Can Learn*. Bloomington: Indiana University Press, 2007.

Feuerstein, Marie Therese. *Burning Flowers, Burning Dreams: Consequences of Suicide Bombings on Civilians in Israel, 2000–2005*. Zichron Yaacov, Israel: Civilian Project, 2005.

Gavron, Daniel. *The Other Side of Despair: Jews and Arabs in the Promised Land*. Lanham, MD: Rowman and Littlefield, 2004.

Gordis, Daniel. *Coming Together, Coming Apart: A Memoir of Heartbreak and Promise in Israel*. Hoboken, NJ: John Wiley, 2006.

——. *If a Place Can Make You Cry: Dispatches from an Anxious State*. New York: Crown Publishers, 2002.

——. *Saving Israel: How the Jewish People Can Win a War That May Never End*. Hoboken, NJ: John Wiley, 2009.

Mandell, Sherri Lederman. *The Blessing of a Broken Heart*. 2nd ed. New Milford, CT: Toby Press, 2003.

Meotti, Giulio. *A New Shoah: The Untold Story of Israel's Victims of Terrorism*. New York: Encounter Books, 2010.

Rabinowitz, Dan, and Khawla Abu-Baker. *Coffins on Our Shoulders: The Experience of the Palestinian Citizens of Israel*. Berkeley and Los Angeles, CA: University of California Press, 2005.

Rosenthal, Donna. *The Israelis: Ordinary People in an Extraordinary Land*. New York: Free Press, 2003.

Wiemer, Liza M., and Benay Katz. *Waiting for Peace: How Israelis Live with Terrorism*. Jerusalem: Gefen Publishing House, 2005.

Index